T0386474

A Guide to In-sessional English for Academic Purposes

A hands-on guide for practitioners, this book prepares instructors to teach in-sessional English for Academic Purposes (ISEAP) higher education courses. As university cohorts become more diverse, there is demand for in-sessional EAP courses not only to support international students, but also increasingly as a provision for all students. This informative resource explores the varying formats of ISEAP courses and how they are embedded within and alongside students' degree programmes in the United Kingdom and beyond.

In accessible chapters, authors Neil Adam Tibbetts and Timothy Chapman present illuminating findings drawn from interviews conducted with experts in the field and highlight the challenges that students and practitioners face. Avoiding prescriptive recommendations, Tibbetts and Chapman address different models and contexts of ISEAP courses at university level and offer guidance and tools for practice. Covering key topics such as pedagogies, logistical challenges, and the wider university context, this book not only provides a roadmap to the often ill-defined but essential domain of ISEAP but also provokes questions and ideas for further reflection, guiding the reader towards a deeper understanding of their role and development in context.

Engaging and inviting, Tibbetts and Chapman's helpful text is a necessary resource for teachers to design and lead successful ISEAP courses.

Neil Adam Tibbetts is a coordinator of in-sessional courses in the Centre for Academic Language and Development (CALD) at the University of Bristol, U.K.

Timothy Chapman is a Senior Lecturer in English for Academic Purposes and Writing Development within the Centre for Academic Language and Literacies (CALL) at Goldsmiths, University of London, U.K.

A Guide to In-sessional English for Academic Purposes

Paradigms and Practices

NEIL ADAM TIBBETTS AND TIMOTHY CHAPMAN

Routledge
Taylor & Francis Group

NEW YORK AND LONDON

Designed cover image: © Getty Images

First published 2023
by Routledge
605 Third Avenue, New York, NY 10158

and by Routledge
4 Park Square, Milton Park, Abingdon, Oxon, OX14 4RN

Routledge is an imprint of the Taylor & Francis Group, an informa business

ISBN: 978-1-032-04543-6 (hbk)
ISBN: 978-1-032-02003-7 (pbk)
ISBN: 978-1-003-19371-5 (ebk)

DOI: 10.4324/9781003193715

Typeset in Bembo
by MPS Limited, Dehradun

To David Gibbon, convenor of the Gibbon Lunch.

Contents

Acknowledgements

The authors would like to thank all those who generously gave up their time and agreed to be interviewed about their practice and thoughts about in-sessional EAP in preparation for this book, as well as their colleagues at CALD in Bristol and CALL at Goldsmiths for their support.

How to use this book

The term 'in-sessional English for Academic Purposes' encompasses a range of activities within a field which is often slightly hidden, undocumented, and largely unregulated. It is a widely varied area of practices and its forms, purposes, design, and delivery are heavily dependent on external factors such as its institutional context and the culture of the EAP centre in which it is based. Consequently, this guide is not designed to be prescriptive as this would hardly be appropriate for such situated settings. Rather, the book aims to survey a range of typical paradigms for in-sessional EAP and takes a research-informed perspective to the possibilities available to a practitioner operating in the field.

The book is primarily intended for in-sessional EAP teachers and course leaders, in order to raise awareness of the particular challenges and affordances of the roles, offering opportunities to reflect on their practice, to develop pedagogies, and enhance the role of in-sessional EAP in their institution. However, as in-sessional academic language development is an integral and emergent part of the contemporary higher education landscape, the book should also be of interest to anyone involved in how academic literacy development interacts with disciplinary knowledge. This includes lecturers with a particular interest in learning and teaching matters, study skills specialists, and those in management roles.

This is designed to be a practical book, informed by published literature and interviews that were conducted with a range of lecturers and practitioners working in different university contexts in different countries. It is largely informed by the UK context, in which the authors work, but with its scope extended to consider a range of other settings. In the book, key issues are discussed in relation to setting up and teaching courses, with consideration of how this has been achieved in a variety of situations. Having surveyed an aspect of practice, each chapter ends with an interactive section with guided questions addressed to the reader, offering opportunities for those practising in in-sessional contexts to reflect on and apply ideas to their own situated practice. These are an explicit invitation to consider one's own setting – its parameters, constraints, affordances, and key environmental factors. This will enable practitioners to decide how best to meet the learning needs of their students.

The chapters of this book are organised into two broad sections:

Section A explores in-sessional practices from within the context of English for Academic Purposes: the specificities of in-sessional EAP (ISEAP) and its varied relationship with disciplinary activities (Chapter 1); how pedagogical approaches from EAP relate to ISEAP contexts (Chapter 2); and the logistics of ISEAP and how best to react to various affordances and constraints (Chapter 3).

Section B takes a wider, more speculative view, looking at the role of in-sessionals within the wider context of rapidly changing higher education policies and practices (Chapter 4); before Chapter 5 focuses on the identity of the practitioner operating in this context and finally Chapter 6 considers the impact of ISEAP on the development of teaching and learning practices in HE, identifying possible future developments based on its unique positioning.

All of the chapters are discrete in their focus, but they do build upon each other to develop a fuller picture of ISEAP. Relationships between chapters are highlighted where appropriate. For this reason, the book is probably best read sequentially, but individual chapters can be read independently, according to the interest of the reader.

Introduction

Introducing ISEAP

This book is intended as a guide to an evolving field of teaching and learning in higher education. As will become clear, the subject matter of this book is not an easily defined, homogenous, or even largely visible area of practice. Therefore, this guide does not intend to be a fully comprehensive 'how-to' handbook with prescriptive recommendations on curriculum design, materials, and content. Instead what follows is an exploration of the often very different ways in which in-sessional English for Academic Purposes (ISEAP) manifests itself in universities in the United Kingdom and beyond. The content is informed by interviews the authors conducted with practitioners and academics working in a variety of contexts. Our aim is not to endorse a single approach or suggest a particular model, but to provide a more open reflective guide for practitioners working in this area, hopefully serving as a useful companion to make sense of, and help them navigate, the range of issues involved in the design, implementation, and management of effective in-sessional academic English courses in university settings.

In the book, we use the abbreviation ISEAP to describe academic English language provision that does not aim to prepare students for future academic study, but rather takes place during the academic year, running alongside the regular teaching and learning activities of the institution. An in-sessional course

DOI: 10.4324/9781003193715-1

is concurrent with students' main study activities. In its various forms, ISEAP may be an optional extracurricular activity, or embedded within the content of students' substantive degree programmes. It should be emphasised therefore that even where they do happen during the normal academic year period, preparatory EAP courses (such as year-round pre-sessional, foundation, or pre-master's programmes) are therefore not within the scope of this book. What is being discussed here is to a large extent the more specific end of EAP: academic language provision that often aligns closely to degree content. In contrast to stand-alone EAP courses, ISEAP often entails a greater degree of discipline specificity in terms of what is taught and how it is delivered, typically requiring closer collaboration with disciplinary lecturers. As we shall also discuss, this is not always the case – more generic EGAP (English for General Academic Purposes) informed in-sessional practices are not uncommon – but the typically enhanced focus on specificity and collaboration of ISEAP offers a particular set of challenges and opportunities regarding curriculum and materials design as well as approaches to teaching and learning.

Pre-sessional and foundation-level EAP courses are characteristically more comparable from one university to another. They are likely to have similarly defined learning outcomes or may make use of course book materials. They are also far more tightly regulated by internal university processes and open to scrutiny through the presence of outside stakeholders, such as external examiners from other institutions. Accreditation schemes for EAP centres such as the British Council's or BALEAP's (prior to 2010, the British Association of Lecturers in English for Academic Purposes, EAP's most prominent professional organisation) have historically limited their focus to pre-sessional activities, although this is starting to change. In-sessional contexts, in contrast, are mostly hidden from view. ISEAP courses are often conceived as a response to particular localised issues, and so may develop independently from more publicly articulated notions of best practice across the EAP sector. All of the above explains why we believe ISEAP paradigms and practices to be worthy of deeper investigation.

One of the key motivations for writing this book then is to address the perceived lack of coherence within this sub-field of EAP and encourage possibilities for the sharing of cross-institutional knowledge. The hidden nature of ISEAP has been recognised, for example by Sloan and Porter (2010: 200), who note the predominance of pre-sessional over in-sessional in literature about the context of EAP practices. In her keynote, at a BALEAP Professional Issues Meeting (PIM) held at the London School of Economics in March 2016, Ursula Wingate bemoaned this lack of awareness and visibility of in-sessional practices within EAP, while also celebrating the quality of specific provision and variety of innovative practices presented at the event (Wingate, 2019). Since then, there have been numerous occasions where the BALEAP JISCMail discussion list (2020) has seen colleagues from the United Kingdom and beyond asking inquisitively about what actually goes on in other institutions' in-sessional contexts. Indeed, as recently as February 2022, at an event hosted by the BALEAP's Academic Literacies Special Interest Group, one of the most notable features of a discussion of pedagogy in-sessional contexts was practitioners from different institutions avidly asking variations of 'So what do you actually do where you are?' This book hopes in some way to shed light on such questions and help redress an oversight in the literature.

The co-authors both work in EAP centres at U.K. universities, which, like most in the sector, deliver in-sessional as well as preparatory academic English courses. In order to research this book, we have supplemented our own knowledge and experience – based on both published sources and a combined experience of over 30 years in EAP – with interviews conducted with 40 practitioners and academics with an interest in in-sessional provision in the United Kingdom and beyond. These interviews were mostly, but not exclusively, one-to-one and lasted around 45 minutes to an hour in length and took the form of informal conversations, practitioner to practitioner. We spoke to centre directors, researchers, curriculum developers, materials writers, EAP practitioners, and subject academics who collaborate with them. The purpose of the interviews was to attempt to gain a broad, but rich understanding of how ISEAP provision has been developed in a variety of local contexts. We were interested in hearing participants' unique and subjective accounts of their practice and context.

It should, however, be noted that our effort was in no way an attempt to survey all in-sessional activities, as this would be is beyond the reach of the book. It is worth mentioning that in 2013 Tribble and Wingate attempted such a project, surveying academic literacy provision in UK universities (cited by Wingate, 2015); they looked at how institutions articulated in-sessional-type activities on 31 UK institutions' websites, finding limited visibility for 'discipline-led literacy work' (2015: 49). This is not to say it did not exist in the institutions surveyed, but rather it serves to underline how ISEAP is often occluded. Our approach has rather been to gain more focussed insight into authentic experiences of the issues central to ISEAP. By attempting to make sense of these issues, we hope to aid others in navigating their own context.

Our findings from the interviews do not offer an exhaustive account of ISEAP, but it is the particularity of different contexts which was often of most interest. The interviews were semi-structured and often discursive in nature, a meeting between peers working within the sector, where we, the interviewers, participated and compared our own contexts with the interviewees'. The interviews in turn led us towards a deeper interrogation of our own experience that has informed the writing of his book. Our approach encouraged participants to reflect on their own practices, and through these discussions we were able to excavate much about the hidden world of ISEAP – a starting point to inform the discussions that follow. Our bank of starting questions can be found in the Appendix. The questions are grouped around six main areas of exploration: the features of localised ISEAP practices, the role of the practitioner in their context, the students themselves, how collaboration with subject lecturers works, the role of wider institutional factors, and finally practical logistical considerations. It is fair to say that among participants there was commonly a desire for greater understanding and knowledge-sharing about how ISEAP manifests itself in different settings.

Throughout the book, we have anonymously quoted from interviews to reveal authentic voices from the field. Often, these quotes demonstrate how concepts from the literature play out in practitioners' actual contexts. We largely rely on speakers' own words rather than paraphrasing; these quotations have been punctuated for ease of reading. We have not followed a specific methodology for analysing discourse and selecting quotations and they have not been selected to support a particular thesis. Rather, it is the ideas themselves that are important: what speakers are able to share about their own paradigms and practices, and the ways that ISEAP is manifested for them. Given ISEAP's often hidden nature, this feature of our book may be a key area of interest for many readers.

What Characterises ISEAP?

The focus of ISEAP is most commonly on developing academic writing skills. Students on most university programmes are still assessed to a greater or lesser extent through written assignments. As writing is a challenging activity for many, it is often implicit that this becomes the key focus of ISEAP provision. However, this should not be taken as a given; Wingate (2015) makes a compelling case for an equal focus on reading skills development, information literacy, and identifying the salient information from complex texts – reading as a basis for writing. In addition, we should not lose sight of the fact that the specific context is all important in ISEAP; being able to express ideas and understanding orally may be just as important an area of development in some disciplinary contexts. Fundamental to ISEAP though is enabling students to develop the skills to participate effectively as members of their academic discourse communities.

As we are writing from our own position as EAP practitioners, it is perhaps understandable that we use 'EAP' as a defining term, but it should be noted that this denotes a somewhat overlapping field of practice and other terms are commonly used in ISEAP provision, such as 'academic literacy development' (ALD) and sometimes 'academic skills'. Often terminology differs according to the entity directing the provision, whether it is an EAP centre or a central service such as the library. To be clear this book's focus is on courses that are taught over consecutive classes, following a bespoke and often discipline-informed syllabus that has been developed with a focus on discourse and developing academic literacy. This is in contrast to various ad-hoc interventions by language specialists that may take place during degree studies, such as study skills advice, one-off sessions, online self-study pages, or writing support tutorials, although these elements may sometimes be present as part of an in-sessional course. Thus, EAP seems the most appropriate term to use, but the variety of terminology, as evinced by our research interviews, will be acknowledged where necessary to ensure clarity and accessibility.

At its heart, in-sessional EAP itself remains ill-defined. Its boundaries are often fuzzy; it is often perceived differently by different stakeholders and paradigms for delivery can vary greatly. Part of the purpose of the book is therefore to recognise these aspects in the in-sessional contexts and, insofar as it is useful, to codify and firm up some of this fuzziness, to identify high-quality practices, and guide readers towards making use of them.

Speaking to practitioners from outside the United Kingdom, it was clear that the nomenclature of 'in-sessional EAP' might not be immediately recognised by all. The term is a commonly used shorthand in the U.K. context (for example, de Chazal (2014: 33) positions it as one EAP's 'two broad types' alongside pre-sessionals.) However, colleagues in Australia suggested the terms 'post-entry' or 'post-enrolment' as more readily identifiable for them. Furthermore, in conversation with a colleague in South Africa it became clear that, in a context where few students are designated as 'international' and where pre-sessional English provision does not exist as such, there is no need to specifically designate activities as 'in-sessional'. In such a context, EAP effectively *is* ISEAP. Furthermore, in English as a Medium of Instruction (EMI) contexts in non-Anglophone countries, such as in a number of European countries, interviewees articulated the primary aim of academic English language provision quite differently, for example focussing on detailed comprehension (reading) over production (writing). In U.K. settings though, where universities typically have a department or centre dedicated to English language provision or academic language and literacy development, in-sessional EAP is a commonly understood key strand of their activities.

We should clarify that in our consideration of ISEAP, we are not including the 'writing across the curriculum' model (WAC) common to many U.S. universities. Such writing courses are often delivered as a separate module with little to no interaction with specific disciplines. As such, this model differs considerably from the kind of cooperative relationship building with disciplinary academics we advocate. It is also less focussed on the specifically academic language, literacy and discourse practices that are fundamental to in-sessional endeavours. Interestingly, one of our interviewees even suggested that changing circumstances in the United States, partly due to increasing numbers of international students, have put WAC pedagogies under a degree of pressure, with some practitioners now looking towards developing more EAP-informed practices.

In the period of researching this book (2020–22), we also must acknowledge some notable external forces that had a significant impact on how we approached our research and the content itself. Obviously, the global COVID-19 pandemic has had enormous consequences for teaching and learning (most notably the sudden implementation of technology-enhanced learning (TEL) or blended asynchronous-synchronous delivery) and the university sector in general (including questions around greater need for sustaining a sense of community in online cohorts). These have had particular implications for how ISEAP is delivered and were widely discussed themes in our interviews with practitioners.

We were also influenced by a number of recent developments and publications within EAP scholarship, in particular a tendency towards more practitioner-based literature that focusses on issues beyond theory and discourse towards a consideration of the role of EAP within wider institutional considerations and the issues facing practitioners. Bee Bond's critical interrogation of the dichotomy between language and content in *Making Language Visible in the University* (2020) has been particularly influential, with its proposals for more collaborative language provision integrated within the curriculums of HE teaching. We also acknowledge the continuing critical interest in the identity, practice, and perceptions of those working in the EAP sector (as exemplified by Ding and Bruce's 2017 book, *The English for Academic Purposes Practitioner*). Our book is primarily aimed as a guide for EAP practitioners and interested fellow travellers, yet like Bond (2020), we believe much of its content should be of wider interest to many involved in teaching and learning in higher education.

The Content of This Book

Although we present a picture of complexity and diversity, insofar as an inherent aspect of ISEAP is the way it is highly sensitive to its context, there are some interesting commonalities and similarities of experience at cross-sector level too. As stated, it is beyond the scope of this book to develop a fully comprehensive guide, or to accurately map all in-sessional provision. And indeed our intention is not to prescribe a particular approach to how this might be achieved. Instead, we hope to contribute to ongoing and emergent discussions about this interesting, interdisciplinary area of practice. The possibility for ISEAP practitioners to be working in isolated contexts without clear guidance or opportunities for co-development is nicely encapsulated by one of our interviewees, who sketched a typical situation:

> I've got this course on my timetable: it says, you're doing 'Year 2 Undergraduate Planning' [in-sessional]. And I look at the materials – I've got last year's materials, ten sessions from last year, semester one. So what do I do? I can find the module specs and module details on our intranet. I can get onto the [Virtual Learning Environment] page. But it was like, all right, I want to contact the module leader to speak to her. But what do I ask her? What do I talk about? What can I ask of her, to do? And I was really nervous about that. I was like, is she interested in my course? Am I wasting her time? All those sorts of things that I was worried about.

The book seeks to provide guidance towards the reader looking for answers to such questions, to help develop a framework to reflect on the issues raised and consider them in relation to their own context. It will hopefully thereby encourage those interested in ISEAP to develop their own practice and seek connections with both others in their own universities as well as practitioners operating in similar contexts elsewhere, to further illuminate the possibilities open to them. Hopefully, it may even serve as a launchpad for scholarship, to conduct further research into this fascinating and rapidly developing area of teaching practice.

The book is divided into two halves, each consisting of three chapters. The first half, **The In-sessional within the EAP Context**, explores developments in ISEAP practices and issues to consider in setting up successful provision. The second half, **In-sessional EAP: Its Role Within the Wider University**, takes a broader view, considering the shifting sands of higher education and how ISEAP can impact, and interact with, multiple stakeholders.

In the first three chapters, we study ISEAP up close. **Chapter 1: The State and Status of ISEAP** examines variations in the ways that ISEAP manifests itself and the forces that affect this. It considers the key drivers shaping its delivery and the sometimes thorny issues inherent within different models of provision. **Chapter 2: Pedagogies and Teaching ISEAP** looks at the theories and approaches that typically inform EAP practice and consider how these relate specifically to ISEAP. **Chapter 3: Logistical Issues** focusses on the practicalities of ISEAP delivery, considering ways of identifying needs, some models for course design and delivery, and the issues inherent in making choices according to the resources available.

In the second half of the book, **Chapter 4: Changing Contexts** discusses how ISEAP is subject to rapid changes in the university, including the pervasive influence of neoliberal policies, the effect of the COVID-19 pandemic and the impact of decolonisation movements on provision. **Chapter 5: The ISEAP Practitioner** considers questions of expertise and knowledge, positioning and status, and roles and attributes of those operating in this sector, with their implications for the identity of the ISEAP practitioner. Finally, **Chapter 6: Beyond ISEAP** by way of conclusion, considers the influence of ISEAP on its surroundings and on emergent teaching and learning practices in higher education.

As the book is intended as a usable guide which promotes further reflection and discussion, each chapter ends with guiding questions. Following each chapter's presentation of guidance based on literature and relevant 'reportage' from our interviews, the focus then turns to the reader, encouraging them to look at their own setting, to consider the avenues and possibilities open to them, and identify the constraints and affordances of their context. These sections are designed to enable those approaching teaching in an ISEAP setting, or interested in exploring ISEAP as a phenomenon in situ, to critically map their own situation. Here we ask direct questions, guiding the reader towards an ongoing development of their own practice. In this way, it is hoped that the themes from each chapter can be applied locally. Ultimately, across a reading of the whole book, a clearer perception of the issues inherent in contextualised academic language provision should be achieved; it is hoped with positive implications for ISEAP practitioners' own course development.

References

BALEAP JISCMail (2020) *Embedded in-sessionals and CEM.* For tutors/lecturers in EAP (English for Academic Purposes) BALEAP@JISCMail.ac.uk.

Bond, B. (2020) *Making language visible in the university: English for academic purposes and internationalisation.* Bristol: Multilingual Matters.

de Chazal, E. (2014) *English for academic purposes.* Oxford: Oxford University Press.

Ding, A. and Bruce, I. (2017) *The English for academic purposes practitioner: Operating on the edge of academia.* Cham, Switzerland: Palgrave Macmillan.

Sloan, D. and Porter, E. (2010) Changing international student and business staff perceptions of in-sessional EAP: using the CEM model. *Journal of English for Academic Purposes*, 9:3, 198–210.

Wingate, U. (2015) *Academic literacy and student diversity: The case for inclusive practice.* Bristol: Multilingual Matters.

Wingate, U. (2019) Introduction in Brewer, S., Strandring, A. and Stansfield, G. (eds.) *Papers from the Professional Issues Meeting (PIM) on In-sessional English for Academic Purposes held at London School of Economics 19 March 2016*, 9–17. Available at: https://www.baleap.org/wp-content/uploads/2019/10/Baleap_Book_Interactive.pdf [accessed 1/9/22].

Section A: The In-sessional Within the EAP Context

Chapter 1

The State and Status of ISEAP

The purpose of this opening chapter is to consider some of the forces driving ISEAP provision and the various ways it manifests itself as a result. We present a complex field, full of interconnecting factors that result in forms that are highly situated. As we shall see, it is not always an easy field for practitioners to navigate, as it can be far from the more homogenous approaches to teaching and learning common to many pre-sessional EAP programmes. After outlining the many factors informing provision, this chapter then invites the reader to reflect on their context in the reflective section that follows, in order to identify how the issues mentioned relate to their institutional setting.

Some form of ISEAP provision is a mainstay of most institutions, in the United Kingdom and elsewhere, particularly where there are substantial numbers of international students. Yet despite this ubiquity, rather than just accepting it as part of the landscape of higher education we should consider the needs it sets out to address, and then by implication whether its various forms best meet these needs. As it takes so many guises and is highly context-dependent, we must also consider localised factors and how these influence provision. It is only by considering these influences, and by recognising considerable inherent challenges, that we then consider the theories that inform its practices and key logistical factors for successful delivery (these two aspects are the focus of Chapters 2 and 3, respectively.)

DOI: 10.4324/9781003193715-3

A useful starting point may be found from one of our interviewees, a director of a large EAP centre in the United Kingdom, who states that all in-sessional practitioners should be asking themselves three fundamental questions about their practice:

> What are you trying to do? Who are you trying to target it at? For what reasons?

As the interviewee states, these are not simple questions to answer, but this essential focus on *what?*, *who?*, and *why?* will frame the development of the chapter, acting as guiding principles around which we will survey some of the considerations central to ISEAP provision.

1.1 'What Are You Trying to Do?'

This section looks at some of the main needs ISEAP courses seek to address, firstly in the United Kingdom, followed by other countries' contexts.

Pinning down the essential purposes of ISEAP is not straightforward. This is partly due to it being heavily context-dependent in its forms and outcomes, further compounded by its often occluded nature. Nevertheless, the beginnings of an answer to the question lies in macro societal processes. It is largely a given that the linguistic nature of EAP has led to a focus on primarily working with international students, and ISEAP in many universities is still mostly directed toward them. Yet this is not a stable situation. In the United Kingdom, as recently as June 2022, the Russell Group (made up of 24 research-intensive universities) released a briefing which made the point that the funding for U.K. undergraduates, capped at £9,250 per student per year, is lagging behind the costs of actually teaching them (Russell Group, 2022). The prestige of Russell Group universities is globally attractive, and so they generally have large international cohorts. The implication of this funding issue, according to a report in *The Guardian*, is that 'some [universities] may end up pulling out of teaching UK students, focusing entirely on international students and postgraduates' (Fazackerley, 2022). These two often overlapping cohorts – international students and postgraduates – are so often the focus of in-sessional delivery. Some common forms of ISEAP develop as a direct result of these categorisations.

In terms of what ISEAP expects to achieve with these cohorts, we need to look at the wider context. ISEAP can be seen as an intervention on the part of an institution to enable students to thrive in their academic environments, which can be particularly urgent on postgraduate taught (PGT) programmes. These are usually much briefer than, for example, undergraduate studies, mostly accounting for just one year of full-time study in the United Kingdom. Students under such time pressure need to perform at a high level quickly, without the 'bedding in' period typical of the beginning of an undergraduate degree. As such, there is an emphasis on speed in transition: students need to quickly develop their abilities, linguistic and cultural, to successfully negotiate their academic contexts. It should also be noted that there is increasingly a strong interdisciplinary or applied studies aspect to PGT study. In recent years, there has been a proliferation in master's degrees and business- or practice-based degrees requiring students to read and produce texts within differing genres, based on different research traditions and academic practices. This increasing interdisciplinarity was recognised as a trend by Feak as long ago as 2011. The brevity of a one-year master's (and perhaps its cost-effectiveness) and often an employment-facing applied focus are factors that in no small way contribute to PGT degrees being particularly attractive to international students.

The designation 'international student' most obviously refers to students from outside the country of study. In many countries, these are students who pay higher fees, and particularly in the United Kingdom they form a large cohort on which the financial wellbeing of many institutions rely. Hadley (2015: 32) notes that this is not solely a U.K. phenomenon: 'many countries have followed the US, UK and others by accepting thousands of primarily Asian students as a means of bolstering their financially faltering university systems.' Although 'international student' refers to students from both anglophone and non-anglophone countries, it should also be recognised that the term is a common shorthand in the United Kingdom and other anglophone countries for students for whom English is a second or additional language. The traditions of EAP are to work closely with international students, most prominently on pre-sessional courses. These are usually the main source of income for a U.K. EAP centre, and its business model probably aligns closely with its institution's international student recruitment objectives. EAP centres are often funded through pre-sessional courses, providing students with a route into academic departments (Fulcher, 2009). Indeed, EAP centres have experienced the sharp face of universities' neoliberal drives (a theme that particularly informs Chapter 4), yet in contrast to pre-sessionals, in-sessionals are rarely an income-generating activity.

This focus on students from non-anglophone countries is enshrined in EAP's history. SELMOUS, the forerunner of BALEAP and the first EAP professional organisation, was an acronym for Special English Language Materials for Overseas University Students. Gillett described the purpose of EAP courses back in 1996 as 'to help overseas students overcome some of the linguistic difficulties involved in studying in English' (Gillett, 1996). This is still a typical orientation in the sector, but is now subject to greater interrogation. Discussions at BALEAP's recent 50th anniversary event (2022) suggest the debate about whether the efforts of EAP should be specifically directed towards 'international' students is still ongoing, but with more voices advocating pitching forms of EAP towards 'home' students. As we shall see, this orientation can easily slip into a 'deficit discourse,' whereby particular cohorts of students are identified as lacking some essential skills, typically linguistic, which inhibit successful study.

A deficit discourse is a more complex issue for in-sessionals than it is for preparation courses. Pre-sessional courses are often explicitly predicated upon raising a students' linguistic abilities, often measured by end-of-course assessment or a recognised test such as IELTS. However, the desired outcomes of in-sessionals are much less defined; rather, in-sessional interventions are often articulated as 'support', put in place so that students can make the most of their studies. Stated learning outcomes may lack the strong linguistic focus of a pre-sessional and are probably less end-goal oriented. The in-sessional curriculum may also be less tightly structured. Outcomes are likely to be dependent on the learning contexts and realistically these will vary from student to student. A more fundamental issue is surely that if in-sessionals represent an ongoing effort by institutions to enable students to perform to the best of their abilities, such a specifically 'international' focus is open to question. International student cohorts are unlikely to be the only ones experiencing difficulty developing the academic literacy to engage fully in their studies. Academic literacy is a more complex set of interrelations than can just be summed up as language ability in itself. Yet it is still common for provision to be articulated around a perceived notion of deficit, in which specific cohorts of students need support in their efforts to acculturate to the norms and expectations of their discipline and institution, which Wingate (2015) presents a thorough critique of in her case for more inclusive provision.

While it is certain that student populations have become more international, the institutions themselves have not necessarily become 'internationalised' (Jenkins and Wingate, 2015), despite many universities' strategic statements to that effect. Internationalisation means rather more than simply diversifying the student cohort; it indicates a more fundamental institutional change, in the way subjects are studied, the types of knowledge valued, and the recognition of a multiplicity of voices. As Ryan and Carroll (2005: 4) remark, the 'the rhetoric of diversity often does not translate easily into practice,' borne out by U.K. universities' elevation of international recruitment over internationalisation per se. However, while institutional practices lag behind demographic diversity, in-sessionals have a clear role to play in this. They are often seen as part of a university's attempts to level a varied field and create equality of opportunity. However, it could also be argued that by targeting international students as a relatively privileged cohort (who are mostly paying higher international fees), then this hardly aligns with a university's hopes for inclusion and equitability. The students targeted may well be unfamiliar with approaches to knowledge, disciplinary discourses, and how to study in an unfamiliar institutional setting, but they are hardly likely to be alone in this.

1.1.1 Increasing Diversity

Beyond international recruitment, student cohorts have become increasingly diverse along many other lines. One factor has been the diversification caused by the multiplicity of degrees, particularly at PGT level, but another major factor has been a widening of access to higher education, with greater re-cruitment of students from 'non-traditional' backgrounds. The language of university strategies and mission statements often reflects this. In addition to the ubiquitous use of 'internationalisation,' terms like 'inclusion,' 'equit-ability,' 'diversity,' and 'opportunity' are employed to articulate institutional strategies. For many universities, such values and imperatives may be more aspirational than an objective statement of reality. Nevertheless, in the U.K. context, a series of policies under the overall heading of Widening Participation have achieved some success in providing access to higher edu-cation to previously under-represented groups. These policies have con-tributed to a more heterogeneous student body; as noted above, those identified as 'international' are unlikely to have a monopoly on unfamiliarity with their discipline's approaches to knowledge, learning and discourse. As one of our interviewees, an experienced EAP practitioner, noted:

> If you start using words like 'inclusivity' and 'equality' and all that sort of stuff, you could get a non-native speaker saying: well, you know I need some help with my writing too.

Ryan and Carroll (2005: 4) make the point that, 'the issues surrounding international students mirror the experience of widening participation per se.'

Using the analogy of canaries in a mine to describe the experience of international students, the writers draw attention to how their experience highlights the kinds of issues in learning and teaching that will likely affect other cohorts in the near future. The implication of all of this is that if disciplinary lecturers can no longer teach to a typical, idealised student then teaching practices in general need to be more inclusive, recognising diverse lived experiences. And if disciplinary teaching is unable to adapt to its new student body, is the answer to the question 'What are you trying to do?' to bridge the gap between students and their learning contexts?

So where does this leave ISEAP, at least in the United Kingdom? It certainly suggests that a traditional focus on academic language development for international students is open to question given current education settings. One of our interviewees articulated the need for ISEAP in order to respond to the problem that '[academic departments'] old normal teaching techniques aren't working.' As we will see, there are numerous models for ISEAP interventions, yet the tradition of the optional 'support' class persists. This has been criticised, for example, by Turner (2011: 34) as being seen as 'a 'cinderella' class,' given the role of tidying-up language issues with minimal visibility. Such positioning of in-sessional activities has similarly been criticised by Wingate (2015: 38) for its 'trivialisation and marginalisation of academic language and literacy': whereby something as central to students' development as the clear and appropriate articulation of their learning and ideas is reduced to an optional extra in this model of delivery. Equally importantly, Wingate (2015: 43) goes on to argue that such an approach is largely ineffective, presenting it as an outmoded model: perhaps suitable for a few struggling students, but not effective at dealing with the realities of a massively expanded and diversified student cohort. There are other shortcomings of this 'support' model: a likely focus on superficial skills and surface features over academic literacy, its implications of remediation directed towards international students, and simply by virtue of it being an optional session, it is unlikely to meet the needs of all the students it could.

There is a tension inherent to ISEAP's role in the wider university: ISEAP needs to be effective at providing access to developmental opportunities so that all students can thrive. This should be a high-profile area of activity, as it aligns closely to interrelated strategic imperatives, yet its visibility and status do not often match this importance. One of our interviewees made the case for the high-stakes nature of ISEAP:

> Even though it is not income generating, there's the possibility of reputational damage if it doesn't exist.

ISEAP is not always a high-profile endeavour; it is also true that it is unlikely to generate income for the EAP centre or institution, yet it does have an important role in enabling students to succeed. Courses should help students to successfully navigate their learning, enhancing their experience, and so increase attainment. They can be essential in students overcoming issues from clarity of expression to academic integrity, arresting frustration, disengagement, and ultimately attrition.

In such a rapidly changing environment, where there is a tension between EAP's traditions of working with international students and wider university drives, the space ISEAP occupies is not easy to negotiate. Returning to our initial question 'What are you trying to do?,' a practitioner's answer will have to consider the broader context they work in as a contributing factor to their own aims in the classroom.

1.1.2 Non-U.K. Contexts

Most of the above considerations relate most obviously to the U.K. context, with its focus on international student recruitment and widening participation, and an EAP centre's potential role to play in supporting students. It is also helpful to consider the drivers behind ISEAP provision in non-U.K. contexts; the term 'in-sessional' might not be used, but academic literacy support is a feature across many countries' universities. The following section will focus on the particular forces influencing provision firstly in Australia and then in EMI (English as a Medium of Instruction) contexts in a range of countries.

1.1.2.1 Post-Entry Courses in Australia

Just like the United Kingdom, Australia is an attractive destination for international students, but a key difference for the role ISEAP needs to fulfil is that Australia's government has implemented a national language policy for universities. ISEAP in the U.K. context can be hard to pin down: it plays a part in filling a vague attainment vacuum, to enhance student learning, and contributes towards meeting grand, if ill-defined, objectives. ISEAP in Australia (or 'post-entry,' as it is more likely termed in this context), on the other hand, has a more explicit purpose: to help meet specific English language outcomes which apply to all graduates. A landmark article by Birrell (2006) contributed to a national discussion about language competence in Australia. Entitled 'Implications of Low English Standards Among Overseas Students at Australian Universities,' he reported that a third of international students obtaining residence visas following graduation did not meet the minimum English requirement for professional employment. This opened questions about Australian universities' entry standards and the extent to which students developed linguistically during their studies. Subsequently, the Tertiary Education Quality and Standards Agency (TEQSA) was formed. Its standards framework specifies not only that higher education providers have 'strong English language requirements,' but that they 'are also required to offer support services that are *informed by the needs of their student cohorts*' (TEQSA, 2019) (our emphasis). This specific requirement for universities to support students' linguistic needs provides a strong impetus for investment into post-entry/ISEAP courses.

The Office for Students (the United Kingdom's equivalent regulatory body) has no such language support requirement. In 2021, it reported that 'inclusive assessment' practices employed by universities (possibly in the spirit of Ryan and Carroll's (2005) suggested approach, outlined above) meant that 'spelling, punctuation and grammar' were not taken into account in assessment, which it reports subsequently contributed to perceived grade inflation (Office for Students, 2021). This claim is arguable to say the least, but what is important for our purposes is that beyond the relatively low CEFR B1 level required for student visas, U.K. regulation of English language is much more 'hands off,' leaving decisions about English language support entirely up to each institution. This means that in-sessional courses operate in a far more variegated landscape in the United Kingdom, with less clearly defined outcomes and subsequently varied levels of investment. Factors like the types of degrees a university offers, its student demographics, the amount of funding available for 'support,' and the relative influence of its EAP centre become important factors in the form ISEAP takes in the United Kingdom.

The implication of the TEQSA regulation is a high level of investment in student support and the form this takes is usually more than a one-size-fits-all approach. Instead, it is likely to be more embedded and based on an analysis of needs, often at modular level. It is not unusual for Australian universities to screen students' English language abilities at entry as a way of identifying this. As an Australian interviewee put it:

> In the standards, it says that universities have to ensure that students who need to develop their language – and I think they use the word English – are identified and that they receive follow-up language development, that they're provided with opportunities. So because that is in the standards, it means universities can be audited for that … We're in the job of making sure that if TEQSA came, if the university got audited, that they're able to say, 'yup, this is what we're doing.'

Such an institutionally driven approach is much less likely in the United Kingdom, due to its lighter regulatory context and less defined language policies – nationally and institutionally. However, in Australia, the likely importance of ISEAP to a university fulfilling TEQSA requirements can provide EAP centres with visibility – for students and staff – and a level of investment that may be unusual elsewhere. Also central to the Australian context is language support not only for international students, but students from migrant backgrounds and indigenous groups. For these cohorts, English may not be the first language, and the TEQSA requirements call for an increasing level of English language support for these too. Another of our Australian interviewees highlighted a stark contrast with the United Kingdom, where the government's interest in language level mainly concerns entry, a deciding factor for granting student visas:

> We can't just be looking at entry. We have to be looking at English language development over the whole period of their study, and so [the institution] had to make a quite convincing statement about entry standards: how students would be supported at the beginning of the course and how they will continue to be supported in academic English over the duration of their study in that particular course, and that relates to what are called 'graduate attributes' that the university has, and communication is a top one there.

Graduate attributes describe 'the skills, knowledge and abilities of university graduates, beyond disciplinary content knowledge, which are applicable to a range of contexts and are acquired as a result of completing any undergraduate degree' (Barrie, 2006, cited by Alexander, 2020). The concept of graduate attributes is increasingly gaining currency as a part of higher education, as well as in EAP, yet there is currently no comparable bureaucratic requirement in the United Kingdom to which universities are accountable. Thus, a key driver for Australian ISEAP provision is towards greater rigour and visibility, in contrast to the sometimes 'cottage industry' tendencies of ISEAP in the United Kingdom.

1.1.2.2 English as a Medium of Instruction (EMI)

Moving on to consider some of the contexts where English is the medium of instruction, it should be noted that it is beyond the remit of our book to provide a detailed look at all localities. Nevertheless, some guiding principles can be sketched out. Firstly, what exactly is EMI? It is a sometimes disputed term, but we adopt Dearden's (2015) definition: '[t]he use of the English language to teach academic subjects (other than English itself) in countries or jurisdictions in which the majority of the population's first language is not English' (Dearden, 2015, cited by Macaro et al., 2017: 231). In contrast to the way that pre-sessionals are integral to the United Kingdom and Australia's drive for international student recruitment, such courses are unlikely to feature prominently in an EMI landscape. Indeed, student cohorts may not be 'international' as such, but rather the majority are probably 'home' (or local) students studying in English, which for most is an additional language. EAP itself in these contexts is for the most part probably some form of ISEAP. The drive for internationalisation, especially in research outputs, has led to whole territories moving – sometimes very rapidly – towards delivering their programmes in English. A key difference compared with many contexts then is scale; while ISEAP is most often targeted towards particular groups in the U.K. context, or possibly identified via some form of screening activity in Australia, in an EMI context the target is more likely to be all students, i.e. it is inherently less targeted when English is not the first language of the vast majority of students. As we shall see, debates are ongoing about the degree of embeddedness and specificity of ISEAP provision in the United Kingdom, with some degrees being supported by quite tailored discipline-specific provision. In EMI settings, there is likely to be less debate: it may well be the case that all students require academic literacy work, and therefore a high degree of discipline specificity is impractical. An interviewee based in Turkey told us that:

> We are trying to imitate what they're expected to do in their departments. But not around the topic of their discipline, but in a general discipline that is applicable … students are mixed discipline-wise in our English classes, but these are general skills: you [students] are expected to do this at university.

There is a greater likelihood that provision will be modularised and credit-bearing, taken by an entire cohort, with a requirement to pass the ISEAP module's assessment. Even where there are efforts to link to disciplinary contexts, by necessity these take a fairly general EGAP (English for General Academic Purposes) approach. An exception to this may be found in Hakim's (2021) work. She explains the process of implementing embedded literacy support for a newly initiated EMI context in Lebanon. Informed by Galloway and Rose's (2021) calls for greater integration of EAP support within EMI disciplinary contexts, she demonstrates the benefits of collaboration with disciplinary specialists and explores the possibilities for discipline-specific provision in an EMI setting. While still relatively rare in EMI, Hakim's case study suggests that a move towards more discipline-informed ISEAP in the United Kingdom and Australia is having an influence.

In South Africa's multilingual context, students on ISEAP courses are largely local, yet English may well be a second or third language (just 9.6 percent of South Africa's population identify as having English as a first language (Khokhlova, 2015). Unlike secondary education, at the university level there is a requirement to study using English as the medium of instruction. Furthermore, access to higher education is widening; both of these factors drive a need for compulsory in-sessionals, which may well be credit-bearing and must be passed in order to graduate. The scale and reach of provision is therefore much greater than is typical in anglophone contexts. As with Australia, it is also more likely to align with national educational agendas. A South African interviewee drew attention to this:

> There's a big drive for multilingualism at the moment in universities generally; the decolonisation agenda is also important, which we think about in a large part of our curriculum development.

Returning to our opening question, 'What are you trying to do?,' this again demonstrates the situatedness of ISEAP: courses' learning outcomes are greatly context-dependent.

In most European EMI contexts, the educational context itself is likely driven by national initiatives aimed at increasing countries' global competitiveness. However, the drivers for ISEAP provision may well be more ad hoc in nature, depending on local university circumstances. In the absence of the national language agendas we have seen in Australia and South Africa, ISEAP may take forms more similar to the U.K. context. ISEAP may find its place by meeting localised needs where identified, often through informal contacts with subject academics. An interviewee in Norway remarked upon a kind of 'institutional invisibility' to their work, which may be familiar to U.K. readers, stating:

> There's no framework [for ISEAP provision]. It's very random and ad hoc unfortunately, very person-dependent.

Without a university language policy that gives credence to the importance of language experts, ISEAP does not necessarily become an integral part of students' educational experience. But this is not necessarily true of all EMI contexts. Another interviewee, an educational developer responsible for language support at another northern European university, presented a much more systematised approach:

> Lecturers decide when and where student support is needed throughout the curriculum, and then the team arrives with the tools.

Here, ISEAP is far more embedded and integral to the students' experience. Subject lecturers might not always be best placed to identify students' linguistic needs; see, for example, the instances of unclear feedback given on students' work by disciplinary experts reported by Lea and Street: 'The conflicting advice received from academic teaching staff in different courses added to [students'] confusion' (1998: 164). However, this approach does perhaps aid the beginnings of the kind of systematised needs analysis integral to successful ISEAP. This will be detailed in Chapter 3.

As EMI contexts differ so greatly, another possible by-product of EMI delivery is limited investment in ISEAP provision, especially where English language proficiency is high among students, as is often the case in northern Europe, for example. Where overall English levels are lower, the pressures placed upon EAP practitioners are similar to many other contexts, with the responsibility for language issues being seen as their domain. An interviewee working in a Turkish EMI context contributed this:

> We have done a lot of work to teach the other colleagues in the subject, professors, in that it's impossible: we cannot be the only ones who teach [English] and you can't just expect the students to be taught it [at the EAP centre] and it'll be okay. It needs to be enforced through your classes, through your feedback, through your consciousness about language issues.

The tensions here between subject lecturers and EAP practitioners highlight some of the issues within certain EMI contexts. The expectation upon ISEAP to be able to 'fix' language issues with limited resources is likely to be familiar to many EAP practitioners. The orientation of EAP towards raising language awareness of lecturers, in addition to students, is an area that will be discussed in more detail as the book progresses. However, the belief that responsibility for language development and awareness does not solely sit with EAP professionals, that all educators have a responsibility for language issues, chimes with Bond's notion that '[l]anguage should be embedded within the taught curriculum' (2020: 176).

Considering the possibility of a more integrated approach to language development in EMI settings, it is worth briefly drawing attention to CLIL: Content and Language Integrated Learning. This area of pedagogic practice focusses on language development that takes place within the delivery of content. It is therefore distinct from EMI, which simply shifts the language of instruction, not working towards distinct language-informed learning outcomes. CLIL is less common in tertiary settings, but it does point towards a way in which the content specialist might also become the language expert. In settings where it gains a foothold, the development of CLIL has the potential to shift the balance away from ISEAP. In-sessional activities will be less relevant if language outcomes are already integral to a curriculum. While not advocating that CLIL is adopted as a pedagogic approach, Wingate (2015) does push towards an integration of literacy development within core subject curriculums. This is not to say that ISEAP should cease to exist, but such initiatives and ideas indicate that ISEAP should not be set in stone; its utility comes from its responsiveness to particular contextual factors, not just about what to teach but whom. This returns us to one of the questions posed at the beginning of the chapter.

1.2 'Who Are You Trying to Target It At?'

In considering who our students are, this section will also look at the associated aspects including identifying and meeting student needs, reaching the desired cohorts, and perceptions and principles of our EAP practice. It will review various ways of working with subject academics in setting up ISEAP courses and then survey some of the common forms courses take.

1.2.1 Student Needs

It should be clear from the discussion above that ISEAP is primarily concerned with linguistic development. But this is unlikely to be the kind of decontextualised easily digested language provision still common on, say, IELTS preparation courses or even universities' pre-sessionals. Rather, ISEAP's focus is on language in the context of academic literacy development. One of our interviewees made the point that:

> English for Academic Purposes is not a student need. It is not something that students ascribe to; it is a label that we give it for convenience. Students don't have general academic needs. They have discipline-specific needs that relate to their particular programme. It's we who generalise, find commonalities, because it is convenient … The only need for the student is: yes, this applies to you.

Students are unlikely to identify themselves as needing EAP, but they may well benefit from a course specifically aimed at developing their ability to participate actively, and perhaps fully, in their discourse communities. Thus, we need to consider where provision should be directed as one of ISEAP's main purposes.

A commonly cited articulation of the aim of EAP is to prepare students for 'the cognitive, social and linguistic demands of specific academic disciplines' (Hyland and Hamp-Lyons, 2002: 2). This emphasis on linguistic demands is key to our understanding of ISEAP, acknowledging not only its roots in English Language Teaching (ELT), but also working with specific disciplinary discourses. As EAP practitioners are unlikely to be, and arguably should not be, experts in specific disciplinary fields, in-sessionals often benefit from a textual-analytical approach. By using a set of discourse analytical tools, ISEAP can serve to identify specific features of a genre. These tools can be taught to students to foster learner independence or students' learning from this process can be applied directly to their own written production. This approach is commonly used in ISEAP, and is one which largely avoids teaching the discrete skills one might expect on a preparation course; instead, the focus is on the actual practices students engage in when they are doing their degree. Most ISEAP courses have a strong focus on the development of students' disciplinary writing abilities, simply because written genres are still the main form of assessment on most degrees. It should also be noted that writing skills do not sit in isolation from reading, a point made forcibly by Wingate (2015), who advocates purposeful teaching of active reading skills as a key part of academic literacy development, to enable students to find appropriate sources, select from them and put them into the service of their own writing. (It is again worth emphasising that reading and writing may not be the exclusive focus for in-sessionals: development of seminar and listening skills may well be an appropriate focus for ISEAP in some contexts.) Methodologies and approaches for ISEAP will be discussed in more detail in Chapter 2, but for our immediate purposes we must ask, if we identify that student needs relate to their programme and are discipline-specific, how do we successfully target our provision?

1.2.2 ISEAP for All?

Despite its roots in ELT, and the fact that EAP centres' income and re-sourcing are often based on preparatory courses for international students, increasingly ISEAP's remit lies beyond solely students for whom English is an additional language (EAL). In many institutions, ISEAP is recognised as beneficial for, and is therefore offered to, all students within a cohort. One of our interviewees was emphatic about the need for in-sessionals to be directed towards, what they called:

> ... the academic literacy needs that *every* [their emphasis] student new to university has.

If all students have academic literacy needs, why direct limited provision towards particular demographics? Bourdieu and Passeron's (1994: 8) epithet that 'academic language is ... no one's mother tongue' is often cited within EAP, and leaving aside discussion about the actual context of this quote (e.g. by Ding, 2019), it is usually understood to signify that fluency in academic discourses is not innate or a 'given,' but rather develops through a process of acquisition *by all students* as they gain fuller membership of their discipline. ISEAP plays a part in this, with pedagogies intended at making the inchoate become clearer and exposing the often hidden underlying knowledge that has given rise to particular practices. Increasingly, universities are waking up to this and reevaluating the nature of their ISEAP provision. They may, for example, have recognised that this aligns well with university strategies ad-dressing attainment gaps and attrition. Access to courses for all students is where we see many of the best practices of ISEAP emerging, yet this still sits in contrast to more common paradigms for delivery. At one of our own institutions, for example, the in-sessional webpage describes courses as being for '[s]tudents who use English as an Additional Language, such as interna-tional and EU students' (Goldsmiths, 2022a).

1.2.3 Academic Literacy or Skills Development?

Whichever model of delivery is adopted – directed at 'international' students or for all – the focus must be on the development of students' academic literacy. This term has been defined variously and is sometimes conflated with generic 'study skills' provision. However, in this book we adhere to Wingate's (2015: 6) definition, that academic literacy is 'the ability to communicate competently in an academic discourse community.' This focus on communication emphasises both its linguistic and social aspects. An obvious corollary of this is a focus for ISEAP on epistemologies, i.e. what counts as knowledge within a specific disciplinary context. Students need to develop an understanding of these aspects in order to begin to grapple with the essential academic arguments of their discipline and develop their own voice and position within them. Academic literacy cannot be reductively presented as simply 'language skills.' The focus on literacy and disciplinary communication inherent in academic literacy is important, distinguishing it from a purely skills-based approach, as exemplified for example by Cottrell's popular *The Study Skills Handbook* (2019) and other publications, which are not informed by any particular discipline, but rather outline perceived good practices of successful students. In the U.K. it is not uncommon for 'academic support' to be shared between an EAP centre, where international students are directed, with a likely perception of deficit, and a skills-based centre (often termed something like a Study Skills, Academic Skills or Student Learning Centre), the latter pitched at home students, assumed L1 speakers of English. Leaving aside for the moment the common division into L1 and L2 users being an overly simplistic distinction, our key consideration here is that a skills-based approach most commonly refers to interventions aimed at improving students' participation and attainment that lack the linguistic discourse-analytical focus that characterises EAP.

As long ago as 1998, Lea and Street presented a critique of 'the study skills approach,' in part because it positions student development within a deficit model. It is based on the (incorrect) assumption that literacy is 'a set of atomised skills which students have to learn and which are then transferable to other contexts' (Lea and Street, 1998: 158). Although the writers recognised in 1998 that a lot of provision had moved on from the crudity of this approach, it is remarkable that even today, skills centres can be found delivering such technicist, decontextualised provision. In 1993, Dudley-Evans highlighted that biologists and engineers follow differing argument structures (cited by Hyland, 2006: 52) yet, perhaps due to the considerable resourcing implications of bespoke provision, such differences are often passed over in skills-based support. Study skills guidance is commonly delivered as one-to-one consultations or as one-off sessions rather than the types of courses common to ISEAP, and it is not uncommon for students to be directed to online, self-study materials offering 'one-size-fits-all' guidance on academic style and generic advice on surface features like linking words and academic vocabulary. The issues with this approach are put succinctly by Turner (2011: 81), who makes the point that '[the] relationship between thinking and writing is at best symbiotic rather than mechanistic,' an intrinsic relationship that is not always recognised by institutional decision makers.

EAP practitioners' reservations about the generic nature of study skills interventions was borne out by some of our interviews. One interviewee described the contrast between study skills advisers and EAP practitioners at their institution. The more specific nature of contextualised ISEAP provision probably demands more of practitioners, students, and disciplinary academics:

> What [study skills advisers] do is assumed to be successful, whether they go and give a lecture on referencing, academics like the idea of, 'oh, there's been a lecture on referencing; everybody will be able to reference now.' Their understanding and confidence in us requires a lot more work.

It is difficult to generalise about universities' activities in this area, and it should be noted that the assertion we make about the prevalence of generic study skills provision is partly based on personal experience. As the limited findings of Wingate and Tribble's 2013 survey for Universities UK (cited by Wingate, 2015) demonstrate, this area of an institution's activities is very often occluded, but what their findings do show is that provision at that time was mostly generic in nature. As Wingate (2015: 48) comments, '[the] fact that most of the support is provided by libraries or study skills units with seemingly no involvement of academics in the disciplines is … unsatisfactory.' Anecdotally, we are aware that there seems to be some movement away from this model, yet an absence of published studies makes it difficult to state this definitively.

The picture we present of skills centres' activities is not to suggest that all are engaged in simplistic, remedial interventions. The divide between EAP and skills provision may not always be clear-cut, and indeed the positioning of EAP centres within university structures varies greatly. Ding and Bruce (2017) consider this at some length, noting that positioning often provides an indicator of the status the university accords to EAP activities: whether EAP is seen as a support service or an academic field in its own right. Nevertheless, it is important to make the point that even if a university explicitly identifies EAP as a service, say as a study skills unit within the library, this does not necessarily mean its provision is simplistic or decontextualised. Our interviews attest to practitioners having developed high-quality collaborative ISEAP *courses* (not just one-off interventions) from within the auspices of the library, finding possibilities for effective provision in spite of where they are positioned within the university. One of our interviewees, a director of a large EAP centre, commented:

> Someone once described EAP units as political footballs in the university. I think that's a very good way of putting it. We're in professional services right now. There are things that really bug me about it, but there are pluses as well.

The pluses in this case stem from the financial autonomy afforded by a successful pre-sessional course, funds from which can then partly be deployed into quality ISEAP provision.

The pitching of ISEAP towards EAL (English as an additional language) students is inherent in how many universities see its international cohorts. However, given the problems discussed above, such positioning is unlikely to be meeting the needs of the many students outside of this designation.

1.2.4 Positioning of ISEAP

When considering how we target our provision, issues of status and visibility for EAP centres become prevalent. Earlier on in this chapter, some implications concerning the limited visibility of ISEAP were discussed, in particular how an institution may see EAP's role as merely tidying up language issues, rather than making a substantive contribution to students' overall learning development. However, even where ISEAP courses are given prominence and are accessible beyond the traditional scope of 'international' students, problems still arise. 'Support' is one of the most commonly used terms to describe in sessional activities, and indeed it is a term that is occasionally used in this book. But we also recognise that it is one that needs careful use. It can inadvertently position in-sessional activities in a subservient role, seen as serving the needs of other departments rather than focusing on enabling learning opportunities for its participants. Raimes (1991) termed this the 'butler's stance,' where practitioners who value disciplinary knowledge over the content inherent in EAP 'see language courses as service courses, in service of the larger academic community' (1991: 243). In using this term, it is EAP practitioners who see themselves as servile, yet this may have knock-on effects on how EAP is understood institutionally. Interestingly, the majority of our interviewees did not see themselves this way; they recognised some inherent institutional factors that encourage such positioning, but it is not how they conceptualised their own ISEAP practices. One EAP practitioner we interviewed put this succinctly and unambiguously in describing the EAP centre's relationship to other departments:

> We are not butlers. We are definitely colleagues.

However, in the same interview, their colleague talked about some of the subtle challenges in navigating this area of practice:

> It's a bit of a tightrope. How do you be perceived as helpful and collegiate versus undermining their [subject lecturers'] expertise and their status? It's a tricky one. I find myself taking one step forward, taking one step back quite often with that.

They went on to suggest that emotional intelligence and diplomacy are key skills for practitioners working in ISEAP, in order to figure out how a relationship will work with particular subject academics. Of course, a necessary starting point is for the latter to recognise the value and expertise EAP practitioners bring, and perhaps this comes indirectly by seeing the effects of ISEAP interventions, from student feedback or in improved work from students.

Awareness of the issue of professional status means that some EAP practitioners and centres may go to great lengths (we ourselves are not immune to this) to avoid 'the s-word'; instead of 'support' in-sessional activities may be articulated as 'opportunities for development,' 'instruction,' and other more empowering terms. But the institutions themselves are unlikely to be as nuanced in their choice of terminology.

Within all of the activities EAP practitioners engage in, it is in ISEAP where this positioning as butlers is most prevalent. A pre-sessional's *raison d'etre* is naturally to prepare students for their actual degrees, yet as it is more or less independent from other programmes – with its own learning aims, syllabus, assessment regime, quality processes, and certification – it is less likely to be seen as a 'butler.' It may too lack the visibility of an in-sessional, often taking place during the summer outside of the main activities of the university. ISEAP, on the other hand, taking place in tandem with disciplinary teaching and more likely to result from some form of cooperative involvement, can more easily be seen in the service of other departments, even by practitioners themselves (as Raimes (1991: 243) argues). This being the case, such a designation of ISEAP activities among senior management and subject academics is also probable. Yet literacy is not a service; developing the ability to express oneself within disciplinary discourses is surely an essential learning outcome on any degree, even if not explicitly articulated as such. As we shall see, best ISEAP practices arise from a reversal of a common 'tendency to work *for* rather than *with* subject specialists'

(Hyland and Hamp-Lyons, 2002: 3). Interactions tend to be more productive if all parties are on an equal footing, rather than having the EAP practitioner placed in a servile position. If it is possible to set such ground rules, they can help obviate the butler's stance.

If being positioned as a service is problematic, an alternative, and perhaps more empowering, orientation for ISEAP teaching practice is to be a 'meddler-in-the-middle' (McWilliam, 2009). On an in-sessional, the EAP practitioner is unlikely to be in a position to 'deliver' content; indeed one would hope that the students themselves might have a stronger, more detailed understanding of disciplinary knowledge. It is entirely expected that students will experience confusion and disorientation at various stages of their disciplinary learning, perhaps especially at the beginning, when in-sessionals may typically be delivered. Rather than trying to resolve this for them, by trying to answer students' questions, the meddler is 'mutually involved with students in assembling and/or dis-assembling knowledge' (McWilliam, 2009: 288). While McWilliam is not writing about EAP, but rather broader pedagogies used to encourage creativity, this active approach to classroom learning is highly suited to discipline-aware in-sessional contexts. Teacher and student enjoy equal status, creating an environment for exploration, of high engagement, where students are critically aware and questioning. In terms of disciplinary discourse and knowledge practices, it offers a framework that enables students to work though, co-theorise, and find answers, as an alternative to their discourse practices being regulated and passively receiving the way things are. As we know from social constructivist pedagogies (e.g. Vygotsky, 1978), this sense of discovery and ownership over one's learning can enable deeper and speedier acquisition.

This approach can be seen as an affordance opened up by the continuities of a weekly in-sessional class; this working through of problems with the students is time consuming, and so is probably beyond the possibilities of a study skills approach or one-off technicist interventions. It is actually articulated as one of the guiding principles in a particular U.K. EAP centre, where one of our interviewees explained the usefulness of meddling to students:

> Just giving students an opportunity to talk about their writing in peer review sessions … A lot of the [subject] academics know that this is a valuable activity. They don't have the time within their programmes to cover that because there's so much quote-unquote 'content' for them to cover.

Meddling in ISEAP is valuable to students as it provides a space for learning and active experimentation that may be lacking in students' substantive programmes, especially with regard to working through and identifying their own discourse practices. It can also benefit the EAP practitioners, moving them away from a service orientation.

Another concept relevant to a discussion of the positioning of ISEAP is that of Threshold Concepts, developed by Meyer and Land (2003). As students encounter the 'troublesome knowledge' of their disciplines, they are likely to experience alienation and a sense of illogicality. While attempting to grasp this, students occupy what Meyer and Land call the 'liminal space' until they cross the threshold into understanding and a sense of ownership over the knowledge. Integral to this way of understanding the learning process is that learning is a 'transformational experience,' a term often used by universities in their mission statements (as in Goldsmiths, University of London's (2022b) for example: 'We offer a transformative experience, generating knowledge and stimulating self-discovery through creative, radical and intellectually rigorous thinking and practice.'). ISEAP can be seen as an attempt to enable students to successfully navigate the liminal space towards transformative learning. In her explanation of Threshold Concepts, Bond (2020: 143) cautions how learners can become 'stuck,' describing liminal spaces 'where there are multiple layers of almost knowing and where a mimicked understanding may become fossilised.'

The meddler-in-the-middle ISEAP teacher can productively work with students at this stage, in co-constructing disciplinary understandings and practices. Nevertheless, in order to gain awareness of some essential principles, some form of collaboration between practitioners and subject lecturers is very helpful to ISEAP curriculum development, and this forms the basis for the section that follows.

1.2.5 Cooperation and Collaboration

However we perceive our work, in order to be most effective at reaching our desired cohorts in ISEAP there is likely to be some degree of working with subject lecturers. Dudley-Evans and St John (1998) make the distinction between '**co-operation**,' '**collaboration**,' and '**team teaching**' to describe different levels at which EAP practitioners can work with disciplinary specialists on the formation of courses.

Co-operation puts the onus on the EAP specialist, according to Hyland (2006: 187), 'asking questions and gathering information about the students' subject course.' This may be informal in nature, with the EAP practitioner as the more active participant, making contact to find out about a cohorts' needs and the discourse practices of the discipline. (A more formal guide to conducting a needs analysis will be presented in Chapter 3 on logistics.) It is the EAP specialist who is then responsible for designing materials and implementing the course. There may well be trade-offs as both parties work towards developing a cooperative working relationship. With inherent inequalities between participants, there is a danger here of placing the EAP practitioner in a subordinate role, i.e. the butler's stance (Raimes, 1991), as discussed in section 1.2.4 above. With co-operation, the resulting in-sessional course is likely to be a standalone, and most likely an optional adjunct to students' main programmes of study. This is not in itself a bad thing, but there are limits placed upon the degree of integration of the ISEAP provision.

Collaboration, as the word suggests, describes a more equal relationship among participants. Here, both parties have input into the creation of materials and course design, yet it is again delivered by the EAP practitioner. This paradigm may offer greater opportunities for washback from the EAP component, influencing the main programme of study through linguistically aware, student-centred pedagogies, and so potentially improving its delivery. True collaboration is more likely to result in embedded provision with perhaps a more nuanced understanding of disciplinary practices and discourses. It is not a given that this would be more useful to students, but Hyland (2006: 88) highlights some advantages:

> More integrated forms of involvement are likely to bring further benefits and we are likely to see more of these pursued in the future, as content and EAP teachers gain greater understanding of each other's work and build up, over time, a working relationship of trust and respect.

His optimism seems well placed: our interviews suggest that in a number of institutions collaboration has become deeper and on an increasingly equal footing, resulting in higher-quality, disciplinary focussed ISEAP provision. We would therefore generally advocate collaboration over cooperation as a means of enhancing in-sessional courses.

Team teaching is where both subject lecturer and EAP practitioner are responsible for the delivery of a course, either by teaching sessions concurrently or designing the course together and teaching different sessions. Division of labour during the course is most probably on language-content lines, with both parties working within their own field of expertise. Dudley-Evans and St John (1998) identify three key elements for successful team teaching: the clear identification of roles, respect for each other's areas of expertise, and finally they suggest that the demands placed on the subject lecturer are relatively low in order to encourage their participation. As one of our interviewees commented (as reported above), navigating this relationship can be 'a bit of a tightrope.' Yet Dudley-Evans and St John's re-commendations can help set up some basic principles to help allay suspicions or fears, and build towards successful teamwork.

Depending on the working context, there may well be limitations on the degree of collaboration that is possible. But as a minimum, in order for a disciplinary focussed in-sessional course to be successful, EAP lecturers will need access to the types of texts students have to read, their task types, and the ways in which information is delivered. And indeed, this is possible through 'mere' cooperation: with subject lecturers acting as informants for the EAP practitioner, the latter can build up a picture of disciplinary literacy practices. Wingate (2015: 58) comments that these three levels can be seen as stages, where EAP practitioners' relationships with subject specialists can deepen over time, moving towards ever greater collaboration, from co-operation towards team teaching.

Interestingly, one of our interviewees – the director of a large EAP centre – highlighted the potentially fraught nature of collaboration. In contrast to a benign relationship between EAP and subject academics, they suggested:

> We need to educate our subject colleagues: not just to work *with* them. And they might think we work *for* them, but rather we need to work *on* them: we need to have a symbiotic relationship. [Italics indicate the speaker's emphasis]

The emphasis here is on educating non-EAP colleagues about focussed work on academic literacy development and the benefits ISEAP can bring to their students' learning experience and outcomes. The different roles adopted by an ISEAP practitioner in the wider institution, and the soft power they can exert, will be discussed more fully in Chapters 5 and 6.

Collaboration amongst different departments in an institution is precarious by its nature. It may be difficult to identify the best person to initiate such a relationship, and also difficult to sustain as initial enthusiasm wanes. Chapter 3, on logistical aspects, will draw on some case studies of successful and less suc-cessful collaboration, in order to reflect upon how practitioners can thrive in their context and deliver purposeful and effective courses.

1.2.6 Integration

A related factor that sits alongside the degree of collaboration is how integrated provision is: is it an adjunct to the main programme of study, or an integral part of it? This has serious implications for the effectiveness of insessional provision. Collaboration, as described above, may open up opportunities for integrated ISEAP provision. Or integrated provision may be developed through the intervention of a 'champion' in senior management. Making the case for integrated and inclusive provision, Wingate (2015: 60) presents a comparison of 'curriculum-integrated' academic literacy development with three other broad types: 'curriculum-linked,' 'additional' and 'extra-curricular.' A table summarising these main features of these types is presented below (Table 1.1).

Table 1.1 Increasing levels of integration

Type	Extra-curricular	Additional	Curriculum-linked	Curriculum-integrated
Location	Outside department	Outside timetable	Timetabled	Timetabled, credit-bearing
Delivery	EAP teachers	EAP teachers	Subject lecturers EAP teachers	Subject lecturers EAP teachers
Collaboration	None	Some input from subject lecturers	Equal contribution to design and delivery	input/advice from EAP teachers
Focus	Grammar, lexis, style, structure, referencing	Literacy conventions, genres, text features	Literacy conventions, genres, text features, argumentation	Literacy conventions, genres, text features, language for the creation of meaning and knowledge
Materials	Unspecific texts	Texts/tasks from the discipline	Texts/task directly linked to classroom content	Texts/task directly linked to classroom content
Participation	Exclusive/ Remedial	Semi-inclusive	Semi-inclusive	Fully inclusive

Adapted from Wingate (2015: 60).

This comparison presents some of the broad tendencies among different paradigms for delivery. The table maps fairly closely to Dudley-Evans and St John's levels of cooperation, aligning other factors in ISEAP delivery with this key consideration. The degree to which provision is integrated, or even embedded, is the other main aspect in this table, which then has implications for the form it takes. We can see some of the key dichotomies of in-sessional provision categorised between two extremes. It seeks answers to questions like:

- Do students have to do ISEAP classes in their own time, or are they an integral part of their disciplinary curriculum?
- Is it a 'cinderella' class, invisible to subject lecturers, or is it referred to by them in their own practice?
- Do the ISEAP learning outcomes align closely to the subject ones?
- Is it an optional or compulsory course?
- Is the course targeted at a specific group (most likely international students, with its implications of remediation) or does it seek to develop academic literacy needs of all students?
- Does ISEAP content relate to students' disciplinary content or does it lack this context?

By grouping these tendencies together, the categorisations present an outline of some of the main forms in-sessional courses take. Wingate herself advocates provision that is as curriculum-integrated as possible, with EAP practitioners working closely with disciplinary colleagues, possibly through secondment to the academic department.

It should be noted, however, that this is not seen as an ideal by all. A longstanding debate in EAP is between proponents of EGAP (English for General Academic Purposes) and ESAP (English for Specific Academic Purposes).

1.2.7 EGAP vs. ESAP Approaches

de Chazal (2014: 38) presents a comparison of the two approaches, re-cognising certain advantages of EGAP. An obvious one is how it places fewer demands on the EAP practitioner, requiring less expertise about specific disciplinary discourse practices. Furthermore, he notes that 'the EAP teacher and the EAP students are responsible for investigating and constructing knowledge of academic practices' (de Chazal, 2014: 36). There are com-monalities then with the 'meddler-in-the-middle' role that teachers might adopt, as described in section 1.2.4 above. This emphasis on student and teacher working as equals in co-investigation can be fruitful and particularly adaptive to disciplinary unpredictability. On the other hand, EGAP is likely to rely on the use of what might be called 'EAP texts' (Alexander et al., 2019: 27) in the classroom, rather than the authentic disciplinary texts students would actually be reading. In this less situated approach, the relevance of the class content may well be experienced as tangential by the students.

Context is as ever a deciding factor: ESAP inevitably requires a greater investment, making use of informants to research discourse practices: it is 'demanding in terms of material preparation and liaison time between EAP teachers and subject lecturers' (Alexander et al., 2019: 29). Even de Chazal, despite being an proponent of EGAP, recognises that in order to address students' needs, an ESAP approach is better suited to in-sessional contexts. Hyland (2006: 12) outlines the essential reasons for this: 'an ESAP view recognizes the complexities of engaging in the specific literacies of the disciplines,' and is broadly representative of the approach taken throughout this book.

Seeking a middle ground between the two approaches, one of our interviewees presented themselves as a proponent of what they termed:

> English for Multiple Disciplinary Academic Purposes or what I call 'tools not rules.'

They expressed an awareness of the dangers of 'training' students to meet specific outcomes, such as individual module assessments, rather than equipping students with the ability to manage multiple tasks and situations. In this paradigm, ISEAP certainly needs to be informed by disciplinary practices, but should not seek to train students towards narrowly defined specific outcomes, rather it should educate students to be able to respond to a wider range of possible disciplinary situations (training versus education is a distinction made by Widdowson (1983), cited by Dudley-Evans and St John, 1998: 42). As we shall see, this is one of the tensions inherent in highly embedded provision; as EAP practitioners develop their disciplinary knowledge, they may be tempted to take on the role of an expert. This can be detrimental; if they are not involved in actual scholarship in the discipline, their understanding may be partial or easily become out of date. In such situations, ESAP could therefore actually be detrimental to students' development. As the interviewee above put it:

> Our [EAP practitioners'] ignorance is useful.

Adaptability, flexibility and agility are key to successful ISEAP practice, whether highly embedded or more general. The following section reviews some of the most common forms of ISEAP course by positioning them on a Cartesian plane.

1.2.8 Types of ISEAP Courses

Wingate's chart in Table 1.1 above aligns different aspects of provision as usually sitting together, e.g. an extra-curricular ISEAP course is less likely to focus on literacy conventions than an embedded one. But this is not necessarily the case. It may also be helpful to consider the form ISEAP provision takes by plotting it on continua between two interconnected axes (Figure 1.1).

In this conceptualisation, it is perhaps easier to identify where one's own ISEAP provision lies. The following paragraphs examine how these forms may play out in practice.

In the **top left** we can find one of the most common paradigms: an **optional extra-curricular course probably directed towards specific cohorts**, most likely EAL students. As this is not a part of students' timetables, to be successful it relies on the students' self-selection and availability. In order to be relevant to students' studies, it is likely to be the result of some form of cooperation from the subject specialist, perhaps providing texts and assignment types. The EAP practitioner will work with what an informant provides to create materials that respond to the disciplinary contexts. Advantages to this

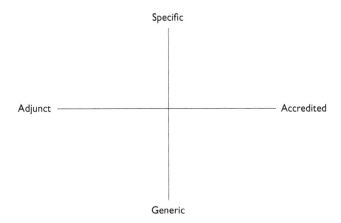

Figure 1.1 Different forms of ISEAP provision.

model include the likely relevance to students' programmes. The EAP lecturer, with the aid of their informant(s), can construct a syllabus that is responsive to student needs. The fact that it is an adjunct, non-credit-bearing course also enables a good deal of flexibility. Areas of practical concern come from the precarious nature of cooperation: it is heavily reliant on the ongoing goodwill of the subject lecturer, someone with a likely interest in teaching and learning matters. If their role changes or they move on, cooperative relations may have to begin again from scratch. As it is extra-curricular, attendance may well be an issue, particularly where students have high demands placed upon them, such as around assignment deadlines. There can be considerable attrition as the course progresses, despite the teacher's best efforts at ensuring relevance. There are also limited opportunities to track the efficacy of the in-sessional intervention; the EAP teacher may know little about students' attainment beyond the ISEAP setting. In fact, they are likely to only have a partial purview of their students; most of the time in this setting, students' contributions are unassessed, and it may be that the teacher is not able to see the students' work in any detail. Some of these issues were summarised by an interviewee as follows:

> The ones that really would benefit from coming don't tend to come; there's kind of a contradiction where we don't want to be 'deficit-y,' but where we're deployed is where people have identified problems, so there's this massive contradiction in our work; and the fact that we don't get marking time … the way that we're structured is not conducive to that.

Such comments were made by a number of our interviewees who were working with this model of ISEAP, and experiencing issues around attendance, attrition and not being resourced sufficiently to fully engage with the work students produce.

The **top-right** quadrant is more likely to be the result of fuller collaboration. The provision here is a **part of the curriculum, aimed at developing the academic literacy needs of all students**. A 'common-sense' separation of language and content may be partially overturned here, with its focus on foregrounding language matters in the expression of ideas. At its best, this form of ISEAP can help create a situation where, to quote Bond (2020: 172) 'linguistic and content knowledge are harnessed to highlight the metadiscoursal features and forms of knowledge communication employed by a particular discipline and genre.' There is the potential to integrate language and content, for students to work with them symbiotically. Provision may be credit-bearing and independently assessed as a module in its own right. Or perhaps attendance is necessitated, with a certificate awarded but work not graded. Sloan and Porter's (2010) CEM (contextualised, embedded, mapped) Model offers a way such provision can be implemented. This model of curriculum development will be discussed in detail in Chapter 3, on the logistics of provision. For some, this top-right quadrant location is an ideal for ISEAP. Such provision may be delivered through EAP practitioners being seconded to academic departments to become embedded in its discourses and practices. Alternatively, it may be organised centrally via committees, often 'championed' by a member of senior management, with cooperative working parties set up. An advantage of this type of practice is that it is easier to track students. Reaching all students means attainment can be compared across years; it may be possible to see the effect of an ISEAP course by comparing cohorts' attainment before and after it was instituted. An obvious disadvantage is that it requires heavy investment on the part of the institution, in order to reach large swathes of students in a cohort. There is also the inherent danger of too narrow a focus on narrowly defined outcomes that lack transferability beyond this to other learning contexts.

The **bottom left** includes more **decontextualised provision**. Courses on 'grammar for writing,' 'listening to lectures,' 'note taking,' and 'pre-sentation skills' are sometimes offered as part of a suite of in-sessional courses provided by an EAP centre, or may be provided by other agents in the in-stitution, such as library service writing centres or study skills specialists. These sessions are optional, with students being able to pick and choose according to their own perceived needs. They are informed by a skills approach, open to students in a range of disciplines, but offer more than just one-off interven-tions. These are most likely to be directed towards EAL students. They may be attractive to students due to their narrow focus; it is more likely that students can identify their own grammar and academic vocabulary issues, rather than messier, more amorphous, aspects of disciplinary discourses. As one of our interviewees put it:

> 'Non-credit generics' run across the two semesters that students from all over the place can come to voluntarily, and they do actually. We all know the problems of teaching that way: we don't know who's coming from one week to the next … But I do believe they have a function, in some ways a social function for the international students, a safe place to

meet. I have seen students make friendships in those groups and it's been quite meaningful for them. Even though I have doubts about the efficacy of that model, I can see there's a place for it.

This neatly sums up advantages and disadvantages of the model. Wingate's (2015) doubts about the usefulness of decontextualised provision seem well founded, yet a place for students to meet with others across the university undergoing similar experiences undoubtedly has some social value. It is of course predicated on a deficit model, but is a cost-effective way for a university to 'support' its students in language matters.

The **lower-right** quadrant takes into account **generic skills-based modules that are compulsory**. Though still relatively few, they are becoming more common, as universities try to enhance academic literacy for all students, especially where students are from a diverse range of backgrounds. ISEAP here is more visible than in its typical positioning, and this model represents an attempt to ensure all students are equipped to succeed. Such modules are not necessarily credit-bearing, but attendance may be noted on student transcripts. The University of Glasgow's (2018) Academic Writing Skills Programme is a case in point. This is largely delivered online to each year's cohort of incoming undergraduate and PGT students, with a mixture of automated marking and bespoke feedback. Other models include optional credit-bearing in-sessional modules, which by necessity are quite general in nature, the learning from which it is up to the students to apply to other modules they are studying. In this optional model, the modules are mainly directed towards speakers of English as an additional language. There is also the large-scale model of 'post-entry' support in place in some Australian universities, as discussed in section 1.1.2.1 above, where language screening takes place to target need where it is perceived to be most called for. In these types of models, the assessed, credit-bearing, or certificated nature provides an extrinsic motivation for students to engage with the course, but this may just be on the surface, particularly if students do not see its value or self-identify as needing this kind of academic literacy development. There may also be a mismatch between ISEAP assessment and assessment on other modules: it is difficult to ensure utility and relevance to disciplinary approaches. The decontextualised nature of provision combined with what is often technology-led tuition in such models may also compound this. It relies on considerable investment from an institution, yet lacks the highly targeted disciplinary focus of bespoke embedded curriculums.

The focus on the more adjunct or generic models is likely to tend towards inducting students into the norms of a new academic culture, however this is defined. This induction may be at a general institutional level or acculturation towards more specific disciplinary practices. However, it does not have to be uncritical. It is possible to undertake Academic Literacies–informed provision (Lea and Street, 1998) or even Critical EAP pedagogy (Benesch, 2001) within such constraints. These will be discussed more fully in Chapter 2, which considers pedagogic approaches for ISEAP, but it is often the case that engagement with issues of power and discourse depend on practitioners' own particular interests and expertise, rather than being entrenched within the strictures of learning outcomes and syllabus design. Of course, situations where ISEAP is more embedded allow for greater work with a discipline's practices and what counts as legitimate knowledge, and thus a deeper engagement with its academic discourse.

The implementation of any of the above models depends not only on the needs of the students targeted, but also on institutional investment and visibility. The relationship between an institution and its in-sessional provision may not always be harmonious; as Alexander et al. (2019: 107) note, '[i]nstitutional attitudes and practices can undermine the best intentions in syllabus design.' Both consideration given to setting these up and implications for their delivery will be discussed more fully in Chapter 3 on logistical matters.

1.3 'For What Reasons?'

Returning to the last of three questions asked at the beginning of the chapter, this final section hones in on what it is hoped students will gain from attending a course: common learning outcomes and how these relate to the syllabus.

1.3.1 The Content of an ISEAP Course

As a general rule, a course's content is driven by its learning outcomes. Yet ISEAP contexts are largely quite free, sitting outside of common Quality Assurance regimes, and so the usual approaches to course development may not apply. Learning outcomes may be vaguely articulated, or not at all. This situation may be partly caused by a lack of institutional interest, perhaps driven in part by an EAP centre's remit being focussed on international students, meaning in-sessional provision is compartmentalised, perhaps interacting minimally with the wider institution and not subject to its usual mechanisms. Where assessment and measurement of the effect of tuition is missing – as we have seen is often the case in the common ISEAP delivery models described in the section above – it reduces the imperative to have clearly defined outcomes. Nevertheless, where provision is embedded and bespoke to particular programmes or modules, learning outcomes are likely to be that much more narrowly defined, relating to learning attainment as articulated in the actual programme specifications.

To choose a more commonplace example, the kinds of learning outcomes typical to an in-sessional that is informed by the disciplinary considerations may include the following:

Students completing the course will:

- *have gained an enhanced understanding of writing within [the discipline];*
- *be able to express themselves using the appropriate discourse for [the discipline];*
- *make effective use of reading in their written work;*
- *reference work using the discipline's system.*

These example aims are authentic, taken from an optional ISEAP course offered as an adjunct to students' main programmes of study and lacking any independent assessment. The focus is clearly on students' writing, and these outcomes inform the course content. Contributions from subject lecturers in this example may be described as towards the cooperative end of the scale rather than collaborative, which may place limits on the EAP practitioner's understanding of the target situation. This leads to some fairly vague articulations of student development. Despite this, they present a reasonable set of purposes for an in-sessional, but there is an imprecision to the aims, meaning that some phrases (e.g. 'using appropriate discourse') do a lot of heavy lifting. In this example, we may well ask a number of questions of these aims: what do we mean by 'appropriate' or indeed 'discourse' here? What are its features? How are these manifested in written and spoken forms? And how will students be expected to acquire it?

1.3.2 Specificities

In seeking answers to these questions, we are led towards greater engagement with disciplinary specifics. Hyland (2006: 2) emphasises that aims should come from a target situation analysis; ISEAP, as a form of specialised English-language teaching is:

> … grounded in the social, cognitive and linguistic demands of academic target situations, providing focussed instruction informed by an understanding of texts and the constraints of academic contexts.

Not only do academic contexts differ enormously across disciplines, but also within them. Disciplinary approaches, key texts, research methodologies, and understandings of what constitutes academic knowledge may well differ according to the characteristics of the institution or the culture of a department within it. Disciplinary fields like business studies or sociology can take many forms and so a 'one-size-fits-all' approach to ISEAP can be problematic for the multiplicity of reasons explained above. Thus, vaguely articulated ISEAP learning aims may also confuse. The creation of more specific and purposeful learning aims, according to Bruce (2011: 46) requires 'exploration of the diversity of disciplinary contexts and their communicative differences.' In contrast to a pre-sessional, the practice of ISEAP is not concerned with preparation for a future target situation, so much as adaptation to a current one. Compared with standalone preparatory courses, the in-sessional curriculum is more likely to be 'backward' (Richards, 2013) in its design, whereby its conception begins with the learning outcomes, which are informed by a detailed needs analysis, with core competencies ideally identified in collaboration with subject specialists from within a discipline. This backward approach to development contrasts with the 'forward' approach more typical of a pre-sessional, where the curriculum is structured around learning events, perhaps following the structure of a course book, ultimately driving the course assessment. As we have discussed above, assessment itself is not commonplace in ISEAP, even if it does exist in some contexts.

An ISEAP curriculum works towards aiding the development of students becoming active participants within the specificities of their disciplinary contexts. Such highly situated learning outcomes means that ISEAP is, to quote Bond (2020: 54), 'localised, contextualised within a specific institution and may be where EAP practice is most obviously influenced by HE practices rather than language teaching norms.' She is writing about content-led EAP more widely, but this is clearly relevant to ISEAP: EAP at its most situated. ISEAP offers opportunities to align EAP practices more closely with the wider academic context in which they sit, as opposed to the often siloed nature of a pre-sessional. If the influence of wider university approaches and practices are brought to bear, the implication is that ISEAP should present more than guidance on conforming to surface discoursal aspects, but rather it should engage with the perhaps messier aspects of disciplinary knowledge production and presentation.

1.3.3 Accommodationist versus Critical Approaches

The general learning outcomes presented in 1.3.1 above are broadly ac-commodationist in their approach, i.e. the focus is on students adapting to perceived disciplinary conventions in a fairly uncritical way. A more co-operative and nuanced engagement with the target situation can enable a more critical approach to ISEAP, encouraging the student to develop their own voice, rather than simply attempting to mimic existing norms. Bruce (2011: 12) takes the view that 'an effective EAP course has to be both ac-commodationist and critical at the same time'; this may well be especially significant for ISEAP, as students are on their journey towards fuller mem-bership of their discourse communities. Reaching a similar conclusion, Wingate and Tribble (2012) recognise the complementary nature of in-corporating the critical focus of Academic Literacies (Lea and Street, 1998) into more neutral EAP pedagogies. A discussion of the blending of EAP approaches will be picked up in Chapter 2.

It should also be noted that disciplinary specialists and EAP practitioners may be divergent in their aims for an in-sessional, yet this disagreement possibly presents an opportunity for the EAP practitioner to assert their own specialist knowledge. Subject specialists are likely to lack the linguistic awareness and meta-language to be able to explain their discourse requirements. Indeed Lea and Street (1998) suggest that they are often poor at helping students develop these skills, and may well see writing conventions as transparent or self-evident. In formulating learning aims, ISEAP practitioners should naturally be informed by disciplinary experts, but also feel confident to assert their own discourse analytical skills in order to identify key student needs.

A further argument against being purely accommodationist comes from Ivanič, whose 1998 study of student writers demonstrates some serious issues related to identity where students experience alienation from their own sense of self as expressed in their writing. This dislocation comes about partly as a result of trying to conform to existing perceived norms. Making the case against strictly adhering to norms, she argues that this literally 'causes people to "change their speech," to take on particular identities' (Ivanič, 1998: 7). This conflict is not always productively experienced by students; she argues that changes in student demographics should in fact be challenging the dominant discourses in higher education. While this focus on identity in writing has not always trickled down to actual pedagogic practices, it is clear that ISEAP has a role in aiding student transition, with an emphasis on stu-dents finding their academic voices.

1.3.4 Beyond Academic Writing

Whether learning outcomes aim towards accommodation or critical engagement, whether they are generally articulated or discipline-informed, the
most common focus for in-sessionals is on developing students' written
production. This is also mostly the focus of EAP more generally, but the need
is often more urgent on an in-sessional, where students are already engaged in
their substantive studies. Understanding and responding appropriately to
written tasks is essential for almost all students, and where time dedicated to
an in-sessional is limited, it may well become the imperative. Yet writing may
not be the sole focus of academic literacy development. Wingate dedicates a
chapter of her book *Academic Literacy and Student Diversity* to the teaching of
reading skills. She notes that substantial independent reading may not have
been a part of students' earlier learning experiences and that, even though
successful academic writing is predicated upon it, 'reading ability is taken for
granted' (2015: 79). This again makes the case for a specific approach to
ISEAP design, towards the use of authentic disciplinary texts, and to encourage a discipline-informed critical response.

Undergraduate in-sessionals may necessitate a different focus from PGT
students though. Bruce (2011: 111) emphasises the 'different content and focus
required at pre-sessional, undergraduate in-sessional and postgraduate in-
sessional levels.' The distinction between in-sessional and pre-sessional is evidenced above, but more than this, understanding the target situation has to
come through collaboration with subject lecturers. One of our interviewees,
whose role focusses on provision for undergraduates, made the point that the
messages from his contacts in university departments is leading to a change in
focus for ISEAP content:

> There is a recognition now that whereas our content focusses on reading
> and writing particularly, what we're hearing from academics is that they
> want students to speak more effectively and to be able to discuss the
> course effectively, and that's what we're looking at at the moment ...
> Especially when collaboration seems to be getting into the curriculum
> more and more, for assessment, it's something we have got to answer.

This focus on oracy may not just be necessary for speakers of English as an
additional language, as may seem to be the most obvious context where this
would be needed. Turner (2011: 37) writes of all students' needing to develop
'the ability to suspend familiarity in ways of speaking and writing in order to

adapt to culturally embedded ways.' All students new to university may share the experience of finding themselves in unfamiliar situations: in seminars, tutorials and advice sessions. Turner (2011: 122) adds that international students are hardly the only ones 'not yet familiar with the subject positions the academic context in a particular language tradition requires them to take up.' This can only be compounded for students from different educational cultures who come to study in a context like the U.K. and who may be completely unfamiliar with, for example, the socratic dialogic principles underpinning Western argumentation.

Bruce (2011: 8) also remarks that '[u]ndergraduate students need to develop the means to interrogate and respond to the requirements of undergraduate assignment genres, which is not a straightforward issue,' citing Johns' (1997) point that some genres are very loosely defined. With increasing interdisciplinarity to be found in PGT degrees, too, particularly with the increased prevalence of applied disciplines, this need to develop genre agility remains an issue for ISEAP more widely. But as ever, it is the specifics of the situated context that have to be at the heart of developing learning aims and so course content.

1.3.5 Multimodalities

Again, we can see that issues central to ISEAP are not as straightforward as they first appear. Designing a course that enables students to develop their abilities in navigating academic discourses may seem simple, but researching the discipline and then making decisions about content may lead to some unexpected turns. A case in point may be that the particular needs of a cohort are not as narrowly defined as subject lecturers might indicate to an EAP collaborator. It is not uncommon for subject academics to identify students' language as a problem, yet be unable to articulate the specifics of the issue in a more nuanced way. This has been phrased '[t]he shock-horror discourse, which erupts when language use is not what is expected' (Turner, 2011: 47). Rather than taking the time to consider a student's actual language use, it may simply be articulated as problematic. Such 'unexpected' use of language may not be restricted to a particular skill. One interviewee describing their own context, drew upon ISEAP practitioners' common foundation in communicative language teaching methodologies, and strongly made the argument to not focus on particular skills:

> Of course language is inherently communicative and we [EAP practitioners] all have a multimodal approach to teaching, because we want our

students to listen, to read, to write and to speak, or to 'discuss' let's say. And I think that's something that a lot of universities don't understand: that if you create possibilities for teachers with multimodal approaches, it can really support active learning in the content teachers' [classes].

Depending on the university context, the remit of ISEAP might well focus on skills beyond writing. Moreover, there are also implications for an ISEAP role in training and lecturer development here. EAP practitioners' expertise in learning and teaching means that they may be able to draw upon a wider range of teaching skills than their disciplinary counterparts. There is a danger of overgeneralisation here, with initiatives focussed on HE teaching and academic development being enshrined within universities, as in the prevalence of universities' own certificates in learning and teaching and the increasing popularity of Advance HE's Higher Education Academy Fellowship scheme; nevertheless, EAP practitioners have the advantage of their focussed attention to pedagogies. But as always in ISEAP, context is an overriding dependent factor for decisions about learning outcomes and course content. The level of investment and time dedicated to an in-sessional course cannot be overlooked. Following a consideration of pedagogic approaches for ISEAP in Chapter 2, Chapter 3 will focus on the practicalities of enacting good practices within the logistical constraints of particular contexts.

Concluding Thoughts

This chapter has presented the major issues to be borne in mind when considering ISEAP provision. The picture is one of much more than just language support for struggling students, as it is often still articulated. Rather, we have presented a picture of radical complexity, of decision making that needs to be done to meet diverse needs of particular students studying particular disciplines in particular settings. This focus on the particular means that it is difficult to provide worthwhile one-size-fits-all best practice. Instead, as will follow with every chapter of this book we have presented a constellation of factors to consider in your own practice, in order to identify the features of your setting, and then how best to set up useful and engaging provision.

Chapter 1 Reflection

Following your reading of this chapter, you may use the following section to reflect on the content and apply it to your perceptions of your own context.

A similar section will appear at the end of each chapter in this book, allowing you to build up a complete map of how the ideas discussed map onto your own specific context.

1. **Key questions**

    Consider the three key questions raised by this chapter and relate them to in-sessional language provision in your context (or in a context you know well); jot down your initial answers to them.

    ISEAP provision in your context:

    A. What are you trying to do?
    B. Who are you trying to target it at?
    C. For what reasons?

2. **Degree of Integration**

    How integrated is your ISEAP provision?

    Consider answers to the questions below if related to your own context:

    A. Do students have to do ISEAP classes in their own time, or are they an integral part of their disciplinary curriculum?
    B. Is it a 'cinderella' class (Turner, 2011), invisible to subject lecturers, or is it referred to by them in their own practice?
    C. Do the ISEAP learning outcomes align closely to the subject learning outcomes?
    D. Is the ISEAP an optional or compulsory course?
    E. Is the ISEAP course targeted at a specific group or does it seek to develop academic literacy needs of all students?
    F. How does the ISEAP content relate to students' disciplinary content? Is there any way that this could be enhanced?

    Look back at Table 1.1 presenting increasing levels of integration (Wingate, 2015) in section 1.2.6 above. Based on your answers to the earlier questions:

    A. Which of these four models is closest to the ISEAP provision in your context?
    B. Does all of the ISEAP provision fit into the same category? (maybe some areas are curriculum linked and some curriculum integrated, for example?)
    C. Where would you like it to be?

3. **Collaboration and Cooperation**
   Look back at the descriptions of the four quadrants on this diagram in section 1.2.8 above.
   Where would you place your provision in this table? Why?

References

Alexander, O. (2020) Retrofitting a syllabus with Graduate Attributes. *EAP Essentials.* https://eap-essentials.com/2020/01/23/retrofitting-a-syllabus-with-graduate-attributes/ [accessed 29/6/22].

Alexander, O., Argent, S. and Spencer, J. (2019) *EAP Essentials: A teacher's guide to principles and practice.* 2nd ed. Reading: Garnet.

Benesch, S. (2001) *Critical English for academic purposes: Theory, politics and practice.* Mahwah, NJ: Lawrence Erlbaum.

Birrell (2006) Implications of Low English Standards Among Overseas Students at Australian Universities. *People and Place,* 14:4, 53–64.

Bond, B. (2020) *Making language visible in the university: English for academic purposes and internationalisation.* Bristol: Multilingual Matters.

Bourdieu, P., Passeron, J-C. and Saint Martin, M. (1994) *Academic discourse: Linguistic misunderstanding and professorial power.* Cambridge: Polity.

Bruce, I. (2011) *Theory and concepts of English for academic purposes.* Basingstoke: Palgrave Macmillan.

Cottrell, S. (2019) *The study skills handbook.* London: Bloomsbury Academic.

de Chazal, E. (2014) *English for academic purposes.* Oxford: Oxford University Press.

Ding, A. (2019) 'Academic language is … no one's mother tongue': Misusing Bourdieu and a 'morally questionable' Hyland. *Teaching EAP* https://teachingeap.wordpress.com/2019/11/01/academic-language-is-no-ones-mother-tongue-misusing-bourdieu-and-a-morally-questionable-hyland/ [accessed 2/6/22]/

Ding, A. and Bruce, I. (2017) *The English for academic purposes practitioner: Operating on the edge of academia.* Cham, Switzerland: Palgrave Macmillan.

Dudley-Evans, T. and St John, M.J. (1998) *Developments in English for specific purposes: A multi-disciplinary approach.* Cambridge: Cambridge University Press.

Fazackerley, A. (2022) UK universities warn tuition fee crisis could mean home student cutbacks. *The Guardian* https://www.theguardian.com/

education/2022/jun/29/uk-universities-warn-tuition-fee-crisis-could-mean-home-student-cutbacks [accessed 29/6/22].

Feak, C. (2011) Culture shock? Genre shock? In Etherington, S. (ed.) *Proceedings of the 2009 BALEAP Conference: English for specific academic purposes.* Reading: Garnet Education, pp. 35–45.

Fulcher, G. (2009) The Commercialisation of Language Provision at University. In Alderson, J.C. (ed.) *The politics of language education: Individuals and institutions.* Bristol: Multilingual Matters, pp. 125–146.

Galloway, N. and Rose, H. (2021) English medium instruction and the English language practitioner. *ELT Journal,* 75:1, 33–41.

Gillett (1996) What is EAP? *IATEFL ESP SIG Newsletter,* 6, 17–23. http://www.uefap.com/articles/eap.htm [accessed 29/6/22].

Goldsmiths (2022a) *Academic Language and Literacies Courses* https://www.gold.ac.uk/call/academic-language/ [accessed 1/10/22].

Goldsmiths (2022b) *Our Mission, Values and Strategy* https://www.gold.ac.uk/strategy/ [accessed 1/10/22].

Hadley, G. (2015) *English for academic purposes in neoliberal universities: A critical grounded theory.* Cham: Springer.

Hakim, A. (2021) Toward University-wide Academic Literacy Development in the EMI Context: Pedagogy, Collaboration and Materials Development. *BAAL and CUP Seminar: Language, Literacies and Learning in the Disciplines: A Higher Education Perspective* https://langlitlearn.files.wordpress.com/2021/06/baal-cup-seminar_hakim-2021-v2.pdf [accessed 01/07/22].

Hyland, K. (2006) *English for academic purposes: An advanced resource book.* London: Routledge.

Hyland, K. and Hamp-Lyons, L. (2002) EAP: Issues and directions. *Journal of English for Academic Purposes,* 1: 1, 1–12.

Ivanič, R. (1998) *Writing and identity: The discoursal construction of identity in academic writing.* Amsterdam: John Benjamins.

Jenkins, J. and Wingate, U. (2015) Staff and Students' Perceptions of English Language Policies and Practices in 'International' Universities: A Case Study from the UK. *Higher Education Review.* 47, 47–73.

Johns, A.M. (1997) *Text, role and context: Developing academic literacies.* Cambridge: Cambridge University Press.

Khokhlova, I. (2015). Lingua Franca English of South Africa. *Procedia - Social and Behavioral Sciences.* 214, 983–991.

Lea, M.R. and Street, B.V. (1998) Student writing in higher education: An academic literacies approach. *Studies in Higher Education,* 23:2, 157–172.

Macaro, E., Hultgren, A.K., Kirkpatrick, A. and Lasagabaster, D. (2017) English medium instruction: Global views and countries in focus. *Language Teaching* (2019), 52.2, 231–248.

McWilliam, E. (2009) Teaching for creativity: from sage to guide to meddler. *Asia Pacific Journal of Education*, 29:3, 281–293.

Meyer, J.H.F. and Land, R. (2003) Threshold concepts and troublesome knowledge: linkages to ways of thinking and practising. In Rust, C. (ed.) *Improving student learning - theory and practice ten years on*. Oxford: Oxford Centre for Staff and Learning Development (OCSLD), pp. 412–424.

Office for Students (2021) Assessment practices in English higher education providers: spelling, punctuation and grammar https://www.officeforstudents. org.uk/media/7c292a54-015d-4638-8c30-18e0eba00bf3/assessment-practices-in-english-higher-education-providers-ofs.pdf [accessed 29/6/22].

Raimes, A. (1991) Instructional balance: from theory to practices in the theory of writing. In J.E. Alatis (Ed.) *Georgetown University round table on languages and linguistics: Linguistics and language pedagogy: The state of the art.* Washington DC: Georgetown University Press, pp. 238–249.

Richards, J.C. (2013) Curriculum approaches in language teaching: Forward, central and backward design. *RELC Journal*, 44: 1, 5–33.

Russell Group (2022) A new funding package for high-quality education. https://russellgroup.ac.uk/media/6070/26052022_external_briefing_sustainability.pdf [accessed 29/6/22].

Ryan, J. and Carroll, J. (2005) 'Canaries in the coalmine': international students in Western universities. In Carroll, J. and Ryan, J. (eds.) *Teaching international students: Improving learning for all.* London: Routledge, pp. 3–10.

Sloan, D. and Porter, E. (2010) Changing international student and business staff perceptions of in-sessional EAP: using the CEM model. *Journal of English for Academic Purposes*, 9:3, 198–210.

TEQSA (2019) English language and support services protecting international students. https://www.teqsa.gov.au/latest-news/articles/english-language-and-support-services-protecting-international-students [accessed 29/6/22].

Turner, J. (2011) *Language in the academy: Cultural reflexivity and intercultural dynamics.* Bristol: Multilingual Matters.

University of Glasgow (2018) *Academic Writing Skills Programme Compulsory for all New Students* https://www.gla.ac.uk/myglasgow/news/studentupdates/headline_606747_en.html#:~:text=The%20Academic%20Writing%20Skills%20Programme,affecting%20any%20of%20their%20grades [accessed 1/10/22].

Vygotsky, L.S. (1978) *Mind in society: The development of higher psychological processes.* Cambridge, MA: Harvard University Press.

Wingate, U. (2015) *Academic literacy and student diversity: The case for inclusive practice.* Bristol: Multilingual Matters.

Wingate, U. and Tribble, C. (2012) The best of both worlds? Towards an English for Academic Purposes/Academic Literacies writing pedagogy. *Studies in Higher Education*, 37:4, 481–495.

Chapter 2

Pedagogies and Teaching ISEAP

In this part of the book we review how in-sessional English for Academic Purposes (ISEAP) is approached – what its underlying pedagogies are and how they are deployed. The first part focusses on what we mean by pedagogy and what has been termed 'the knowledge base of EAP' (Ding and Bruce, 2017; Bond, 2020) and its particular relevance to in-sessional contexts. This is followed by a review of key points on pedagogy beyond what are typically considered to be the key theories of EAP, based on what we uncovered in our interviews with ISEAP practitioners in preparation for this book. In this way, this chapter aims to provide more than just an abstract theoretical overview of what language specialists operating in ISEAP contexts might draw on by also offering a snapshot of what actually goes on in ISEAP in university settings, to explore how pedagogy may be enacted in practice.

The key message regarding pedagogy, however, is that there is no one key guiding theory. In practice practitioners often pick and choose different aspects of main EAP theories, add in some ingredients from what they bring to their practice and adapt to their specific settings and circumstances. It is worth pointing out before reading Chapter 2 that Chapter 3 discusses aspects of how ISEAP may be contextualised, embedded, and mapped, considering the logistics and set up of provision. Given that a key point of this book is that specific context is of paramount importance for how ISEAP develops in practice, what

DOI: 10.4324/9781003193715-4

follows in this chapter should therefore not be considered in a vacuum, but in the light of the detailed look at practicalities of context that follows.

2.1 ISEAP's Pedagogical Complexity

It might be assumed that ISEAP pedagogy, as a result of it being a branch of EAP would probably follow the key traditions of English for Specific Purposes (ESP) or an EAP-informed approach. However, as the previous chapter showed there are a number of dimensions within which ISEAP practice may evolve, all of which depend largely on context. It must also be recognised that in-sessional provision often occurs 'under the radar' in universities and that it is a situated area of practice delivered by practitioners who may arrive with a range of previous teaching experiences and language-teaching knowledge. Thus, it should be pointed out from the start that this chapter does not aim to prescribe any one theory or approach to ISEAP over another. The complexity and diversity of ISEAP can be demonstrated by the fact that when we asked practitioners what their 'underpinning pedagogy' was, what emerged was far more varied and wide-ranging than anticipated. Moreover, the answers to our question on pedagogy (see Appendix for a copy of the standard questions we asked interviewees) were often a little fuzzy, not clearly defined, and brought in some concepts from beyond what might be considered a specific EAP 'canon.'

So the first point to make in this chapter for anyone new to teaching in this context is that there is no one clear pedagogy or clear choice to be made between different pedagogical camps in ISEAP. This is perhaps not surprising in what is often acknowledged more widely in language teaching as today's post-method 'pedagogy of particularity' (Kumaravadivelu, 2001), and it is a natural response to working in a heavily contextualised setting such as in-sessional EAP teaching. In fact, it appears that there is often a conscious decision on the part of those developing or delivering ISEAP to approach it with 'principled eclecticism' (Larsen-Freeman, 2000; Mellow, 2002). Also, there may even be variety within the different parts of in-sessional provision within one institution, even if run by one centre, as for example one of our respondents, the director of an EAP centre in a large U.K. university, commented:

> I don't think there's any one particular area of EAP research or knowledge that is holistically applicable in every single situation. I think you use principled eclecticism depending on the aims and learning outcomes and audience and purpose of each provision.

Consequently, when working in this branch of EAP, there is a need for reflection and 'agility' on the part of the practitioner; a willingness to constantly learn and adapt to context as a teacher and course designer. The framework established by BALEAP for teachers of EAP states that all practitioners, whatever the context, 'should show a commitment to continue to develop professionally,' which, among other considerations, 'means finding time to keep up with developments in the EAP field and related fields such as education or applied linguistics in order to understand how the knowledge base of EAP is expanding' (BALEAP, 2022). In the case of ISEAP, where courses are typically embedded in content more closely than pre-sessional or foundation courses, that is coupled with the need to adapt to different disciplines and practices in the partner courses we collaborate with, as the Teaching English for Academic Purposes (TEAP) handbook goes on to state in the section on scholarship and professional development:

> While EAP practitioners may not have allowance in their workloads for primary research, they are expected to engage in scholarship to become aware of new developments in discourse processing and its implications for academic literacy, as well as the research and teaching practices of the disciplines their students will study.
>
> (BALEAP, 2022: 14)

As a result, we think it would be wrong to suggest that ISEAP should necessarily adhere strongly to any one particular approach, which is in line with what one of our interviewees, director of an EAP centre in another large U.K. university, told us:

> I think that will be problematic, a recommended approach – the problem with that is that it implies that there is a similarity in the universities and that is not the case – in the same way that degrees are not structured the same. It is very different behind the scenes … it's a hyper complex behind the scenes area which has always fascinated more than other areas – visually if you look at the in-sessional in higher education it's a complex overlapping area, which is quite fascinating, which is why some of the answers are quite tricky.

2.2 What Do We Mean By 'Underlying Pedagogy'?

Variability in pedagogies is a reaction to this complexity. Moreover, in ISEAP what makes the picture even more complex is that the resulting pedagogical choices are down to the practitioner. When we asked another of our respondents, who has published widely in EAP research, what they imagined answers from other institutions would be to our pedagogy question, they suggested:

> They are likely to differ quite considerably based on the knowledge and beliefs of the person responsible for in-sessional.

Part of the problem may be the term 'pedagogy' itself. What exactly are the differences between this term and 'approach,' 'theory,' 'methodology,' or even 'ideology'? In fact, if one who works in EAP considers their own response to alternative questions such as 'What is your approach?' or 'What is your methodology?,' these alternative questions suggest either a wider consideration of educational theory or a narrower focus on specific classroom practice. A focus on 'underlying pedagogy' enables us to explore a broader, richer picture of the complex, contextualised, dynamic, and emergent nature of what informs ISEAP in practice.

It is worth considering that answering this question would probably not be that easy for anyone teaching in higher education (HE) contexts, not just for EAP practitioners. Carlile and Jordan (2005) state that although a lecturer's awareness of pedagogy is enshrined in their practice, they are not typically conscious of what it consists of or derives from without a good deal of reflection:

> Consciously or unconsciously, you hold theories of learning since all action is based on assumptions which may or may not have been articulated or tested. These have been developed through your own years of formal education, of learning things on your own, and of developing learning strategies for students. You may not be aware of what your theories are, and they may never have been challenged.
>
> (Carlile and Jordan, 2005: 11)

Conscious reflection on how a teacher's pedagogy continues to evolve over time can also aid further conscious development when teaching in HE settings where typically there is less of a predetermined approach to teaching, compared to further education (FE) or school contexts. This point is noted by Nicholls (2021) in a case study examining the expertise of ten experienced EAP practitioners working on subject specific language provision. She notes that in their practice they 'consider a range of linguistic, pedagogic and contextual factors and their expertise emanates from research, practice and continuous evaluation' (Nicholls, 2021: 187). There should be an emphasis therefore not just on looking back; pedagogy is not static but in constant development.

ISEAP in particular is informed by ideas from across a wide range of theories, with practitioners picking and choosing ideas from different traditions to inform their approach rather than adhering strictly to one particular stream. Our conversations with practitioners confirmed that it is indeed a complex field of practice, highly context dependent, and variable in terms of approach adopted from one institution to another and sometimes even from one provision or section of provision within one institution to another. Indeed, different practitioners working in the same ISEAP provision may bring different concepts of pedagogy into their practice. One of our interviewees who had been working for a year or so with colleagues in ISEAP in a large U.K. institution commented:

> We have a genre approach, so my colleague says. I queried it though, I try to bring in elements of SFL [Systemic Functional Linguistics]. We all have DELTA [Diploma in English Language Teaching to Adults] backgrounds and come from communicative language teaching – we build in that ... Down the line will I be able to switch the way I teach depending on which department I'm working in?

ISEAP is an applied field of practice embedded in diverse settings within a variety of discipline areas and thus the way it is taught will be naturally diverse and emergent. At first this might appear to be a sign of weakness, or lack of coherence; however, as Benesch noted in relation to EAP in general: '[t]he strength of EAP has been its sensitivity to context' (2001, 23). Hyland and Shaw also observe that 'EAP draws its strength from a broad and eclectic range of different ideas, and its effectiveness lies in employing the ideas that offer the most for understanding communication and for classroom practice' and even suggest that this has benefitted EAP research by 'tempering a possible overindulgence in theory with a practical utility (2016: 2).

As this section has shown, practitioners in ISEAP have a wide variety of choices in terms of what to incorporate in practice. The following section will look firstly at what has been termed the 'knowledge base of EAP' practice in general and consider how these core theories relate to in-sessional practice in particular, before considering in more detail what our interviews revealed about underlying pedagogies in ISEAP.

2.3 Defining the Knowledge Base of EAP in In-sessional Contexts

According to many who have provided overviews of its knowledge base (e.g. Charles, 2013; Ding and Bruce, 2017), EAP essentially developed out of English for Specific Purposes (ESP), itself a specialised branch of English Language Teaching (ELT), and draws upon a distinct range of underpinning theories particular to itself. ISEAP, as a sub-field of EAP, would therefore be expected to use more or less the same knowledge base. On exactly which theories form the EAP 'canon,' there is no clear definitive list, but rather much literature in this field presents a developing and expandable list of key theories, possible sources of pedagogical knowledge (Ding and Bruce, 2017; Bond, 2020), sometimes these are categorised or grouped (e.g. Charles, 2013; Wingate, 2015) and some authors have suggested a different focus altogether on what underpins EAP teaching practice (e.g. Hyland and Shaw, 2016; Bell, 2022).

Some authorities list a number of different key theories which exist concurrently, as in two influential texts published in the last few years, especially for EAP in the U.K. HE context. In *The English for Academic Purposes Practitioner*, Ding and Bruce categorise EAP as a 'theory and research informed field of academic English language and literacy education' (2017: 83) and acknowledge that 'EAP practitioners have turned to an ever-broadening knowledge base of theory and research to inform their practice' (2017: 84). They suggest five key pillars of knowledge: Systemic Functional Linguistics (SFL), genre theory, corpus linguistics, Academic Literacies, and critical EAP (Ding and Bruce, 2017). Bee Bond's *Making Language Visible in the University* (2020) defines EAP as having a specific focus on 'identifying linguistic and discursive norms in academic communication' (2020: 168) and broadens the list above by adding in discourse analysis as a separate category, and including a more recent addition, Legitimation Code Theory (LCT) introduced by Maton (2014).

Aside from listing key theories, Ding and Bruce (2017) also comment for each one on whether it seeks to develop specifically social, generic or textual competence or a combination of these (after Bhatia, 2004). Other categorisations focus more specifically on writing, which is often the main focus area of in-sessional language work, and consider the primary focus of instruction on student produced texts. Charles (2013) for example, identifies three clear strands when referring to areas of EAP research: corpus-based (so related to precise analysis of language), genre-based, and approaches focusing on social context. Similarly, Wingate (2015) examines previous categorisations of academic writing teaching by Lea and Street (1998), Hyland (2002), Ivanič (2004) and reconfigures them in three broader categories based on whether the focus of academic writing instruction is primarily text-oriented, writer-oriented, or reader-oriented. Ultimately, Wingate (2015) proposes a re-modelled list of five overarching 'approaches': the skills approach, process approaches, genre approaches, social practices approaches, and 'the social political approach' (2015: 17–23).

The skills approach to teaching academic writing breaks the subject down into a series of 'atomised' skills. Although there is criticism from both Ivanič (2004) and Wingate (2015) of such a de-contextualised and generic approach to teaching writing, they both suggest that a lot of this may go on within practice, even if it is not the espoused pedagogy of the practitioner (see Chaper 1 for a discussion of the factors informing ISEAP course development). Indeed, we did have a number of references made to a skills approach in our interviews. What Wingate refers to as process approaches are those more focussed on the writer, which Hyland (2004) refers to as 'writer-oriented' approaches. Under this classification Wingate (2015: 19) includes approaches that promote more creative expression and a generalised approach to teaching writing (she links this to U.S. composition courses), again suggesting problematic areas, such as the emphasis placed on the individual taking the focus away from situated, em-bedded academic communication. Social practices are more 'reader-oriented' and focus specifically on audience and writing as social interaction. Wingate identifies the key difference between this and genre approaches as the greater ethnographic research basis and the lesser focus on textual analysis in practice. Finally, what Wingate (2015: 22) terms 'socio-political' is essentially what Ding and Bruce (2017) and Bond (2020) identify as critical EAP.

The type of overarching categorisation in Charles (2013) and Wingate (2015), which groups key theories might be helpful as a way to break down EAP research informed teaching for anyone new or unfamiliar with EAP, rather than having a list of apparently separate entities (e.g. Ding and Bruce, 2017; Bond, 2020). However, it might suggest there are clear links between disparate theories where the individual strains have key conceptual differences between them. For one approaching EAP pedagogy with a view to con-sidering suitability of application to ISEAP practice, the list of key theories may appear daunting, however it can be beneficial to explore each theory individually in order to assess its relevance. In this book, rather than espousing a particular approach or suggesting specific combinations of theories, we suggest that it would be worth considering what applying any of these key theories would actually look like in practice and how it would translate to a specific ISEAP context with a specific cohort. The reflection at the end of this chapter will therefore suggest some questions an interested practitioner might consider in a comparison of the key EAP theory areas. The section that follows will give a brief overview of these key pillars of EAP knowledge, and consider how they relate specifically to teaching in-sessional courses based on what we learned from our conversations with ISEAP practitioners. But to decide for themselves, readers are advised to read more deeply the key texts associated with each theory and follow up some suggestions for further reading which appear in the reflection section of this chapter.

2.4 The 'Pillars' of EAP and How They Relate to In-sessional Contexts

The following section provides a discussion of how some of the key pedagogical research theories of EAP relate to in-sessional settings. There is not the space for a full discussion of theory in this book, but each subsection suggests key texts and written accounts of each theory in practice for readers who wish to deepen their own knowledge of them further. All of the theories presented below were mentioned by our interviewees, although, as previously stated, there was a wide diversity of response and answers typically provided a generalised mix of one or more, or included other less specifically EAP concepts (see section 2.5).

This section will look at genre analysis (including a note on discourse analysis), corpus linguistics, SFL, Academic Literacies, critical EAP, and LCT. We based our selection of these pillars on the numbers of mentions in our interviews. Genre theory was by the far the most common response to our question about underlying pedagogy, although how it was enacted in practice was typically the least clearly defined, whereas the mentions of corpus linguistics and LCT were less frequent but their precise application more clearly explained. It should be pointed out that our selection of interviews is not intended to be a fully representative sample, but we believe the individual comments help to illustrate the possibilities of the theory in question. As previously stated, our aim in this book is to encourage reflection and application of ideas in the reader; what follows then is an attempt to provide more of a practitioner view of the EAP knowledge base in practice, based on what we found in our investigation into the world of ISEAP.

2.4.1 Genre Analysis

This was the most commonly mentioned influence in our interviews, although it was not always clear what particular form of genre theory approach was being used. In genre theory, the work of John Swales, especially his defining book *Genre Analysis* (1990), is considered to be fundamental. The definition of genre from Swales is as follows:

> A class of communicative event, the members of which share some set of communicative purposes. These purposes are recognized by the expert members of the parent discourse community, and thereby constitute the rationale for the genre.
>
> (Swales, 1990: 58)

The ideas of membership and experts provide a link between linguistic concepts of discourse communities (Swales, 1990) and broader sociological theories such as communities of practice (Lave and Wenger, 1991). The field of genre theory is large and encompasses a number of different strands. According to the literature (e.g. Hyon, 1996; Bruce, 2011; Charles, 2013; Wingate, 2015), there are broadly three approaches to genre. However, the labels attached to these fluctuate somewhat from one author to another. In most classifications, there is a basic distinction made between more purely linguistic approaches primarily focussed on text, often referred to more broadly as genre analysis, and more socially contextualised ones – closer to what Wingate (2015: 21) considers under her term 'social practices approaches' and more informed by sociological, ethnographic research traditions. Bruce (2011) summarises these differences in terms of how they relate to 'operationalization of genre knowledge'; he divides the EAP research strains by their focus: either on the socialised nature of genre, analysis of organisational features of 'conventionalised' texts, or on categorisation of genre by rhetorical function, e.g. argumentation or reporting (2011: 162).

Genre analysis is highly influential for teaching English in in-sessional ESAP contexts, where discipline-specific understandings of language are key. Indeed, one of our interviewees acknowledged this when asked about their pedagogy:

> I think genre is very strong in terms of the idea that there are specific communicative purposes, and there are structures, and there is language connected to that.

Bruce (2011) defines genre as 'a classificatory concept referring to a pro-
ceduralised way of using language in a certain context, the linguistic trace
of which is a written text or the transcription of a spoken event' (2011:
162). He proposes a model of social/cognitive genre analysis which examines a wider concept of discourse in terms of how texts are considered
and his analytical frameworks examining context, epistemology, writer
stance, and content in texts are an attempt to blend all elements of genre
theory to create a clear pedagogical approach (Bruce, 2011). Although this
has its influence, some commentators have suggested such frameworks are
difficult to apply in practice in EAP classroom practice; for example, Bond
comments that although it is interesting to employ cognitive genre frameworks for text analysis, it 'is a complex process and one which few
practitioners have the knowledge, training, confidence or time to enact'
(2021: 169).

In terms of what typically goes on in ISEAP practice, most of our interviewees who cited genre as a key influence tended towards a more broadly
text analysis or rhetorical 'step' analysis approach, where disciplinary specificity is explored with learners in a discovery approach through analysis of
examples of written production. With a looser pedagogical framework,
Swalesian-influenced approaches focus on analysing discipline specific 'authentic' texts for common 'moves' or schematic structures (Hyland, 2013:
98). The use of research by Swales into the typical 'moves' or rhetorical stages
in research articles, such as the Introduction Method Research Discussion/
Conclusion (IMRD/C) approach or Create a Research Space (CaRS), are
well-known and widely used applications of genre theory in ISEAP contexts
(Swales, 1990). In terms of how this works in practice, EAP teachers will get
students to look at a text, either exemplars of published 'expert' disciplinary
specific material (as in the original research which informed the theory) or
samples of students' own work or previous students' work. The instructional
focus is then on examining typical moves or stages linking language to
rhetorical function, for example, and on raising learners' disciplinary genre
awareness. By getting students to appreciate the typical organisational patterns or
rhetorical 'moves' within authentic texts it is hoped this will help them both
understand better the ways knowledge is communicated in their discipline and
to develop transferable skills and knowledge to apply to future contexts in their
own writing. Training students to become discourse analysts in their own right
is a typical ISEAP technique, and clearly has links to broader educational
concepts such as promoting learner autonomy and student-centred learning. For

example, one of our interviewees explained how this related to what they teach students in their context:

> We're not just looking at a piece of work; we're looking at training them in the skills of analysis that they could apply to something else in the same year or something else. It's that whole methodical approach to a text and to what it is which makes the implicit explicit: I think that's a really core thing.

In our interviews, in terms of how genre theory is enacted in ISEAP teaching practice, genre and discourse analysis were often mentioned in relatively vague terms. 'Discourse analysis' (regarded by Bond (2020) as a key theory in itself), is another term that has varying interpretations; it may imply more of a focus on literary aspects or may be linked to more social practices of critical discourse analysis (Fairclough, 2010). However, in general, the idea of raising awareness of textual and linguistic features in line with genre approaches is a key technique, commonly employed in ISEAP.

In one interview, a practitioner working in an arts-specific context discussed how they were able to conduct a deep ethnographic investigation of the context in which students operated in order to inform their ISEAP practice, a broadly social genre approach. They were invited in by a content lecturer they were collaborating with on discipline-specific provision, including what happened in 'crits,' where creative arts students had to defend their work. They commented on how their approach was informed by:

> Being able to see those sorts of things and just talking to people and observing and seeing those linguistic nuances between people and just seeing how that communication's happening. And simple things like in the crits: we always tell them to take questions at the end [of presentations], but that's absolutely not the case for crits: they can be interrupted at any point. We focus so much on presentations being structured and ordered, but these presentations are based on a drawing and they can start anywhere. No real structure. When [collaboration] does happen you get these real insights into things.

This is an example where there is particularly close collaboration between EAP practitioner and the content lecturers and such opportunities for ISEAP practitioners are not all that common. Indeed the interviewee noted later in the interview that in their teaching context there was a move away from this type of ISEAP arrangement to one of more multi-disciplinary EGAP workshops open to all students on a sign-up basis. As a consequence, the 'real insights' that appear to have been so rewarding for the practitioner and the learners in their provision for the arts students are no longer possible.

It is not unusual for EAP centres to have a mix of more general and more discipline specific provision (see both Chapters 1 and 3 for fuller discussion on this). This does not mean that genre theory no longer has influence, but suggests there are different ways to apply it. One respondent suggested their ISEAP pedagogy was 'genre-based,' but they went on to explain the focus is rather broad and actually seems quite unfocussed:

> And if we think about our EGAP, it's very genre based, for example, 'essay writing for social sciences', but we are looking at social sciences background, etc. and then going into essay writing.

In another modified genre based approach, two heads of EAP departments in two different large U.K. universities suggested the value of including some EGAP provision in a way which deliberately gets learners in multi-disciplinary cohorts to analyse texts and compare conventions across disciplines.

In terms of criticisms of a genre approach, these tend to come from Academic Literacies or critical EAP–informed theorists (e.g. Lea and Street, 1998; Ivanič, 1998; Benesch, 2001), who suggest there is a tendency to apply genre as a fixed, immutable 'monolithic' concept rather than a dynamic one, ignoring the wider implications of the situated nature of writing practice in the university and what the students themselves bring to their learning. Although Swales' (1990) concept of genre, and subsequent developments in genre research acknowledge and seek to rectify these issues and suggest the need for a greater focus on ethnographic research considering the picture beyond texts, there are still those who level the charge of genre approaches being essentially 'accommodationist', not allowing enough consideration of students' own contributions to influence the evolution of disciplinary genres. Moreover, there is another complication especially for text-based genre approaches: in contemporary international HE contexts, there is more blurring of 'specific domain boundaries' of genres and more instances of multimodality and interdisciplinarity, which have led some to call for explicitly blended genre approaches to enable learners to cope with increasingly complex and mutable circumstances (e.g. Sancho Guinda, 2015).

2.4.2 Corpus Linguistics

When someone from a non-linguistics background thinks of 'genres,' they may typically think of distinctly different types of text and this leads into a consideration of approaches which place the greatest emphasis on close investigation and analysis of the language used in disciplinary communication, in line with the more rhetorically focussed and text-based applications of genre theory mentioned above. Corpus linguistics (CL), which involves the use of technology for linguistic analysis of text, is an underlying body of linguistic research that can inform ISEAP pedagogy in a number of ways. It can be worth considering it as a key theory in its own right but it can also be seen as an aspect of data driven learning (DDL) approaches to teaching methodology (Bell, 2022).

As mentioned above, Charles (2013) lists corpus linguistics as a branch of genre theory and there is indeed crossover between these different pillars of EAP. In their highly influential text in the area of textual analysis, Nesi and Gardner (2012), identified 13 key genres of academic writing that commonly occur across different disciplines. Their research was based on the BAWE (British Academic Written English) corpus (a corpus being a databank of authentic text samples from a particular field which is then analysed by use of concordance software that enables comparative searches for linguistic lexicogrammatical features and frequency). Viana and O'Boyle (2022) make a case for greater use and application of corpus linguistics in EAP practice as well as in research on the basis that it provides 'evidence' for research-informed teaching and may even be seen as providing more equity for different Englishes, as corpora of student writing reflect what is actually written or spoken rather than a prescribed or fuzzy notion of genre as enacted in text. Therefore, this suggested benefit of CL could also be seen as aligning EAP teaching practice with decolonising the curriculum, and in particular with the concept of English as a Lingua Franca (ELF) as it provides a knowledge base for EAP which takes into account 'English in changing academic landscapes' (Viana and O'Boyle, 2022: 11). CL analysis can provide answers about language use, create academic vocabulary lists, and examine differences between general language use and discipline-specific contexts. Key affordances of using CL directly in pedagogical practice therefore are that it allows for genre comparison, an analysis of differences between general and academic English and variation between and within disciplinary language use, even contrasting between specific user groups. Viana and O'Boyle go on to point out that it is specifically useful for investigating examples of 'occluded genres' (i.e. examples of text production within discourse communities that may not be accessible to anyone outside specific contexts; typically examples include student emails or communication around research proposals) or largely unexplored discipline areas (Viana and O'Boyle, 2022: 58).

CL can thus feed into a more richly informed textual-focussed approach to genre and discourse analysis. Work in this area has been very influential on EAP practitioners in general and useful in in-sessional contexts. One of our interviewees specifically highlighted the usefulness of Nesi and Gardner's (2012) identification of different genres:

> Nesi and Gardner's 2012 book has been really useful … we did a genre analysis using the genre framework of all the core modules across these eleven degree programmes we support at postgraduate level in the business school just to do a revision of priorities and to see what students are doing. And that framework was absolutely crucial for that and in the team more people than not speak in terms of those genres … empathy writing, design specification, writing for professional purposes: all of that has just become the terminology that we use.

Moreover, the use of concordancers has the capacity for generating detailed textual analyses which can be used not only by practitioners for research and materials preparation, but also accessed by students themselves as text analysts in their own right, helping them to develop their own understanding of what academic communication in their discipline area is. In terms of how CL might be applied, one key area is investigating disciplinary specific or genre specific use of vocabulary. An extremely influential work in this area is the *Academic Word List* by Averil Coxhead (2000). Many general and specific EAP textbooks have been produced which make use of concordance data and, for example, encourage learners to notice instances of core items from the list when they occur in texts, as this is seen as a way of raising the consciousness of typical linguistic features in academic English in general. Alternatively, this can also be applied at a discipline specific level for learners of academic English.

In terms of how a CL approach might be used directly in an ISEAP teaching context, one of our interviewees wholeheartedly espoused this method (reinforcing the idea that pedagogical choices often come about as a result of a practitioner's personal preferences). In a U.K. university context, teaching English in a specific context for law students, concordance software was used to do corpus analyses of texts as the basis for a session with students where both they and the teacher would be analysing discourse to investigate its features more deeply:

> I know they have problems with law reports – in a class I approached this in addition to a 'reading for purpose' perspective. They sent reports they were reading and I also looked for frequent vocabulary – lots of linking phrases, e.g. 'so as to' and 'in accordance with.' It raised awareness for me and for the students.

Moreover, a key feature for the busy and constantly agile ISEAP practitioner here is facility of use. This practitioner commented that a 'quick and dirty analysis' could easily be done, even just in advance of teaching a session. The use of CL in this practitioner's practice was also explicitly presented as a technique which students themselves should add to their academic practice. It was employed on an in-sessional vocabulary module open to all students and billed as 'an introduction to data driven learning' where:

> ... students explore vocab of their own: [they] start off with the Academic Word List, then start looking at concordance lines. There is a need for more knowledge about vocabulary.

The practitioner explained that they would typically get students to use a free online concordancer programme, a link being provided on the teaching materials, and look at texts, produce a vocabulary list and discriminate between items based on frequency of occurrence and to make choices about where to focus their learning. They also commented that they would like to go back to check with their students in the future to see if they were still using concordancers as an aid to reading and as part of their practice. As one of their students had written after the ISEAP course had finished to ask if they could still access the software through the module VLE, this suggests there was still interest and that it had therefore been an effective intervention.

This was however the only one of our interviewees who specifically mentioned using CL in their ISEAP teaching practice, but the significance of CL as an influence on ISEAP pedagogy is likely to be present in most ISEAP contexts in terms of practitioner's awareness of it, even if it does not constitute the key feature of teaching methodology. This case, therefore, is likely to be a prime example of where a practitioner's preferred theory, one they are personally very familiar with, is highlighted in the resulting ISEAP pedagogy. The fact that this was present as part of a vocabulary module may suggest a specific context in the type of ISEAP provision in this context that allowed for it to be operationalised in this way.

2.4.3 Systemic Functional Linguistics (SFL)

SFL derives from Halliday's rhetorical research in the 1970s onwards and developed as a pedagogical tool for analysing functional and structural systems in texts, 'connecting features of language with the social actions with which they correlate' and providing 'fine grained analysis' of texts (Ding and Bruce, 2017: 70). As a pedagogical approach, SFL developed in Australian contexts in the 1980s onwards, and is sometimes known by the alternative name of the 'Sydney School' of genre-informed approaches. According to Wingate, the fourth generation of SFL focussed specifically on HE contexts, whereas its earlier focus was on schools and had a widening participation principle behind it, working to empower underprivileged student cohorts (2015: 28). The idea behind it was to provide learners with tools and an analytical framework to unpack the language conventions of genres, which would enable students to understand 'varieties and linguistic choices that are available' and thus be able to apply this knowledge to their own practice (Wingate, 2015: 31).

One of the often-cited advantages of SFL as a pedagogical theory in which it contrasts favourably with broader genre analysis, and especially with Academic Literacies and critical EAP, is that it has a well-developed and documented methodological approach, based on 'schematic structure modelling, joint negotiation and independent construction of text' (Bruce, 2011: 30). This is known as the 'Sydney School Genre Pedagogy' (SSGP) cycle or the Teaching and Learning TL Cycle (Martin and Rose, 2008; Purser et al., 2020). It essentially involves a guided analysis of 'successful' examples of text from within a specific target genre in a phase of 'deconstruction,' then a teacher works with students to re-create a similar text (the 'co-construction' phase) and finally students, by themselves or in collaboration, then develop their own texts applying their newfound knowledge in the 'reconstruction' phase (Purser et al., 2020).

In terms of what might be applied from this approach in an ISEAP context, in a chapter in *Pedagogies in EAP* edited by MacDiarmid and McDonald, a practitioner operating in an arts-specific ISEAP context at a university in Canada presents an enthusiastic account of introducing some of the key tenets of SFL theory to her practice (Walsh Marr, 2021). These include examining experiential, interpersonal, and textual metafunctions through field, tenor and mode analysis, and 'judicious deployment' of SFL maxims such as 'form follows function' and 'language as choice.' The author notes that this constitutes 'a departure from my previous form-focussed teaching contexts, where grammatical form was prioritised over practice' (Walsh Marr, 2021: 44). For anyone unfamiliar with SFL terminology though, it is clear there is a lot for the practitioner to unpack in this theory.

A common criticism of SFL pedagogy is the level of complexity and concerns about the extent to which the metalanguage of the approach should be shared with learners; indeed Walsh Marr (2021) talks of the necessity for providing 'a curated selection of metalanguage.' Monbec (2020) claims however that SFL is highly applicable and devised her own response to developing a student friendly application of SFL, the 'table of instantiation' tool which she applied to an ISEAP context. One of the key hopes of SFL is that it can empower the practitioner, strengthening their confidence in their own linguistic knowledge base, for example enabling feedback on language to students which is not vague but based on a shared understanding of linguistic and rhetorical description. That said, even in Monbec's study that examined teacher and student perceptions of the use of the table of instantiation tool, a teacher commented that it might be overwhelming for students and a student commented that the terminology used might be difficult to remember or understand (Monbec, 2020: 9). Monbec states that 'the purpose of the EAP module is not to teach SFL theory – but with the way it benefits their writing and achievement in tertiary education'; making use of terminology of Legitimation Code Theory (LCT) (see section 2.4.5), she claims the semantic range used 'does not have to reach very high' and 'incursions into the abstract concepts are followed by text analysis and writing tasks to contextualise the concepts in authentic texts' (2020: 10–11).

It might be construed that SFL is oppositional to, and therefore difficult to combine with, other theoretical bases of practice such as Academic Literacies, but that is expressly denied by some advocates of the SFL tradition (e.g. Gardner, 2012; Monbec, 2020). Purser et al. (2020) list some of the 'big ideas' of SFL which have an influence on EAP practice, and indeed this was acknowledged by approximately a third of the ISEAP practitioners we interviewed as being influential on their practice. For example, one in particular mentioned the influence of 'language as choice' as a guiding tenet of their ISEAP pedagogy, aiming to get students 'making effective choices in writing.' There were few specific references to the application of SFL however and one interviewee we spoke to suggested that SFL was too detail-obsessed for practicable use. It is clearly influential though and, as this comment from a practitioner demonstrates, may be useful where ISEAP exists in non-discipline specific contexts:

> I've been looking at Monbec's work using SFL on transfer and she talks about you can teach how language works without it being tied to a particular discipline or assessment. Teach it so that students have a theoretical understanding of the knowledge and apply it to their disciplines.

2.4.4 Academic Literacies

After genre theory, this was the most cited influence by our interviewees, and like genre the application of the theory in practice was often not clearly articulated. This suggests the theory has a broad influence and applicability in ISEAP but the practice of it is less clear. The landmark article for Academic Literacies (AcLits) theory is Lea and Street (1998). The focus in AcLits is more on the writer rather than the text itself; in other words on the students themselves, their backgrounds, what they bring and how they develop. Indeed, key terms associated with AcLits are 'development,' 'transformations,' and 'identity,' and there are links to be found with broader theories which may underlie pedagogies in the ISEAP arena, communities of practice (Lave and Wenger, 1991) for example, but also threshold concepts (Meyer and Land, 2003) which implies a role for the ISEAP teacher less based on guided discourse or text analysis, but more about guiding learners through their transitions in identity. One of our interviewees from a university in an Australian context reported their approach which relates to this point and has implications for the positioning of the teacher in ISEAP contexts too:

> We need to induct them into the culture of the discipline – they need to gain that knowledge. I feel like the person in the middle – it's boundary crossing.

The above quote could be seen as also linked to ideas of academic socialisation, and with Hyland's classification of reader, rather than writer-oriented social practices approaches to EAP (Hyland, 2002). This stated 'induction into the discipline' might be seen as tending more towards an accommodationist approach, where students are taught to fit in with expected conventions and norms of the university. However, 'boundary crossing' is suggestive of something more linked to identity. AcLits is usually interpreted as having more of a focus on the development of the individual's own identity within discourse communities and considering their prior knowledge and experience, rather than an idea of preparing students as novices entering the academy (e.g. McGrath and Kaufhold, 2016).

AcLits perhaps provides an answer to criticisms that genre theory, including SFL and CL, may all be too fixed in terms of the concept of genres that students encounter and need to gain mastery of, especially in the context of more interdisciplinary courses and multimodal assignment types:

> From a student's point of view, a dominant feature of academic literacy is the requirement to switch practices between one setting and another, to control a range of genres appropriate to each setting, and to handle the meanings and identities that each evokes.
>
> (Hyland, 2013: 97)

AcLits is posited as a more satisfactory response than genre or text-oriented approaches to EAP pedagogy to address an essentially more complex and diverse pattern of language use and communication practices in academic contexts where 'HE literacies are in flux' and students face a 'bewildering range of explicit requirements, shadowed in many cases by an equally complex range of unarticulated expectations' (Tuck, 2018: 2-3). As one head of a U.K. EAP department commented in one of our interviews:

> I think the main principles that are, for me, really important is to make sure that we do keep in mind is taking an Academic Literacies approach. First of all, making sure that we're not making assumptions about what's expected in a discipline and trying to relay those to students.

In a study where two practitioners, one of the genre tradition and one who identified more closely with AcLits, worked together to deliver ISEAP provision, a number of key differences distinguishing AcLits from genre approaches are recorded (McGrath and Kaufhold, 2016). Genre typically focusses on rhetorical, lexical features of texts and consciousness-raising, evaluation of texts, then performance, all towards developing learners' control and a sense of demystification, making the academy open to students (McGrath and Kaufhold, 2016: 936). On the other hand, AcLits approaches are transformative, take into account historical elements such as students' prior experiences and backgrounds, more explicitly embrace heterogeneity within genres and employ critical perspectives to focus on negotiated development of the learners (2016: 937). There is a sense therefore that AcLits makes up for some of the shortcomings of 'genre only' approaches in terms of a wide view of context and a more critical, less 'accommodationist' stance.

A frequent criticism of purely writer-oriented AcLits approaches is that conceptualisations of how it would translate into practice are lacking. McGrath and Kaufhold's answer to this is an attempt to blend elements of the two traditions in a 'best of both worlds' model' (2016). This is in line with the recommendations of adopting a pedagogical approach that is both 'discipline and context specific,' as recommended in Wingate and Tribble (2012).

AcLits was a fairly commonly mentioned underlying pedagogy by the ISEAP practitioners we spoke to, but often there may be limits to how successfully it can be applied in practice due to logistical constraints. As a practitioner from a South African university context where courses are operated on a very large scale told us:

> Lea and Street, Academic literacies, yes as a team we're all within the AcLits thinking space, but the courses as they operate, due to operational constraints … I don't want to say academic skills, it does have elements of socialisation, but it is bordering on more general skills. But we're trying not to do that as much as possible. That's where I'm at.

This suggests that AcLits is not only difficult to apply in ISEAP because it lacks a clear pedagogical framework, but also because of constraints of the context in which ISEAP operates, such as class-size or lack of time to allow for teachers to negotiate identity development with all their cohort. However, it also reveals that AcLits was perceived as a desirable direction of travel and one which this practitioner and their colleagues shared as essential background.

Another explicitly writer-centred approach one of our interviewees mentioned, however, which suggests an application of AcLits-inspired, writer-oriented pedagogy in a more EGAP, non-discipline-specific context, was described as follows:

> One of the tasks I get them to do is to write about an assessment task that they have completed in their discipline area and they have to describe the academic practices that they have used in answering that task so I give them a framework of conceptualising, formulating, revising, and reading.

2.4.5 Legitimation Code Theory (LCT)

An area of research which has been gaining a lot of ground in its influence on EAP especially in the U.K. context in recent years is Legitimation Code Theory (LCT), developed by Maton (2014), which has a much wider knowledge base and potential applications than just EAP, as it relates less specifically to language and more to knowledge construction and sociological aspects of learning. It is in fact not a theory as such but more of an analytical framework or 'social realist toolkit dedicated to investigating knowledge practices in a wide range of contexts' (Monbec, 2020: 10). However, it 'can seem forbidding, in part because of its ambitiousness: it provides a toolkit for understanding how knowledge is constructed out of field specific processes of legitimization' (Solli and Muir, 2021: 69). It is multifaceted and adaptable to different contexts, examining knowledge in a range of different 'dimensions.' In Solli and Muir's study (2021), where it is employed together with AcLits approaches and even storytelling for teaching doctoral students in an ISEAP context, the 'specialisation' dimension is applied as an analytical tool.

In EAP teaching the aspects of LCT's 'semantic dimension' and the examination of 'semantic waves' has typically had more influence on teaching academic writing. This, for example, is described as an analytical tool for research in the SFL study by Monbec (2020). The application of this for analysing text (written or spoken) can be a visualisation, like plotting a graph of 'semantic waves' through a text and examining how effectively a produced text waves up and down, between exemplification, explanation and detail and abstract, theoretical concepts. It can be used to identify how smoothly links between these different levels are accomplished. For this reason, it is, similarly to SFL, an analytical framework which can aid detailed analysis of texts and arguably has even greater potential to be used to investigate other aspects of different genres. Therefore, its applicability to typically discipline-specific and more EGAP iterations of ISEAP contexts is immediately apparent.

In recent years, Steve Kirk, based at Durham University in the United Kingdom, has been one of the key exponents of this approach for EAP. In a recently published chapter (2022), he suggests that LCT may even be a solution to the potential threat of 'fragmentation' within EAP practice, as a uniting theory. Although he acknowledges that, to date, published accounts of how it has been applied in EAP practice are still relatively rare, he suggests that the capacity of analytical frameworks which 'reveal the rules of the game' in terms of how knowledge is constructed within disciplines has potential to be applied to course design as well as teaching practice (2022: 89). In terms of teaching practice, Kirk (2022) recounts an analysis of 'semantic gravity' in a pre-sessional EAP session, examining how the session's structure waves up between contextualising taught academic language concepts and down to abstract level discussion of lexicogrammatical functions, providing insights into how EAP itself may be delivered more effectively.

LCT was not mentioned explicitly by many of our interviewees, which perhaps highlights its novelty as a theoretical underpinning of ISEAP practice. Also, like SFL, the unpacking of complex theory for learners in an in-sessional classroom may be problematic, and perhaps also for practitioners, as one of our interviewees observed:

> It's a very complex theory – there are three different levels, where you have semantic gravity, semantic density. We've been using it looking at PhD students' writing. We use it for reflective writing, where we have the grounded level and you can go up to generalisation and up to theory. It talks about waving between those. [One particular colleague] has the most knowledge about this; we all try to use it, but it's not something we all feel extremely comfortable with – but there is now emerging in EAP literature about how we can apply it in different aspects of our teaching.

However, it certainly may appeal to practitioners wanting to feel their practice has a stronger theoretical basis that perhaps offers a more systematic way of developing academic literacy, as this comment from a U.K. based practitioner from one of our interviews shows:

> I have read Steve Kirk – on training students to become discourse analysts. Sometimes I want to feel like I want to teach a body of knowledge that's more transferable, less tied to the module. With embedded in-sessional you analyse the assignment – what kind of language you'll be using: that sometimes feels a bit circular rather than cumulative.

2.4.6 Critical EAP

Critical EAP is essentially what Wingate (2015) refers to under the umbrella of 'socio-political' approaches, and it is an area which provides impetus to debates on identity and positioning of students within the academy, challenging power relationships and structures within the wider university context. It can therefore be seen as similar to AcLits in terms of its focus on the transformation of the individual, but in critical EAP (CEAP) this transformation has a purpose of effecting change also on the contexts in which the individual is studying. Another similarity between these two key theories is the criticism that there is a lack of clear applied coherent teaching methodology (e.g. as observed by Harwood and Hadley, 2004: 365). Despite the fact that many acknowledge the significance of critical approaches on how EAP has developed, for example Wingate includes it as a key theory in her 'inclusive model of academic literacy instruction' (2015: 128), how it is actually applied in EAP teaching practice is less clear (Ding and Bruce, 2017: 81).

Key figures associated with critical approaches specific to language teaching and EAP are Pennycook, Benesch, and Canagarajah. Pennycook used the term 'vulgar pragmatism' to describe the willingness to limit the pedagogical focus on 'technical, everyday concerns of students' academic study' (Fenton-Smith, 2014: A23). Instead, he endorsed 'critical pragmatism' to challenge bigger questions of 'values, norms and hierarchies' (Pennycook, 1997; Fenton-Smith, 2014: A23).

Benesch in the 1990s urged EAP practitioners to go beyond the traditional content of academic courses and deliberately include more controversial topics in the classroom, related for example to social injustice, unequal power distributions, and problems students may face in their own lives (Mendes Ferreira, 2022). Canagarajah suggested a language teaching approach that was very writer-situated, encouraging learners to critically explore the material conditions of their context and reveal issues of cultural and institutional power (Canagarajah, 2002, in Mendes Ferreira, 2022).

A key aim of critical EAP is the revealing of hidden ideologies, and this may be achieved simply by specifically selecting controversial topics and themes for a curriculum, as indeed was the case in Mendes Ferreira (2022), who reports not on an in-sessional context, but a summer intensive course. It is arguable that in ISEAP contexts, where there is a closer link to subject lecturers and the topic of study is typically already 'chosen,' there is less room for practitioners to have so much influence on what is discussed, perhaps instead there may be more opportunity for a focus on how it is discussed. It may also be felt that in in-sessional contexts the students are not 'our students' in the same way as for a preparation course, and depending on the relationship with the departments the practitioner is collaborating with in ISEAP contexts, challenging the hidden assumptions of the academy may not be an approach their colleagues will warm to. These might seem like accommodationist excuses for not implementing CEAP, however; as Fenton-Smith asks in his article exploring the place of CEAP, 'Is this a reasonable expectation of EAP instructors who may have legitimate fears about job security?' (2014: p. A26).

There may be room for CEAP in ISEAP though. In a discussion of Benesch, Fenton-Smith (2014) explores how a critical approach was applied in an ISEAP context (described as 'paired ESL-Psychology'), where part of the process, 'challenging,' involves content lecturers engaging with students' questions in a capacity as visitors to the language class, in a kind of reversal of typical lecturer-student power relations.

CEAP was mentioned explicitly by a couple of our interviewees; for example, one person linked it to the increasingly important decolonising the curriculum agenda:

> It is a huge area to explore, which is why I find it quite exciting. I'm just at the beginning of unpicking these areas and figuring out ways of bringing them together in practice, but a lot of that involves opening up that space in any classroom for students to reflect on their own experiences and backgrounds, and to look at the differences in those, in terms of this expectation that it slots into some sort of hierarchy where some things are valued and recognised and some things aren't. That's really a foundation of decolonising pedagogy: to elevate the significance and the centrality of individual experience, which is likely very different from the assumption of what the norm is, on which a lot of our intellectual processing is based.

As mentioned, the usual criticism of CEAP (for example Wingate, 2015; Ding and Bruce, 2017) is that it lacks a clear pedagogy. However, the above quote (and the popularity of articles in EAP journals on this topic over the last 10 to 15 years) suggest it is influential even if more as an underlying pedagogical concern, rather than an enacted one, and therefore definitely merits a mention in the knowledge base of ISEAP. Fenton-Smith (2014) suggests that it 'entails a radical reassessment of everything one does as an educator, and why one is doing it' and lists three useful questions which it raises for the EAP practitioner, which are interesting to mention in any discussion of pedagogy.

1. Should I be better informed about the nature of the industry I work in?

2. Should I be more aware of the ideological bases of my teaching?
3. Should the curricula I design and implement have a more critical edge?

(Fenton-Smith, 2014: A23–24)

2.5 Beyond the Pillars

As the discussion above shows, it is not always easy to categorise ISEAP pedagogy as it is enacted into one of the key EAP traditions, nor is there an expectation of following one as opposed to any other as the best approach for ISEAP or indeed any EAP setting. There are other ways of considering what the knowledge base of EAP consists of beyond this focus specifically on well-defined research traditions. In our interviews with practitioners we found underlying pedagogy may often relate to singular practices, concepts or wider values which inform practice, methodologies, or classroom teaching. Some influences may derive from prior teaching experience (typically English language teaching (ELT) and others arise as unique responses to context and cohort specificity. This final section of the chapter will focus on these other influences on ISEAP pedagogy in practice.

Firstly, it should be stated that in EAP literature, there are other conceptualisations of the EAP knowledge base that do not rely on the same kind of list or classification of key theories as in section 2.4 above. Hyland and Shaw (2016: 3), for instance, looked at underpinning theory in a different way, examining four wider ideals EAP enshrines in its practice: 'authenticity' (in terms of materials and tasks), 'groundedness' (closely linking research and teaching practice), 'interdisciplinarity' (acknowledging 'the eclectic range of theories and methods'), and 'relevance' (teaching based on an analysis of needs). These ideals perhaps also relate to wider considerations of why we are doing what we are doing in EAP in general and ISEAP in particular, i.e. research-informed language practice focussed on specificity, working closely within situated disciplinary settings with learners.

On a more practical note, and one that speaks more to the idea of EAP practitioners bringing prior teaching knowledge theories to bear, Bell (2022) suggests there is some value in reappraising a list of six pedagogical approaches identified in an earlier survey of practice by Watson Todd in 2013: inductive learning, process syllabuses, learner autonomy, use of authentic materials, technology-enhanced learning, and team teaching (Bell, 2022: 6). Although these approaches are not necessarily considered to be specific to ISEAP, EAP, or even language teaching per se, and are not necessarily prevalent streams of current academic research in the EAP field, most EAP practitioners would no doubt acknowledge at least two or three of these as having a formative influence on the evolution of how they teach. Team-teaching, technology-enhanced learning, process approaches, and authentic materials were all mentioned by our interviewees; and team-teaching and authenticity relate particularly to ISEAP as a collaborative, embedded area of practice.

The following section will pick up on a number of these key points and explore how they relate specifically to pedagogy in an ISEAP context.

2.5.1 ISEAP and Authenticity

The use of authentic materials could be perceived as relating to genre, discourse analysis, corpus linguistics, and Academic Literacies as part of the investigation of disciplinary specificity. However, authenticity was often mentioned in our interviews without it necessarily being specifically linked to one of the key traditions of EAP research in the section above. For example, in one of our interviews with two colleagues who work in the same university, we had this comment, demonstrating the perceived relevance of how a facet of pedagogy can transcend classification:

> I definitely use exemplars and my focus is on students being able to achieve all of that they can achieve, especially for international students. In my focus I use a combination of pedagogies and processes that are practical so the students can see what is going to make a difference.

Exemplars used in ISEAP contexts might be taken from published material from the disciplinary context (journal articles perhaps), or authentic samples of work by previous students, sometimes with extra insight in the form of feedback provided by the subject lecturers on the text. Tutor feedback and commentary on student work can add further contextual information about what is considered effective disciplinary specific communication, as this comment by the colleague of the interviewee above shows:

> I like the module leader to say 'this is a good piece of work, these are the features that we like: I don't like a flowery introduction, I don't want any filler, I want you to get to the point.' So that stuff informs my practice, I find that an easy way to teach – especially with refer/defer students: they don't have a lot of time to get up to speed.

Evidence supplied by authentic tutor feedback and input enables the ISEAP practitioner to make explicit what is implicit in terms of what the lecturer expects as effective communication in the discipline. Its use might be seen as too accommodationist perhaps, and as running the risk of teaching to a specific assignment or task, rather than delivering a comprehensive academic language and literacy syllabus. However, if presented as only part of an approach where learners themselves investigate the parameters of their own discipline, and if care is taken with stressing transferability to wider literacy development, such problematic aspects can be avoided.

The authentic text approach can certainly be aligned with genre approaches which take into account a wide range of contextual information, and can be helpful to the practitioner in the process of developing a comprehensive needs analysis, as in this example:

> Times I have done it, e.g. organised short courses for a specific module, and it's tremendously hard work, as you do a whole set of materials based on a course that up to that point you didn't really know. For bespoke materials, you need to do the research, the course, the genre, the discourse, try to get some models: three times two-hour sessions. It was the most rewarding teaching I've ever done on in-sessional, because I'd researched the course; it was new to me but it was fascinating.

This comment also reveals the amount of work that has to go into the preparation of truly tailored ISEAP provision, more of which will be discussed in Chapter 3. It shows how a non-specialist language practitioner can enter into a genre, as well as how satisfying ISEAP can be for the teacher in providing such situated, specific courses. This also introduces another practical question related to the use of authentic materials: the need for access. The most common way for ISEAP practitioners to get hold of authentic exemplars for use in ISEAP is to request samples from content lecturers they work with. This can, at times, be problematic, and failures in this area may lead to ISEAP content being less well informed and EAP practitioners having to be more innovative in what they use as the basis of their provision, as one interviewee commented:

> It's in the minority of cases that you can rely on the departments to give you all the information and all the texts and what you need, and more often than not we are doing all the chasing and we are inventing to fill the gaps.

It is not clear exactly what 'inventing' actually involves. However, what is clear is the need for a flexible and inventive approach to pedagogical design in ISEAP. Moreover, it shows that a proactive approach (i.e. 'chasing') is often required. One of our interviewees, who is based in the library of the institution where they work, told us that their team was working on building a repository of student work related to different disciplines they work with, with the ultimate intention of making this available to students as well as to all subject lecturers: a nice example of reciprocal cooperation between language specialist and subject lecturer.

Since moving much ISEAP delivery online, hastened by the experience of lockdown and COVID-19, a now more common means of obtaining access to key course module information and documents which then can be used in the ISEAP classroom is via course virtual learning environments or other module sites. This can help facilitate tighter integration into the target ISEAP context and solve any issues of access, as one of our interviewees noted:

> What's really helped with things going online: I can look at modules and see exactly where students have got to each week. It gives me an idea of the timeline assessments, report deadlines, when first drafts are going in […] I can see what students have done – first draft, second draft, the feedback they got and mark they got. You can almost do that journey with them. You can take excerpts, anonymise them. You can cherry-pick. It's that sharing of information.

This not only effectively enhances learning by ensuring relevance to the students but it is also puts the ISEAP practitioner in a place where they can understand the learning context of the students from a privileged position or vantage point within the learning experience as it takes place (for more on this unique vantage point of ISEAP practice, positioning, and effect on practitioner identity, see Chapter 5). It also reveals links to another of the six approaches mentioned by Bell (2022): process approaches to teaching writing, which look at planning, drafting, and refining written work over a period of time.

Process approaches may seem like an atypical feature of ISEAP contexts, where the EAP course is not the main focus of the cohort's attention and it is not always possible to follow students through all stages of their programmes of study. In fully embedded paradigms, there is typically a strict avoidance of adding to student's workload so this would preclude building in formative, draft writing tasks for instance. Students in in-sessionals are already concentrating on completing summative assignments and tasks and so homework is rarely a feature of most ISEAP courses. On the other hand, getting students to submit drafts of their own work in progress for assignments they are doing on their substantive programmes and sharing this as an authentic resource is a more familiar approach. The example that follows displays a very well-integrated ISEAP use of student input:

> We ran a few sessions a couple of weeks ago where students were able to look at work they had done, a large thesis, a fifty-page thesis in computer science, very technical, very heavy. And we were able to go through the handbook and the marking criteria and have them look at the work they were doing, midpoint, work in progress: look at some samples and really help them out.

Beyond 'authenticity,' this kind of approach to ISEAP provision also ensures 'relevance.' Moreover such a deep level of embeddedness within a specific authentic discipline also serves to further distinguish ISEAP pedagogical practices from other EAP contexts.

2.5.2 ISEAP Modes of Delivery

Team-teaching, which featured on Bell's list of approaches (2022), can be a very beneficial practice when the opportunity arises in ISEAP contexts to develop not only a very close, well-integrated and relevant provision, but also one which is developmental and sustainable over a period of time, for example in this comment on practice by a U.K.-based practitioner:

> The undergraduate work that I do that is part of their core module, so I go in and teach three one-hour sessions, so more of a lecture; they have the first half with their subject lecturer then I come in and do the second half, so I develop a relationship not just with the lecturer but also with the students ... [my work is] closely tied to the assessments, even duplicating slides from their lectures to demonstrate the relevance of what I'm teaching them.

The example below from another U.K. university describes an online team-teaching paradigm that has arisen since the days of the COVID-19 pandemic, where there was a sharing of teaching within the sessions with responsibilities for different phases of the class with specific interaction patterns (there is a mention of online break-out rooms):

> One other idea is that the online element in the last year and a half has placed us in a different realm as well. I had one module: I had a lecture where the lecturer was live, I was online, the teaching was happening. When it broke out, I was interacting with the online group.

It should be observed that this last example might raise some questions about the effect on the status and positioning of the ISEAP practitioner relative to the subject lecturer though, since their responsibility is as a facilitator of discussion. This illustrates an important issue for team teaching as part of ISEAP practice; the need to be clear about the role of the EAP specialist and to avoid becoming simply a teaching assistant to the content lecturer.

In terms of the mode of delivery, the use of either bookable or drop-in one-to-one tutorials giving feedback on draft student writing as part of the mix of ISEAP provision might not be considered ideal. There may be a perceived tendency in such sessions to focus primarily on language accuracy and thus identify this as a deficit practice. Moreover, having language practitioners perform this function could be perceived as reducing the content-embeddedness of their provision and placing them in a specifically adjunct position. However, in many cases, tutorials are included as part of an embedded ISEAP provision. Even in the case where tutorials are available to anyone from across the institution who signs up or drops in, it could be construed as a deficit approach and a reduction in the status of ISEAP to that of a 'tidying up' role, but this does not necessarily have to be the case. As one of our interviewees from a U.K. context, which has this as part of their provision, observed:

> We also do things like feedback on writing where students would access a set of contextualised materials on the programme learning page, and they would then have the opportunity to submit work for feedback to a Dropbox if they wanted.

Although they admitted to misgivings about the provision of feedback in such a decontextualised form, a discussion with a colleague made them realise that actually this has a place in ISEAP practice, as they observed that providing discoursal and linguistic feedback was very much within the skillset of ISEAP practitioners.

Furthermore, in the case above the interviewee went on to underline the reach this enables for the ISEAP provision and the EAP centre's own standing within the institution as perceived by students. This was considerable, as apparently the take-up of this feedback provision was very successful.

In terms of delivery and technology enhanced learning (TEL), the period of lockdowns due to the COVID-19 crisis (2020–22) clearly added greater impetus to the roll-out of online and technology enhanced modes in all areas of HE pedagogy, including ISEAP delivery. Online and hybrid teaching may have a longer term impact on how ISEAP provision is delivered, as another U.K. university practitioner noted:

> I think blended learning has taught us ways in which we can shape lectures and I think we're going to see different models appear in the next few years.

Overall, there was no typical mode of ISEAP delivery evident from our conversations with practitioners. There were however frequent mentions of workshops. Similar to one-to-ones and feedback on draft writing, this could potentially be seen as an example of decontextualised language provision rather than a specifically ISEAP approach as workshops suggest sign-up, EGAP and decontextualised EAP practices. However, using workshops may be a response to contextual constraints in some universities and can be made to work, perhaps in conjunction with discipline specific content. The case below, from an interview with an ISEAP practitioner in the United Kingdom, suggests the benefits of generic EAP workshops as they provide a solution to improving student recruitment in a context where ISEAP provision is not fully embedded in the timetable:

> We have a core set of workshops that students at all levels could access at any time – this helps us maximise the number of people who could attend. They are highly interactive, student-centred, accessible, and inclusive.

Also in this example below from another U.K. setting, open workshops sessions can be included as part of the ISEAP mix and may be an effective way to promote student recruitment, where that is necessary:

> We thought if we can offer more support like that – maybe that would be more effective. Booking a shorter workshop psychologically might be

more appealing rather than signing up for a whole module – a different method of accessing them.

In terms of how workshops are used as part of delivery in specific contexts, there may be potential for developing workshops open to wider audiences, even within specific ISEAP courses, and in the example below this may even have the effect of widening the remit of ISEAP provision and adding to community building across an institution. One interviewee from a Scandinavian context commented on how workshops are blended into their ISEAP provision:

> I work with doctoral students: we offer things for doctoral students who want to come to us. They [the workshops] are open for any faculty members too ... Also, non-credit workshop things: on writing disserta-tions, etc. ... We announce it and people sign up for it.

2.5.3 ISEAP and Language Teaching

Although ISEAP is not to be confused with simply teaching English language in academic settings, it is worth considering as a part of the pedagogical mix where more general theories related to language teaching have influence. In Englsh language teaching (ELT), often the background of many practitioners coming into ISEAP, the four skill areas of reading, writing, speaking and listening are often addressed as equal parts of the curriculum. In terms of the 'language skill area' of ISEAP sessions where influence from language teaching methodology was sometimes noted by our interviewees, writing was unsurprisingly the primary one. A greater focus on academic writing is in-herent in many genre-based EAP approaches, certainly SFL and corpus lin-guistics. Many U.K. pre-sessional courses still have a language skills focus as a defining concept of their syllabus and assessment models, even if in a number of institutions there has been a concerted move away from this. In ISEAP the specific focus on text production and writing tends to dominate. However, sessions on reading were frequently mentioned by our interviewees, as was speaking and there were a couple of references to a focus on listening. Aside from language skill areas, incorporating specific work on critical thinking was mentioned, as were grammar and vocabulary. Wingate's categorisation of atomised skills and a language-course study skills model implies that in-troducing these elements as separable skills areas is not advocated by her for

ISEAP contexts, but she notes that elements of this may still be prevalent within what actually goes on in practice in university EAP departments, even if practitioners and departments claim to follow a more Academic Literacies informed developmental approach (2015).

In our interviews, the word 'skills' was often mentioned, but not always specifically suggesting a skills approach. Occasionally though, in line with Wingate's point about the lingering influence of deficit approaches, we found non-discipline-specific grammar or academic speaking workshops were provided, albeit often as part of a wider mix of ISEAP provision.

Bell (2022: 8) suggests that the question of teaching methodology generally receives 'insufficient attention' in EAP research literature and questions whether 'methodological transfer' from EFL teaching has a positive or negative influence on what we do in EAP practice. Indeed, more practical guides to teaching EAP, such as Alexander et al. (2019) and de Chazal (2014), list a number of the items already identified in this chapter from the knowledge base of EAP, but also include theories of teaching which relate to classroom practice in general language teaching. For example, Alexander et al. discuss applications of task-based learning and an 'input into output' focus on grammar, alongside genre-based 'rhetorical consciousness raising' in their section on methodology (2019). de Chazal includes a list of influences on teaching practice and at the top of the list is ELT, asking the question: 'What aspects of general ELT methodology can we use in our EAP context?' (2014: 276). This can be seen as making a link between the origins of most EAP practitioners who arrived in this field from ELT contexts, as acknowledged by Ding and Bruce (2017). Consequently, it is important to acknowledge that the eclectic mix of what informs a practitioner's EAP pedagogy can include influences from prior teaching knowledge and practical language teaching techniques, even if these pedagogical traces are likely to need some modification and adaptation to fit for the specifics of teaching ISEAP.

One example of a very specifically EFL pedagogy in our interviews was a mention of the Dogme ELT approach to teaching. Accredited to Scott Thornbury (2005), Dogme methodology essentially suggests that the form of a language teaching session can be dictated purely by what the learners themselves bring with them, organically developing from what they wish to focus on at the time. One of our interviewees employs this in the case of EGAP, open-to-all drop-in ISEAP provision, where they come prepared only with a selection of generic PowerPoint slides and exemplars which they can draw on to facilitate illustration of a point, but the session itself is not based on any predetermined learning outcomes or scheme of work. This was developed as an approach very much in response to the particularity of having to teach sign-up sessions, with no formal tie to any particular discipline and where any student, undergraduate or postgraduate, could just turn up. Although the set-up is not ideal in ISEAP terms, this use of Dogme ELT seems highly appropriate given the constraints of the particular teaching context.

This example also demonstrates the importance once more of reflection on the part of the practitioner, questioning what underpins their practice from their own background and considering what elements of it they can bring with them into the more specific sphere of ISEAP; will their previously learned pedagogy still be applicable and suitable here? Chapter 5 will explore more of this in a section on practitioner identity.

A more commonly discussed example of a throwback to pedagogy from prior language teaching backgrounds which emerged in our interviews was communicative language teaching (CLT). This approach, which became the dominant focus of EFL instruction in the last 30 years, is based on social constructivist theories of learning and implies greater focus on communicative competence rather than on language accuracy or, in the case of speaking, attempting to emulate some standard form of pronunciation. CLT is mentioned as a key pedagogical underpinning for EAP for example in both Alexander et al. (2019) and de Chazal (2014), and a surprisingly large number of our interviewees cited it as an important influence. The most prominent example of this came when one head of department in a large U.K. university, who commented:

> The communicative approach to teaching is broadly what people think we're doing, and what we *are* doing as far as I know as I am not in every class. The bedrock is effectively communicative; do they adopt another approach for ESAP teaching? Fundamentally no.

It may be that for any language specialist, adopting a communicative approach to teaching comes naturally, as one interviewee in a Scandinavian context suggested:

> We [EAP practitioners] all have a multimodal approach to teaching, because we want our students to listen, to read, to write and to speak, or to 'discuss' let's say.

It is interesting to observe that CLT was relatively frequently mentioned in our interviews (more than corpus linguistics, LCT, or critical EAP, for example). Many noted the practical advantages of using it in their practice in order to create more engaging ISEAP sessions. For example, another interviewee stated:

> I actually think that CLT is no bad thing because it gives such a different experience in a workshop, getting students to do something rather than just sitting there listening to someone drone on.

Kirk and King (2022) however suggest there is a tension between CLT, with its emphasis on the 'how' of communicating socially in a broader sense (i.e. 'communicative competence') and EAP practice, where the attention is ideally trained on enabling students to grapple with the 'what' of academic discourse and practices. If we are labelling ISEAP pedagogy, is explicitly identifying our approach as CLT in such contexts really appropriate? Does CLT have a place beyond pure language course settings in an area where the subject matter is more concerned with language and literacy, and applied and complex knowledge?

One comment from a U.K. university head of department was:

> We need both theories of language and theories of learning; the latter is basically social constructivism – albeit in the guise of communicative language teaching.

This suggests that CLT is an example of a teaching technique from a broader language teaching background which can still be useful when applied to ISEAP classroom practice, essentially acting as an enabler for the practitioner to enact wider pedagogical aims. If not considering the sense of having the same underlying motivations for use or intentions in what it aims to teach, CLT is then applicable to ISEAP contexts as a handle for explaining a methodological approach, and can be seen as similar to other 'practical' modes of teaching such as team teaching or encouraging learner autonomy, from Bell's list (2022).

2.5.4 ISEAP and Wider Philosophies of Education

Social constructivism, as in the last example above, was sometimes mentioned by our interviewees as an ideological basis for ISEAP practice, although it appears there may be blurred lines between areas of pedagogical inspiration which arise from wider philosophies, such as constructivism or cognitivism. CLT in ISEAP contexts could be seen as an example of where practitioners take a familiar language teaching methodology and then translate that to how they enshrine key educational concepts and achieve their pedagogical aims. Perhaps, in this way CLT, a very familiar approach to anyone coming into EAP from a language teaching background, could be appropriated or at least translated into part of a mixed ISEAP pedagogy on an indirect basis, essentially related to teaching methodology, foregrounding interaction and collaborative learning as part of a social constructivist ideology. This may manifest itself in a reduced focus on grammatical accuracy, more on effective communication, or in the classroom encouraging discussion and promoting peer-to-peer feedback discussion on writing, for example.

Promoting discursive, collaborative learning, where learners work together to reach an understanding of their discipline's discourse was typically mentioned as part of ISEAP practice. As another interviewee from a U.K. institution stated:

> One of the things that I think is most valuable about [our in-sessional courses] is the discursive element, the chance to talk about writing, to share those questions.

Such approaches are common in ISEAP and this may be down to the typical origins of EAP practitioners, attempts to enshrine wider conceptualisations or philosophies of education such as social constructivism, or as a response to peculiar aspects of teaching in the ISEAP context. For example, one interviewee from a U.K. arts-based context commented that they were trying to enshrine ideas related to specific pedagogical concepts in their teaching approach:

> Situated learning, as in Lave and Wenger [1991], underpins the decision for how we're running it. We've had, for example, first and third year Animation students together – it was brilliant: promoting a community of practice, where they share practice, experiences and strategies. There is a novice-expert dynamic. We facilitate and plug gaps.

Moreover, they observed that this fitted well with their university's concept of community building, which introduces another aspect which ISEAP provision often attempts to address: taking pedagogical inspiration from institution-level principles. They went on to mention that these students often wanted 'a chat, not a didactic experience.' This indeed shows the value of ISEAP provision having a social function, beyond purely linguistic pedagogical aims, of promoting social interaction across boundaries. As another U.K.-based interviewee stated:

> Some students want to meet people from other countries. It creates a sense of community, we have writing retreats … it gets different types of writers together, especially at PGR [postgraduate research] level. It's like a support mechanism.

There are a number of implications of integrating teaching and collaborating with content lecturers which influence the pedagogical philosophies behind and the modes in which in-sessional language is taught. For example, some of our interviewees team teach or develop fully integrated and embedded sessions with content specialists. Others (as in the case of the previously mentioned practitioner who employed a Dogme ELT approach) are essentially on their own and have to make the best of completely decontextualised sessions where they are unsupported and have a floating population of potential attendees. The next chapter will discuss aspects of how context shapes ISEAP provision, and suggest ways in which practitioners can navigate this. Flexibility and fit with context are indeed important factors in deciding a pedagogical response in ISEAP. Along with the left-overs from practitioners' prior experience, and applications of wider ideological, methodological or simply key aspects of EAP theory, this section has further demonstrated, however, that a description of ISEAP pedagogy cannot rely simply on what are typically perceived as the key EAP theories. Diversity and complexity is at the heart of any truly representative picture of ISEAP pedagogy.

Concluding Thoughts

As we make clear throughout this book, ISEAP is by its nature a situated field of practice and therefore pedagogies cannot be considered in isolation from their contexts. Moreover, as previously stated, our interviews were not systematically organised as a research project, but as a series of informal conversations between practitioners. The points we make above are intended to serve illustrative purposes. Also, our interviewees were operating in universities in diverse locations, in the United Kingdom, Europe, Australia, South Africa, and Asia and this also needs to be taken into account. It cannot be assumed that the ISEAP provider will always have consistency in terms of the exact cohort they teach from one session to the next or the modes of delivery which are open to them within the context of the department and the institution where they operate.

For all these reasons, agility and adaptability are paramount in determining ISEAP pedagogy. There is clearly a benefit of having solid familiarity with methodologies and teaching techniques which support classroom management and engagement, as well as allow for differentiation between individual students within a class. However, ISEAP is an arena which demands further development and reflection on developing innovative pedagogical responses fit for context.

Bell (2022: 9) observes that teachers new to EAP contexts go through 'a process of enforced on-the-job learning.' The complexity of ISEAP contexts as demonstrated above suggests that the same is true for the sub-field of in-sessional teaching. This chapter ends with reflective questions, which aim to help navigate some of this complexity. In terms of the importance of ongoing reflection, Ding and Bruce note that 'part of the appeal of reflective practices lies in the perceived inability of theoretical or abstract knowledge to deal with the contingencies and complexity of practice' (2017: 143).

Indeed, as a final point on how to deal with the complexity of pedagogical options, it should be stressed that for ISEAP practitioners, continuous reflection on their practice is also advised. An interesting approach to this was mentioned by one of our interviewees' examination of pedagogy undertaken as a group project:

> Last year we did write some principles: how we think about ourselves and our ideologies and the way we think about our practice. We did write it down – Academic Literacies and supporting students in an enhancement way. But at the moment we don't have a departmental culture where everybody's on board with one way of doing things. Everyone in our team is very much versed in genre theory and Academic Literacies, and CLT – these underpin everybody's practice; LCT, SFL are more niche areas that some people are more interested in and other people aren't.

In a similar way, holding academic reading circles (Seburn, 2016) can provide a means for ISEAP practitioners to revisit a selection of key texts from the EAP knowledge base areas; participants discuss how their existing practice and teaching materials relate to these texts. Such forms of explicit reflection on pedagogy, whether collaborative or individual, in preparation for teaching in

ISEAP contexts or used retrospectively can help to make sense of the complexity.

This chapter has aimed to touch on as many of the different aspects informing ISEAP pedagogy as space here would allow, without specifically endorsing any of them. It is suggested that the reader engage with the reflective questions that follow to make their own decisions. It is clear that ISEAP pedagogy and how provision is taught should not be based solely on pedagogical choices made in a vacuum. The impact of contextual features, such as specific content areas, topics to cover, or the makeup of the cohort, even constraints over which the practitioner or EAP department have varying levels of influence or control over (such as modes of delivery and classroom or online set up) are all key features in determining the approach to teaching ISEAP. These logistical issues will be the focus of the chapter that follows.

Chapter 2 Reflection

1. **Examine the key theories of EAP as identified in this chapter.**
   The table below shows the key EAP theories as discussed in section 2.3 and for each one a couple of key texts explaining the theory are suggested as follow-up reading. You can use the third column to add notes on how the theory relates to your own specific context.

Theory	Key reading	Specific example of how this relates to your ISEAP practice
Genre theory	Swales (1990) Hyland (2004)	
Corpus Linguistics	Nesi and Gardner (2012) Viana and O'Boyle (2022)	
Systemic Functional Linguistics (SFL)	Martin and Rose (2008) Monbec (2020)	
Academic Literacies	Lea and Street (1998) Wingate and Tribble (2012)	
Legitimation Code Theory (LCT)	Maton (2014) Kirk (2022)	
Critical EAP	Benesch (2001) Fenton-Smith (2014)	

2. **Consider your personal pedagogy.**

   Before reading the next chapter, answer the questions below:

   A. What are your origins as a teacher? How familiar are you with in-sessional teaching at universities? What do you know about ISEAP?

   B. How did you get into EAP?

   C. How does ISEAP relate to your previous teaching practice?

   D. What can you bring with you, and translate into your teaching in in-sessional university contexts?

   E. What are your key personal values and beliefs about teaching? Which of those do you bring to bear in the context of teaching EAP?

   F. Which of the EAP pedagogical traditions in the table above do you most closely subscribe to? Which do you not know so much about – what might you like to try?

   G. How do your answers to questions A to F above influence your pedagogical approach to teaching in in-sessional contexts?

   H. Do you plan to make your pedagogical approach explicit to learners/collaborators/colleagues working in your department? If so, how would you communicate this?

References

Alexander, O., Argent, S. and Spencer, J. (2019) *EAP Essentials: A teacher's guide to principles and practice.* 2nd ed. Reading: Garnet.

BALEAP (2022) *BALEAP TEAP Individual Accreditation Scheme 2022 Handbook.* https://www.baleap.org/wp-content/uploads/2022/04/BALEAP-TEAP-Handbook-2022-edition.pdf [accessed 1/10/22].

Benesch, S. (2001) *Critical English for academic purposes: Theory, politics and practice.* Mahwah, NJ: Lawrence Erlbaum.

Bell, D. (2022) Methodology in EAP: Why is it largely still an overlooked issue? *Journal of English for Academic Purposes,* 55:2022, 1–11.

Bhatia, V.K. (2004). *Worlds of written discourse: A genre-based view.* London: Bloomsbury Academic.

Bond, B. (2020) *Making language visible in the university: English for academic purposes and internationalisation.* Bristol: Multilingual Matters.

Bruce, I. (2011) *Theory and concepts of English for academic purposes.* Basingstoke: Palgrave Macmillan.

Canagarajah, A.S. (2002). *A geopolitics of academic writing.* University of Pittsburgh Press.

Carlile, O. and Jordan, A. (2005) It works in practice but will it work in theory? The theoretical underpinnings of pedagogy. In O'Neill, G., Moore, S. and Mc Mullin, B. (eds) *Emerging issues in the practice of university learning and teaching*. Dublin: Aishe.

Charles, M. (2013) English for Academic Purposes. In Paltridge, B. and Starfield, S. (eds.) *The handbook of English for specific purposes*. Oxford: Wiley and Blackwell, pp. 137–153.

Coxhead, A. (2000) A New Academic Word List. *TESOL Quarterly*, 34:2, 213–238.

de Chazal, E. (2014) *English for academic purposes*. Oxford: Oxford University Press.

Ding, A. and Bruce, I. (2017) *The English for academic purposes practitioner: Operating on the edge of academia*. Cham, Switzerland: Palgrave Macmillan.

Fairclough, N. (2010) *Critical discourse analysis: The critical study of language* (2nd ed.). Abingdon, Oxon: Routledge.

Fenton-Smith, B. (2014) The place of Benesch's critical English for academic purposes in the current practice of academic language and learning. *Journal of Academic Language & Learning*, 8:3, A23–A33.

Gardner, S. (2012) Genre and registers of student report writing: An SFL perspective on texts and practices. *Journal of English for Academic Purposes*, 11:2012, 52–63.

Harwood, N. and Hadley, G. (2004) Demystifying institutional practices: Critical pragmatism and the teaching of academic writing. *English for Specific Purposes* 23:4, 355–377.

Hyland, K. (2002) *Teaching and researching writing*. Harlow: Pearson Education.

Hyland, K. (2004) *Disciplinary discourses: Social interactions in academic writing*. Michigan: Michigan ELT.

Hyland, K. (2013) ESP and Writing. In Paltridge, B. and Starfield, S. (eds.) *The handbook of English for specific purposes*. Oxford: Wiley and Blackwell, pp. 95–114.

Hyland, K. and Shaw, P. (2016) Introduction. In Hyland, K. and Shaw, P. (eds.) *The Routledge handbook of English for academic purposes*. Abingdon, Oxon: Routledge, pp. 1–4.

Hyon, S. (1996) Genre in three traditions: implications for ESL. *TESOL Quarterly*, 30:1996, 693–722.

Ivanič, R. (1998) *Writing and identity: The discoursal construction of identity in academic writing*. Amsterdam: John Benjamins.

Ivanič, R. (2004) Discourses of writing and learning to write. *Language and Education*, 18:3, 220–245.

Kirk, S. (2022) Legitimation Code Theory: Addressing Fragmentation in EAP. In Ding, A. and Evans, M. (eds) *Social theory for English for academic purposes: Foundations and perspectives*. London: Bloomsbury Academic, pp. 87–112.

Kirk, S. and King, J. (2022) EAP teacher observation: Developing criteria and identifying the forms of pedagogic practice they afford, *Journal of English for Academic Purposes*, 59, 101139.

Kumaravadivelu, B. (2001) Toward a postmethod pedagogy. *TESOL Quarterly*, 35:4, 537–560.

Larsen-Freeman, D. (2000) *Techniques and principles in language teaching* (2nd ed.). Oxford: Oxford University Press.

Lave, J. and Wenger, E. (1991) *Situated learning: Legitimate peripheral participation*. Cambridge: Cambridge University Press.

Lea, M.R. and Street, B. (1998) Student writing in higher education: An academic literacies approach. *Studies in Higher Education*, 23:2, 157–172.

Martin, J.R. and Rose, D. (2008). *Genre relations: Mapping culture*. London: Equinox.

Maton, K. (2014) *Knowledge and knowers: Towards a realist sociology of education*. Abingdon, Oxon: Routledge.

McGrath, L. and Kaufhold, K. (2016) English for Specific Purposes and Academic Literacies: eclecticism in academic writing pedagogy, *Teaching in Higher Education*, 21:8, 933–947.

Mellow, J.D. (2002) Towards principled eclecticism in language teaching: The two-dimensional model and the centering principle. *TESL-EJ*, 5:4, 1–18.

Mendes Ferreira, M. (2022) Using Developmental Teaching to Promote Critical EAP in an Academic Writing Course in English. In MacDiarmid, C. and MacDonald, J. (Eds.) *Pedagogies in English for academic purposes: Teaching and learning in international contexts*. London: Bloomsbury Academic, pp. 75–90.

Meyer, J.H.F. and Land, R. (2003) Threshold concepts and troublesome knowledge: linkages to ways of thinking and practising. In Rust, C. (ed.) *Improving student learning - theory and practice ten years on*. Oxford: Oxford Centre for Staff and Learning Development (OCSLD), pp. 412–424.

Monbec, L. (2020) Systemic functional linguistics for the EGAP module: Revisiting the common core. *Journal of English for Academic Purposes*, 43, 100794.

Nesi, H. and Gardner, S. (2012) *Genres across disciplines: Student writing in higher education*. Cambridge: Cambridge University Press.

Nicholls, K. (2021) Illuminating expertise in academic language development: English for Academic Purposes practitioners in the UK. *International Journal of English for Academic Purposes: Research and Practice*, 2021 (Autumn), 167–191.

Pennycook, A. (1997) Vulgar pragmatism, critical pragmatism, and EAP. *English for Specific Purposes*, 16:4, 253–269.

Purser, E., Dreyfus, S. and Jones, P. (2020) Big ideas and sharp focus: researching and developing students' academic writing across the disciplines. *Journal of English for Academic Purposes*, 43, 100807.

Sancho Guinda, C. (2015) Genres on the move: Currency and erosion of the genre moves construct. *Journal of English for Academic Purposes*, 19:2015, 73–87.

Seburn, T. (2016) *Academic reading circles*. CreateSpace Independent Publishing Platform.

Solli, K. and Muir, T. (2021) EAP Pedagogies for Doctoral Students in Professional Fields. In MacDiarmid, C. and MacDonald, J. (Eds.) *Pedagogies in English for academic purposes: Teaching and learning in international contexts.* London: Bloomsbury Academic, pp. 59–74.

Swales, J. (1990) *Genre analysis: English in academic and research settings.* Cambridge: Cambridge University Press.

Thornbury, S. (2005) *Dogme: Dancing in the Dark?* Available at: http://nebula.wsimg.com/22eaea86234146ac3105f57698b06b75?AccessKeyId=186A535D1BA4FC995A73&disposition=0&alloworigin=1 [accessed 2/10/22].

Tuck, J. (2018) *Academics engaging with student writing: Working at the higher education textface.* Abingdon, Oxon: Routledge.

Viana, V. and O'Boyle, A. (2022) *Corpus linguistics for English for academic purposes.* Abingdon, Oxon: Routledge.

Walsh Marr, J. (2021) Moving from Form to Function: Leveraging SFL Metalanguage to illuminate features and functions of texts in First-year University EAP. In MacDiarmid, C. and MacDonald, J. (Eds.) *Pedagogies in English for academic purposes: Teaching and learning in international contexts.* London: Bloomsbury Academic, pp. 43–58.

Wingate, U. (2015) *Academic literacy and student diversity: The case for inclusive practice.* Bristol: Multilingual Matters.

Wingate, U. and Tribble, C. (2012) The best of both worlds? Towards an English for Academic Purposes/Academic Literacies writing pedagogy. *Studies in Higher Education*, 37:4, 481–495.

Chapter 3

Logistical Issues in ISEAP

Having considered some of the essential complexities inherent in the context of ISEAP provision and the pedagogical options open to the practitioner, this chapter looks more closely at the practice of in-sessional delivery. It draws on case studies, both published and from our interviews, to help enable practitioners navigate practicalities in the shifting sands of in-sessional provision. Practitioners are likely to be working beyond the confines of the largely unified syllabus of a pre-sessional, with its clear learning outcomes and academic support structures. Instead, they are probably interacting more closely with the wider institution, perhaps with senior management, in implementing courses, or with disciplinary colleagues, trying to find the best solutions to further develop the language and literacy of their students. Or indeed practitioners may be working without any support in deciding the learning outcomes, designing both syllabus and materials, and in delivering the course itself. Nevertheless, in-sessional activities probably situate the EAP practitioner within wider academic cultures beyond the EAP centre. For these reasons, of all EAP teaching settings, ISEAP can sometimes be the most demanding of the EAP practitioner. We have seen some of the advantages that an EAP practitioner's background in ELT can bring, with a suite of pedagogic approaches to draw upon, yet Pitt et al. (2019: 76) highlight a possible disadvantage of this: they note that for practitioners from a language teaching background, 'adapting to the culture of academia can be daunting.'

DOI: 10.4324/9781003193715-5

By focussing on some of the practicalities, this chapter aims to make the essential complexities of this situation rather less daunting.

As we have already outlined, probably the most effective paradigm for delivery is for language and literacy development to have a disciplinary focus, and as far as possible, to be embedded as a part of students' overall learning. As we might also imagine, this requires the highest level of investment on the part of an institution, to enable EAP practitioners to maintain a high degree of collaboration and to engage as fully as possible with disciplinary approaches and practices. But as Wingate (2015: 62) comments, such a highly integrated approach is unusual as it needs the support of university managers and what she terms 'considerable structural changes.' There is evidence, based on our own experience and on our interviews with practitioners, that such structural changes are taking place in some disciplines at some institutions. But to give an idea of the kind of investment needed to set up such a 'best practice' model, Pitt et al. (2019: 75–76), explaining the implementation of an embedded in-sessional model, itemised the likely work that needs to be done:

> For even a single hour-long lecture or seminar within a module timetable, it is not unusual to invest considerable time in reading module handbooks, exploring assignment briefs, getting to know the discipline, and to then spend many hours liaising with local lecturers and designing bespoke materials which are pitched to meet the needs of a diverse cohort.

This summarises some of the reality of collaboration. It may well be intellectually stimulating and creatively satisfying work, but within common EAP workload allocation models, it is sometimes a luxury to have 90 minutes to prepare an hour of teaching. It is indeed likely that many practitioners work in less than ideal settings with regard to the level of institutional support and investment in ISEAP, so the work of this chapter is to help practitioners make the choices that best utilise the resources available. Nevertheless, even where provision is not highly embedded, one should not underestimate the workload attached to ISEAP. As one of our interviewees put it:

> Implementation in a busy university year is tricky … as I'm sure you know, there is a lot of behind-the-scenes work: from focus groups to genre to scheduling to, if you can, needs analysis. Behind the scenes that's a lot of work compared to other areas of things we do.

This interviewee goes on to compare in-sessionals to 'a blancmange,' emphasising their inherently messy qualities. This chapter then aims to present a recipe for the blancmange, raising the visibility of hidden aspects of preparing and producing a course. Balancing the challenges of a high and challenging workload against something more positive, this same interviewee reflected back on their earlier experience teaching in-sessionals:

> I find it a very curious experience in many ways. It literally was some of the most interesting, rewarding teaching that I've done in the twenty years when I was doing a lot of teaching. But also if you asked me to do a cline of the least rewarding, it would also be it.

We aim to help the reader navigate the setting so that their experience is at the most rewarding end of this cline. The chapter follows a typical progression of developing a course: from information-gathering and conducting a needs analysis, to its actual implementation, often through collaborative partnerships, to issues surrounding its delivery.

3.1 Information Gathering and Needs Analysis

Given the highly contextualised nature of ISEAP, a needs analysis is even more important here compared with other EAP courses. It is essential to gain detailed insight into how language is used in disciplinary settings and consequent expectations about student performance. Given the variation among disciplinary approaches, there can be no 'common core' of discrete language needs applicable to all situations. However, conducting a needs analysis is highly dependent on the resources available and the level of cooperation possible with the disciplinary department. The approach we present below is specific to ISEAP, but is informed by the approaches presented by Hutchinson and Waters (1987) for English for Specific Purposes (ESP) and Jordan (1997) and Dudley-Evans and St John (1998) for EAP, as well as Hyland's (2006) and Bruce's (2011) discussions and development of these. As Hyland (2006: 74) notes though:

> EAP courses rarely provide enough time to meet all identified needs, nor adequate time to collect and analyse needs data, which means that teachers typically write their courses on the basis of incomplete information.

With this in mind, the approach we present is adaptable according to different logistical constraints and the degree of collaboration possible.

The first question one may ask is 'What do we mean by need?'; Jordan (1997: 22) notes that needs analysis is an umbrella term encompassing a potentially complex array of approaches: 'target-situation analysis, present-situation analysis, deficiency analysis, strategy analysis, means analysis, language audit and constraints.' However, in order to be as usable as possible, we adopt a streamlined approach that is centred upon the target situation. Hutchinson and Waters (1987: 55) think of needs in terms of 'necessities,' 'lacks,' and 'wants' in the approach to needs analysis they recommend for ESP courses. Our starting point is their necessities: 'observing what situations the learner will need to function in and then analysing the constituent parts of them.' This is essential to ISEAP, understanding the context in which language will be used; this will be considered under the heading **Target Situation Analysis**. Hutchinson and Waters (1987) further describe 'lacks' as relating to the existing proficiency of learners – what they do and do not know – and 'wants' as relating to learners' own awareness, what they themselves think they need. Some insight into both of these is essential to a needs analysis, and will be considered under the heading **Present Situation Analysis**. There may be tension between these elements, but all of them are important to identify a rounded picture of need.

In their needs analysis, Hutchinson and Waters (1987: 58) state the following ways that information can be collected:

questionnaires;
interviews;
observation;
data collection, e.g. gathering texts;
informal consultations.

This is a good starting point for our purposes. To this we would further add that *interviews* should ideally be with subject lecturers and *gathering texts* takes place through cooperation with them. *Observation* of lectures and/or seminar interactions is undoubtedly beneficial if it is an available option. To this list we would also add:

collecting assessment briefs;
examples of student work.

Like Hyland, we caution against over-relying on *questionnaires* for needs analysis, which may well offer 'restricted reliability and [a] one dimensional picture' (2006: 78). The needs data collected in this way may be overly reductive. We recommend more than one means of data collection to create a fuller picture of needs, for example *interviewing* or *consulting* a subject lecturer and *gathering relevant texts* and *assignment briefs*; the opportunity to *observe* a class can only enhance the reliability of data gained.

As is often the case in academia, consultation is often quite informal in nature, and connections get made via a variety of means. One of our interviewees effectively illustrated the highly personal way such collaborations can form, describing an EAP colleague:

> He collaborated with somebody from Economics, but apart from being colleagues in the same university they were also jazz fans. So they had a friendship based on the mutual like of jazz, so that made the collaboration easier.

Despite the informality of the relationship described above, there is no reason for a consultation to be completely unstructured. However one meets with an informant, discussions should be entered into in a structured way with a clear idea of the questions that need to be answered. There may be comparatively few opportunities for such discussion, so having a clear idea of the type of information required is essential. It can yield a personal understanding of an academic department's cultural practices, revealing insider knowledge that is difficult to gain through other means. In consultation with subject lecturers, there is also no reason not to assert one's specialist EAP knowledge. The interviewee above emphasised the discourse awareness that EAP practitioners bring to such conversations:

> The discipline-based academics don't tell us what their students need. Of course not, because they don't know in our terms what the students need.

Thus, it aids collaboration if one is able to meet disciplinary experts on an equal footing, recognising the specialism, knowledge and experience both parties can bring to understanding and analysing the students' target situation. It may be that, as Hutchinson and Waters (1987: 60) argue, that subject lecturers exaggerate the need for English due to their own personal investment in making the case for a high level of English required in their discipline. Balancing this against other data sources like an analysis of typical texts, task types and examples of student production will help identify a more satisfactory picture of the language needs in the target situation.

3.1.1 Target Situation Analysis

The following table takes Hutchinson and Waters' target situation analysis as its starting point, centring the key areas of investigation around five of the essential questions in their framework. A difference in our model compared with theirs is the change in tense from future to present, as the target situation in ISEAP is concurrent to students' learning on the course. Furthermore, the sub-points have all been adapted to specifically ISEAP contexts, informed too by Hyland's (2006) adaptations as well as our own. The second column offers an indication about where the information can be sourced from, depending on the learning context. The questions presented here will go on to inform course design, investigating the target situation before teaching begins (Table 3.1).

In using this table, it is important to recognise that in order to gather information about, say, *where* the language is used, practitioners are not restricted to administrative data sources; consultation with subject lecturers is likely to be an invaluable source of information in answering many of the questions. When conducting the target situation analysis, it is important to be aware of what Bruce (2011: 27) calls 'the meta-knowledge of academic settings,' that is localised factors such as how a course is organised, how its content is presented to students, departmental communication practices and how assessment is conducted. Deconstructing course documents will provide insight into how students experience their degree.

This research process has the potential to be wide and lengthy, depending on the quantity of data sources available. In-sessional activities can be compared to an iceberg, given the amount of hidden activity that goes into worthwhile course design. Indeed, such a detailed analysis may well be beyond the scope of a single EAP practitioner. The opposite situation is also possible: where resources are restricted and choices need to be made about the most important information needed. It is worth referring back to advice offered in Chapter 1; as a minimum an understanding is needed of:

the types of texts students have to read;
their task types;
and the ways in which information is delivered.

Table 3.1 Target situation analysis

Information needed about the target situation	Possible information sources

Why is the language needed?
• programme of study:
  • participate in seminars;
  • give presentations;
  • collaborate with peers;
  • understand lecture content;
  • read particular genres of text;
  • navigate interdisciplinarity;
  • write assignments: essays, reports and others genres;
  • perform in examinations.
	Discussion(s) with subject lecturers about the learning setting and the functional use of language in context;
	Focus group(s) with previous cohorts of students.

How is the language used?
• medium: reading, writing, listening, speaking;
• channel:
  • face-to-face classroom setting;
  • online meeting rooms;
  • message boards;
• types of discourse:
  • epistemologies;
  • academic texts: articles, books, essays, reports:
    • typical structure of these texts;
    • discourse analysis, genre analysis;
    • disciplinary referencing conventions;
  • lectures, seminar interactions:
    • typical forms;
    • discourse analysis, salient features;
  • emails;
  • informal conversations, tutorials.
	Access to:
	• past assignment briefs;
	• past examination papers;
	• past examples of student writing;
	• examples of feedback and grades awarded.
	Virtual learning environment (VLE).

What are the content areas?
• academic discipline(s):
  • an applied disciplinary field?
  • interdisciplinarity;
• level of study: PG, UG, Foundation.
	Student handbooks; programme and module specifications;
	Access to key texts from reading lists;
	Quality Assurance Agency (QAA) subject benchmark statements or equivalent.

Who does the learner use the language with? • classmates and lecturers; • L1 and/or L2 speakers of English; • level of knowledge among participants: expert, intermediate; beginner; • relationships: peer, superior, subordinate.	Observations of the learning settings, to see interactions – face-to-face and/or online; Access to course enrolment stats and registers if available.
Where is the language used? • physical setting: classroom, lecture theatre, studio space, or online spaces; • human context: alone, among peers, with lecturers; • linguistic context: overseas or home/EMI setting.	Departmental administration and timetabling.

Adapted from Hutchinson and Waters (1987: 59) and Hyland (2006: 75).

It should also be noted that this is not what Hutchinson and Waters (1987: 59) call a 'once-for-all activity'; rather, as de Chazal (2014: 267) emphasises, it is part of a cycle of activity that continues into curriculum design and materials development, before returning to the needs analysis, to consider whether the course design fulfils these needs. A fuller picture of needs necessarily takes time to coalesce. With an understanding of the demands of the target situation, we should now turn our attention to the 'lacks' and 'wants' of the learners themselves by focussing on the present situation analysis.

3.1.2 Present Situation Analysis

In order to find out about the learners themselves at the point of entry onto an ISEAP course, we have again based our approach on Hutchinson and Waters' (1987: 62–63) essential questions and Hyland's (2006: 75) adaptations. We have adapted the questions to an ISEAP context and have added a column to the table indicating the likely sources of information. Students' 'wants' and 'lacks' are explicitly engaged with in this consideration of why students are taking the course and their existing knowledge and abilities (Table 3.2).

At the heart of analysing the present situation is the learners themselves. Time dedicated to understanding the diversity of learner needs, their prior learning experiences, and the expectations for the course are invaluable to its success. In an environment that is often focussed on deficit – 'how can we improve their language?' – and producing outcomes in a limited timeframe, it may sometimes seem that the voice of the students themselves gets lost. The distinction between target and present situation can be slightly clouded in ISEAP, simply because it is not a preparation course: learners are engaged in the target situation on their degrees while engaged in the present situation of the in-sessional. By focussing on these two separate aspects of the needs analysis, it ensures the presence of the student voice in the process. As with the target situation analysis, the present situation should be revisited where possible, negotiating the curriculum in some way to maintain its relevance and student engagement. In the following section, we hear from some of our interviewees about some of the practicalities of conducting their own needs analyses.

3.1.3 Voices from the Field

The target and present situation analyses outlined above potentially entail the collection of a detailed wealth of information, and naturally this may not always be straightforward in specific institutional instances. A cautionary note was

Table 3.2 Present situation analysis

Information needed about the present situation	Possible information sources
Who are the learners? • age, gender, nationality, L1/L2 speakers of English; • what do students already know about the target situation's linguistic requirements? • disciplinary knowledge learners already have; • their attitude to their discipline; • socio-cultural background.	Enrolment information Discussion with admissions tutors Pre-enrolment discussions with students Possible knowledge from pre-sessional course
Why are the learners taking the course? • compulsory or optional; • apparent needs. **Wants:** • What do the learners expect to achieve? • academic goals – what do they want from an ISEAP course? • What is their attitude towards the ISEAP course? • Do learners have the time to dedicate to it, with reference to the other commitments at different times of the academic year?	Pre-enrolment activities: • 'placement' testing; • reflective writing; • questionnaires. Speaking to the learners themselves at key moments during the course: • focus groups; • in-class discussion activities.
How do the learners learn? • learning background; • experience and conceptualisation of teaching and learning; • appropriate methodologies – size of ISEAP groups is a factor here; • learner strategies.	
What do the learners know? • literacy abilities; • writing and/or seminar experience. **Lacks:** • linguistic proficiency; • apparent needs; • discoursal awareness; • familiarity with key academic genres.	
When will the ISEAP course take place? • scheduled around learners' disciplinary studies; • time of day (are students on campus/able to get online?); • mapped to points of key need; • students' availability.	Best answered from data collected during the target situation analysis

Adapted from Hutchinson and Waters (1987: 62–63) and Hyland (2006: 75).

struck by one of our interviewees, who coordinates in-sessional provision at a large U.K. university. Underlining the importance of needs analysis as a foundation for ISEAP design and development, they explained some of the consequences when detailed information could not be gained about the target situation:

It's fine from an operational point of view, because you can still get the thing up and running. Where I find that it does become challenging is that for the people on the team teaching those modules and working with those departments it can start to feel a little bit dispiriting, where they feel that they're supporting these students, they're trying to do the most useful thing for these students, but they can't quite get the information that they need. And so then as a programme director that obviously needs quite careful management to manage the expectations of people in your team, make sure they have got some guidance on what they can do with the students, perhaps directing them to other resources they can look at, but it does become more challenging all around.

An absence of information at this stage can have knock-on effects on morale, management of teaching and learning, and ultimately on the relevance of the curriculum to students' actual learning needs. As our interviewee states, operationally it is possible to run a course, but its usefulness becomes much more open to question.

There is no doubt that gaining detailed disciplinary information can be a daunting task. Gathering information about an unfamiliar discipline and interacting with disciplinary experts demands a high level of engagement from the EAP practitioner. Another of our interviewees spoke about the demanding nature of performing a needs analysis, working alone to set up content-informed ISEAP:

It's tremendously hard work, because you're doing a whole set of materials based on a course that up to that point you didn't really know. And then you're making bespoke materials: you have to do the research on the course, the genre, the discourse, try and get some models. To be honest, it was the most rewarding teaching I've ever done, because I'd researched the course; it was new to me but it was fascinating. And I looked at the way articles were written. I looked at the way students wrote, and we discussed genre and discourse and they just wanted to learn.

Even though the detailed needs analysis laid the foundations for a successful course, in the end limited resources meant that the course could not be sustained in this instance. Again, a practitioner comments on the rewarding nature of highly specific ISEAP teaching, yet they were not the only interviewee to comment on the challenges of sustaining an ESAP approach. The risks inherent to an approach based on personal relationships again become apparent. In contrast, where there is a culture of content-led ISEAP within an institution, having clear systems can greatly help this kind of data collection. When asked about how needs analysis was conducted in their institution, another practitioner was able to explain their systematic five-point approach:

> It involves:
>
> 1. Desk research: finding module specs, looking at the VLE [virtual learning environment] and looking at materials.
> 2. Getting in touch with the department, asking 'can I be on the VLE module?,' and checking that things haven't changed.
> 3. Going to departments with a suggested syllabus: 'do you think these are the areas … ?.' You need to show you've done work already rather than expecting them to tell me.
> 4. Looking at module reviews, identifying where students have performed well or not.
> 5. Meeting the students: this is what I really want. It is constantly evolving. A cohort is not fixed, and needs change.

Here we have a streamlined and practicable procedure for needs analysis, which aligns closely with the approach explained above: points 1 to 3 gain an understanding of the target situation, and 4 to 5 hone in on the present situation, including students' needs and wants. More ethnographically informed means of information gathering like classroom observations are notably missing, but further data sources can be added where resourcing allows. The five-point plan described is likely to be within the means of a busy EAP department and enables courses to be aligned closely to student needs. It is also important to underline again that needs analysis is not finished when a course begins, but is subject to fine tuning and ongoing responses to changing needs.

The involvement of students is central to the approaches we recommend, and in-sessional practitioners need to be adept at managing competing preconceptions and understandings, which may differ among stakeholders. As Hyland (2006: 79) notes, '"needs" will be defined differently by different stakeholders, with university administrators, subject tutors, teachers and learners having different views.' Benesch (2001) focusses on the ideological and instrumental aspects inherent in the concept of 'needs,' and instead advocates a 'rights analysis,' focussing on the students' voices and their active participation in the direction of the course. A full rights analysis may be beyond the resources of a busy EAP practitioner, but it highlights the importance of including students in decision making, especially in an environment where many stakeholders may be seeking a 'quick fix.' Indeed, the very concept of a needs analysis would imply a deficit model to many of the stakeholders Hyland (2006) lists above. However, once the analysis of needs (and possibly rights) has been understood and performed, the next stage is to work with the information gained to create actual provision.

3.2 Implementation

Moving from identifying needs to delivering a course that actually meets those needs is not a straightforward undertaking. An influential concept in in-sessional course design is the CEM Model (Sloan and Porter, 2010), a framework for collaboration that has been drawn upon for many univiersities' provision. Developed at Northumbria University for international PGT students at its business school, even where it has not been fully implemented, the underlying principles of this model have become common currency among practitioners developing discipline-informed in-sessionals. Many of our interviewees referred explicitly to these principles and explained how they worked with them, or adapted them, to their own institutional context. Their voices will be considered after an outline of the model itself.

3.2.1 The CEM (Contextualisation, Embedding, Mapping) Model

Recognising the complexities inherent to in-sessional provision, Sloan and Porter (2010: 199) describe the CEM Model as 'practice-based,' specifically created 'to improve the management, design and delivery of EAP through establishing a stronger working partnership between EAP tutors and business tutors.' It offers a framework through which in-sessional provision can be integrated closely to disciplinary learning. The model presents three interconnected elements which should all be present: contextualisation, embedding, and mapping. The authors present these graphically as a Venn diagram (Figure 3.1).

It is most straightforward that Sloan and Porter (2010: 202) explain the three elements:

> *Contextualisation* [...] relates to the context in which the learning and teaching of EAP was presented and communicated to the students;
> *Embedding* [...] reflects the position of the EAP programme within the

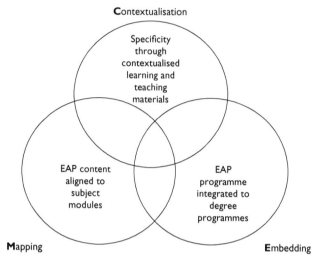

Contextualisation

Specificity
through
contextualised
learning and
teaching
materials

EAP content
aligned to
subject
modules

EAP
programme
integrated to
degree
programmes

Mapping   Embedding

Figure 3.1 The CEM Model (Sloan and Porter, 2010: 205).

overall degree programme and the position of the EAP tutor in the
academic business team; and *Mapping* [...] involves coordinating the EAP
teaching with student learning needs and outcomes throughout the
academic year.

Beyond their immediate context of Northumbria's business school, **contextualisation** concerns a move away from more generic EAP approaches.
Instead, there needs to be effective collaboration between EAP and subject
lecturers to create contextualised in-sessional teaching materials. The focus is
on academic literacy within the disciplinary field, mainly through working
with specific texts and tasks from the discipline, often at a modular level. By
collaborating with a module leader, the EAP practitioner will have a more
nuanced awareness of epistemologies, disciplinary conventions and assessment
practices. The purpose is for learners to see the relevance of this disciplinary-
focussed EAP *and* then to be able to transfer their language and literacy acquisition to their learning on other modules. A detailed target situation
analysis based on a high degree of involvement from disciplinary specialists
reaps rewards here.

The purpose of **embedding** is to change perceptions of both students and
subject lecturers, so that ISEAP is not seen as a peripheral adjunct, but rather
an integral part of their learning. It repositions the EAP practitioner as part of
the degree's teaching team, not as a 'visitor', which is intended to change

students' perceptions of the in-sessional. To make embedding effective, Sloan and Porter (2010) advise that the in-sessional course must be presented to students at the programme induction; the EAP tutor should be identified as part of the disciplinary team; and the ISEAP sessions should appear on the students' timetables. There should be similar clarity about the start date and student groups. (A reason for the failure of an in-sessional programme is sometimes because a student cannot find it; its promotion is not always clear and students often experience difficulty navigating institutional structures.)

Mapping concerns the appropriate timing of key areas of input. Sloan and Porter (2010: 203–204), referring to an earlier decontextualised in-sessional programme, note that it 'did not deliver EAP seminars on dissertation writing skills at a time in the academic year when students felt those inputs were appropriate.' Instead, the CEM Model advocates a targeting of provision at the point of need, such as around particular assessments or activities. In order for mapping to be effective, regular two-way communication needs to be maintained between EAP and disciplinary specialists. Again, being seen as a part of the disciplinary team is helpful; attending teaching and learning meetings enables such timely interventions. The implication of mapping is that in-sessional delivery may not take the form of weekly classes, but may instead be strategically timed within the main programme syllabus.

3.2.2 CEM in Practice

Many of our interviewees spoke about aligning their activities broadly with CEM principles, if not implementing the model per se. To take one example, a director of a large EAP centre explained:

> When I came in post, there was no overarching model, no overarching set of principles. Although all of them, I would say whether they knew it or not, were based on the CEM Model.

The essential tenets of CEM often underpin how in-sessionals are conceived and positioned, whether this is explicitly articulated or not. However, among our interviewees, just one institution fully and explicitly implemented the model, like at Northumbria with a business school, and likewise targeting provision towards international students. The predominance of international cohorts in U.K. business schools is perhaps ideal for implementing such a thoroughgoing model. The in-sessional leaders in this instance highlighted the advantages of adopting the model, in particular so that students did not experience difficulty trying to navigate university support for themselves. Instead, the students have one clear place to go to, a specialist who can work with drafts, exemplars, key linguistic features, referencing, and academic integrity issues in 'one tidy place,' as they put it. They added:

> That's why the CEM Model is really good, because of that embeddedness within the module: it's clear where they should go. They see us in their classes, they hear about us from their lecturers, we offer things on their module site, so it's clear where the best support can come for that particular module.

The course was not presented as an adjunct, but rather a non-credit-bearing certificated module, which experienced good attendance and positive effect on student attainment. Fundamental to this university's success in implementing the model has been the presence of an institutional champion. Indeed, Sloan and Porter (2010) highlight the role of a champion in their original article. In this instance:

> [A member of the senior management team] was actually at the forefront of promoting the CEM Model, because she went to a conference and heard about the CEM Model from Diane Sloan and thought it sounded very positive and useful. So she started it off probably.

Embedding and mapping in-sessional provision requires more than simply cooperating with like-minded disciplinary academics. Rather, it requires a number of institutional units to cooperate and actively promote the approach (timetabling, curriculum development, wider academic teams), which often need the presence of a champion to lead. Indeed, in a later article, Sloan, Porter and Alexander (2013: 292) note, '[t]he CEM model would not be adopted very easily without the support of senior management.' This article details attempts to implement the CEM Model within various disciplines at Heriot-Watt University in the United Kingdom. A particular stumbling block was the level of investment from subject specialists; this was at times vague and information conflicted; without a clear idea of what they were teaching, the EAP specialist was unable to map in-sessional provision effectively. In most disciplines, the provision suffered attendance issues fairly common to adjunct in-sessionals. But contextualised provision, embedded and mapped, was successful on the degree in Translating and Interpreting, where the in-sessional maintained a high level of student engagement. The writers put this down to clear investment in the provision by the disciplinary team, facilitating open communication with the EAP team and students; they recommend that this success 'should be built on as exemplar for other programmes to illustrate the benefits of collaboration' (Sloan, Porter and Alexander, 2013: 293). Fundamentally though, this highlights the challenges facing mapped and embedded provision. If there is a lack of institutional drive, it will not work. As another interviewee put it:

> It does depend on the students, the EAP teachers and the institution buying into it. If all the institution wants for students, and all they want, is additional time in conversation with native English speaker teachers, then the CEM Model is largely redundant.

3.2.3 Critiques of the CEM Model

Like conducting a needs analysis, implementing CEM is not a 'once-for-all-activity' either. Disciplinary practices, texts, and assessments are subject to ongoing change. Without ongoing collaboration, there is a danger for the ostensibly embedded in-sessional to become ossified in out-of-date disciplinary practices, potentially becoming detrimental to students' development, rather than enabling it. Highlighting in-sessional courses' 'extreme situatedness,' one interviewee highlighted concerns about the fluidity of specific academic contexts, engaged as they are in knowledge creation as a matter of purpose. Regarding CEM, they also noted:

> Embedding carries risk. It can be overly narrow, looking at a module, say, in isolation.

They expressed concerns about CEM being too limited in its focus, effectively 'training' students to respond to specific assignments or tasks, rather than educating them to develop abilities that they can apply to a wider variety of assignment types. For them, CEM principles are 'aspirational,' rather than a model to be strictly adhered to. Coupled with this is the issue that the more tightly focussed provision becomes, the more one is likely to be aware of the gaps, the aspects of a degree curriculum where the needs of students are not being met on the in-sessional.

Embedding provision can also be a logistical challenge. This is highlighted by Benson and Anderson (2019), who describe the challenges of using the

CEM Model to implement a dissertation writing course for education students at the University of Edinburgh. The course could only be partially embedded and mapped: it was not fully integrated into the degree and could not be fully mapped to students' learning due to resourcing issues.

Beyond these practical considerations, the fundamentals of the CEM approach is not without its critics. As well as describing it as 'not rocket science,' in a blog post the EAP Archivist (2015) has a more fundamental critique:

> I am sure it is not their intention but Sloan and Porter compound the notion of EAP tutor as 'servant to the discipline' in their positioning of the EAP tutor as deficient in knowledge, dependent on the subject-specialist to give meaning to their courses.

Again we return to debates about the positioning of EAP as remedial and practitioners as butlers, an ongoing concern in ISEAP. In the institution mentioned above that had successfully implemented the model, we asked interviewees directly about this issue, to which they emphasised the need for equal respect for all participants' expertise:

> I feel that by building up a proper relationship with the lecturer you get away from that [the butler's stance] because they see your value and expertise. I rarely get asked to do photocopying!

3.2.4 Approaches to Embedding

The above discussion of the CEM Model largely concerns targeting ISEAP towards international cohorts. However, a number of interviewees explained how they used its underlying principles to develop provision for all students. This aligns with Murray and Nallaya's (2016: 1296) position in an article outlining embedded academic literacy provision at an Australian university: '*all* students require tuition that helps them develop conversancy in the academic literacies of their particular disciplines.' Embedding is more transparent, and perhaps easier, where there can be no perception of a particular subset of students identified as having a deficit.

Although Murray and Nallaya (2016) make no mention of CEM, their embedding is similarly based on a high degree of collaboration, where academic literacies staff were provided with appropriate texts and authentic resources and the process was supported by a champion, in this case, the Deputy Vice Chancellor: Academic. Interestingly, the flow of texts between collaborators was two way: subject academics were provided with readings on academic literacies, underlining their importance beyond EAP. There was an attempt to gain consensus on what the literacies pertinent to their disciplines are. As one might imagine, this was not a smooth process in every discipline. Familiar inhibitors to full collaboration made their presence felt: territorial considerations and, as the authors note, 'training that academics had undergone in the past appeared to both dictate and constrain their understanding of academic literacies' (Murray and Nallaya, 2016: 1305). Furthermore, there was scepticism with regard to the inseparability of content and literacy, a belief surely at the heart of the embedded provision, which chimes with Bond's (2020: 191) questioning of the language-content dichotomy in order to 'locate language within the reality of a TPG [Taught Postgraduate] curriculum.' It is clearly challenging to embed provision, but this is where the role of a champion can be invaluable, to reach consensus about the nature of the in-sessional intervention, its aims and the concepts underpinning it.

Murray and Muller (2019) offer a more encouraging case study of embedded provision, tailored to students in nursing studies. In this example, the academic literacies specialist was fully incorporated into the School of Nursing and Midwifery and managed within its own structures. A particularly positive outcome was raising awareness among disciplinary specialists about the challenges students faced in academic communication, 'and with it the possibility of more sensitive and empathetic pedagogy' (2019: 1360) within departmental practices. One of our interviewees was bemoaning the common issue of ISEAP being identified as a service, provided as an adjunct for international students. In the interview, they recalled an earlier, more satisfying, teaching experience where they too were embedded teaching healthcare professionals. In this setting, EAP was an assessed part of the curriculum, where the cohort consisted of people with limited educational experience. Many had left school early and gone into nursing:

> They just hadn't had the opportunities really to develop. They wanted to go further in the health service and really needed help with their academic development, writing essays. They'd never written, not for years, maybe women in their forties. We got embedded and we were really trying to encourage their development, so we were part of modules that were being produced and built into. The assessments were elements of what we were doing in EAP, and that made us more of a player; it was taken more seriously. You felt as if the students could see the point of it and it was helping them. It was satisfying all round. For tutors it was

satisfying, and you have more regular meetings with module leads and programme leads and you're part of that grouping, as opposed to seeing you as a service.

This successful embedding of provision was based on mutual respect among participants, incorporation of EAP elements into the disciplinary curriculum, well maintained channels of communication, and clear identifiable needs among the whole cohort, not a specific group identified for special provision.

3.2.5 Getting Out or Staying In?

In another case study on embedding academic literacies and educational development at Middlesex University in the United Kingdom, Pitt et al. (2019) cite Shrives and Bond's (2003) three stages for educational development consultancy: getting in, getting on, and getting out. While this approach is not specific to EAP, the writers make use of the model to conceive and implement embedded in-sessional activities. The focus here is on working closely with disciplinary partners, becoming embedded in the subject settings, and then when a form of cultural shift has occurred within the discipline and subject academics have integrated academic literacy development into their own pedagogic practices, vacating themselves. Resourcing is often an issue in EAP, and as a largely non-income generating enterprise, in-sessionals may not be funded as well as preparatory courses. Thus, this offers a seemingly efficient way of targeting needs, so that the EAP team will not be 'channelling energies where they are no longer needed' (Pitt et al., 2019: 77). Wingate's (2019: 11) notion of curriculum-integrated provision aligns closely to this, where literacy work is 'mainly delivered by subject lecturers.' At Middlesex, as well as raising the agenda for academic language and literacy within disciplines, a positive corollary has been an enhanced awareness of the EAP centre's expertise among the wider university. Some of the wider roles that EAP specialists might adopt in the university will be more fully explored in Chapters 5 and 6.

Macnaught et al. (2022) also report on the experience of embedding provision and gradually handing over the academic literacy work to disciplinary lecturers. This 'getting out' took place during a four-year period over multiple iterations of a course. The writers emphasise the importance of this extended timeframe – as well as 'an extensive initial collaboration period' (2022: 8) – in order to make this handing over a success. It should be noted that some disciplinary lecturers did not feel they had the expertise to teach literacy work, expressing preference for a team-teaching model. However, the overall findings indicate that a smooth transition of responsibility could occur as long as this was done gradually. A key finding was an enhanced level of insight on the part of disciplinary experts into the specific writing demands placed upon students in their assessment tasks. McGrath et al. (2019) similarly noted that subject academics' understanding of literacy demands was mostly tacit and undertook a project to improve their knowledge and understanding of genre, in order to better teach what they expected from students.

A keen awareness of the heavy resourcing attached to in-sessionals led one of our interviewees towards developing 'legacy relationships' with academic departments, so that the mantle of literacy development was passed on:

> We'd like to be able to support as much as we can, but we can't continue just coming in and doing sessions year-on-year and then they [departments] tick the box that we've done that session with their students. We're going to try to move towards giving them more agency. We can do something for them but then the lecturers can also start to take control a bit more.

Even though 'getting out' has been successful in some cases, most of our interviewees questioned whether disciplinary academics are best placed to develop literacy and discourse awareness in learners. As one put it:

> It's a bit like asking EAP teachers to be subject specialists, isn't it? I think it's a big ask, especially for a lot of teachers who've never thought about language before, and that's probably the majority of people.

This is not to suggest that subject specialists are not teaching inclusively. However, in contrast with the team at Middlesex, most writers advocate some form of getting in, getting on, and *staying in*. The nature of academic language and literacy acquisition is that it is rarely a quick or even a smooth process. We referred to Threshold Concepts (Meyer and Land, 2003) in Chapter 1 to highlight the troublesome experiences of learners transitioning to new ways of being and knowing. Thus, there is a strong case for the particular skills set of EAP specialists deserving a more longitudinal place within departmental teaching teams. Wingate (2015) recognises that the likely outcome of subject lecturers teaching literacy without contributions from EAP specialists will be unsustainable workloads and diminishing interest. Thus, there is the opportunity for them to stay in and integrate closely with the disciplinary teaching and assessment.

This embedding of EAP practitioners within departments may still not be common practice, but it was presented as a working model by one of our interviewees. They described a system of embedded ISEAP which was not so reliant on the CEM Model's exercise of power by a champion. Rather, it demonstrates how embedding is possible from the bottom up through a 'hub and spoke' model, where practitioners do much of their work in satellites separated from the main hub:

> We work with schools that ask us to work with them. If the school asks us to work with them, we have a secondment model so we've got a member of staff who goes and works in that school, for a maximum of four days a week during the semester teaching time, and they are connected to modules where the school identifies they want them to be – it's only really taught postgraduate. So depending on the school, the capacity, the student numbers, it starts off as open to all; it's added into all students' timetables.

What is notable here is the disciplinary school seeing the value that EAP expertise can bring by initiating the collaboration. The high level of collaboration is evident in the physical relocation of the EAP practitioner for much of their teaching, as well as the ability to timetable EAP sessions close to other teaching activities. They went on to describe how the seconded EAP practitioner helped inform the design of, and become fully embedded in, a new master's degree:

> When they were planning the programme, getting it through all of the university structures, they built us into their core modules, so we're named on the module and all students have an EAP class.

Even where there is no champion as such, the institutional structures need to be in place to support such embedded provision. As we know from earlier discussions, it can be a challenging task for EAP practitioners to engage with the particularities of disciplinary cultures at first; such collaborative relationships can also be precarious, especially in the early stages where both parties need to be able to see the benefits of the time invested (the contribution of the EAP practitioner 'need[s] to live up to expectation,' as Pitt et al. (2019: 74) put it.) The advantage of a hub–and–spoke approach is that practitioners can build up expertise and specialisations, which should enhance the quality of the ISEAP students' experience. Potential issues stem from practitioner identities though. The balance between content and language may be hard to negotiate. As practitioners become more knowledgeable about the discipline, does this affect what they think they should be teaching? Is there a danger of becoming fossilised in the academic departmental culture (the spoke), away from the CPD opportunities of the EAP centre (the hub)? Might they simply become lonely? What if the disciplinary department adopts them as their own? And what if they leave? Does all their accrued knowledge then get lost? These questions are inherent to the approach, and are not easy to resolve.

A contrasting approach to this culture of secondments responding to interest in ISEAP as it develops is one which is more centrally managed, with stakeholders across the institution contributing. An interviewee described a series of committees at various levels providing structures through which stakeholders could contribute to the development of provision. This committee structure allows for co-development of ISEAP, with the EAP centre having a strong voice in a shared decision-making process, with less reliance on a single powerful champion. Within this structure, discussions take place about the kinds of embedded provision needed, not only at its inception, but feeding into the provision on an ongoing basis. The advantage of the committee structure is that it may mitigate some of the risks present in the secondment model: it is far less reliant on specific individuals and the development of an individual EAP practitioner's expertise. On the other hand, the level of embeddedness and specificity of language and literacy provision is likely to be that much more general. As one interviewee put it:

> We're working currently with one school that was formed by the fusing together of four or five different schools into one big 'super school.' So actually in effect there's really five departments. So as we go and offer in-sessional, do we try to develop one for each department, each programme, or do we try to do some sort of school focus? In short, it's going to be school focussed. It's politically and administratively more embedded, but in terms of the context of our materials it's going to be a compromise.

Much of the potential for precarity of the hub and spoke model is ameliorated or resolved here, yet the provision itself is likely to be less specific and relevant to students' actual language and literacy practices. More positively, this committee-structured framework is likely to be less resource intensive. Another interviewee explicitly questioned the seconding of EAP practitioners: with a smaller 'hub' (i.e. practitioners situated in the EAP centre) they saw the possibility for a weakened standing of the EAP centre within the wider institution. The institutional considerations of these two models will be explored more fully in Chapter 4: Changing Contexts in ISEAP. Both models clearly have their risks and their comparison underlines some of the essential tensions inherent in the practicalities of trying to embed tailored, specific ISEAP.

3.2.6 Enhancing Collaborative Relationships

We have emphasised how both needs analysis and implementing the CEM are rarely complete activities. Listening to informants and making subsequent alterations to provision are essential to most ISEAP paradigms. In order to strengthen a bond of trust between EAP practitioners and subject academics, some of our interviewees highlighted the benefits of sharing their EAP materials. One of the inhibiting factors to fuller collaboration is a misconception on the part of disciplinary lecturers as to what actually happens in an ISEAP class (as we have seen, technicist notions like 'a quick fix,' 'top study tips,' and 'brushing up students' English' can be alarmingly hard to shake). Team-teaching can be labour-intensive to set up and requires a trusting relationship and appropriate resourcing, and is only possible after overcoming such misunderstandings. It may seem exposing to share one's materials, particularly if the EAP practitioner does not feel confident about their knowledge of the discipline, or even their EAP experience. Yet as Campion (2016: 67) found in her study of teachers transitioning to EAP, 'learning to teach EAP took them a considerable amount of time, and occurred through a wide variety of means.' Sharing materials may provide such a learning opportunity. Practitioners who have done this attest to its benefits, ultimately creating openings to become a fuller participant in students' education. In this extract, an interviewee explains how this provided a way of fostering a relationship with a subject academic:

> One of the big things for me was sharing my materials with [subject specialist academics]. I was like: is this even what I should be doing? There's no published in-sessional materials, so what am I comparing it to? There's no *New English File for In-sessional*, so I didn't really have a point of comparison. What I found in the second semester: there was one guy who was so open, asking me questions about what he could do. So because of that I started to share mine: so this is what I'm doing this week. He would go through it and give me comments, and I would make changes.

In this process, we can see the EAP materials being enhanced and more strongly related to students' disciplinary studies. In this instance, the co-operation went beyond sharing and led to the EAP practitioner's ideas about learning and teaching influencing how the 'content' was delivered. This interviewee goes on to explain:

> Sometimes he would change his materials as a result as well. After the class I would send a follow-up email, a couple of sentences saying, 'they found this difficult'; 'they asked about this.' We would quite often have a bit of back and forth about any particular issues and that for me really built my confidence, feeling like I'm actually doing something useful and that's valued by the tutors. It was the feeling of legitimacy.

Rather than being positioned as peripheral to students' learning, here we see a trajectory of ISEAP becoming increasingly influential and 'legitimate,' with positive reinforcement of the EAP practitioner's identity. This kind of cross-pollination should not be a surprise; another interviewee – an educational studies expert – was emphatic about the quality of teaching EAP practitioners bring to the institution; they described them as:

> The most trained teachers that are ever going to be found on any campus.

While this may seem hyperbolic, as in most contexts there is the possibility for subject lecturers to study for an in-house certificate in learning and teaching; nevertheless this is much less training than a diploma-qualified (so-called 'TEFLQ') English language teacher has, a common qualification for many EAP practitioners. Sharing materials and entering into pedagogical dialogues highlights the value EAP practitioners can bring to wider university agendas. It is often simply important to recognise one's expertise as a way into a more egalitarian, less service-oriented dialogue. This was something another interviewee felt they needed to remind themselves of:

> I'm trying to stop starting my emails with: 'Sorry to bother you about this again.'

This is surely sound practical advice. Another interviewee argued that engagement in scholarship enables the EAP practitioner to be taken more seriously by disciplinary academics; it provides the means to develop an appropriate discourse for collaboration. Subject academics are likely to develop a more nuanced understanding of EAP as a result:

> If they start to talk in the way people are treating them, actually they realise they've got quite a lot of knowledge. I think it's also those people are the ones who engage most with scholarship because it's made them think 'I need to know' and they've got a genuine focussed interest. It's not just all EAP stuff: 'am I interested in reading or writing?.' It's actually 'I want to know what Design does.'

3.2.7 Developing Collaboration

It is difficult to provide a formulation for how best to foster collaborative partnerships with disciplinary departments. As noted, these are often personal in nature and dependent on highly localised contextual factors. And we have seen, a well-placed champion can open doors and provide conditions for collaboration. Without this though, there are still many possibilities. We have seen two departmental cultures above – one via secondments and the other through university committees – that enable this also. From our interviews with EAP centre managers, most recognised the issues attached to relying on personal relationships, and as one put it:

> It [ISEAP] needs to be systematised in order to be sustainable.

Yet there is no one system that can be applied to all contexts. So a central issue for ISEAP coordinators is the building up of a system that serves to future-proof the provision. In larger centres and universities, this may be hierarchical in nature. Another centre manager described the multiple layers of management in their centre, including roles with responsibility for the organisation of each individual course, as well as further layers, all engaged in operational management as well as course development in collaboration with schools. The number of staff members involved in developing and sustaining the provision, each with demarcated responsibilities, makes the provision more resilient, and less susceptible to damage through a single point of failure. This is an ever-present danger in more informal collaborations. What is also clear from interviewing managers is that this work of collaboration is never completed, whether the relationships are formalised or casual. One spoke of their work as:

> Helping people to continuously understand what we do and why it's important.

This work may be familiar to many EAP practitioners, a reminder of the legwork involved in constantly highlighting the importance of developing students' language and literacy in the wider institution.

Related to this is a consideration of the culture of the institution, and individual departments, towards their students. Is there a willingness to resource frameworks that support students in their disciplinary learning? Where there are only more informal opportunities for collaboration, making use of the institution's teaching and learning networks and schemes like the Advance HE's Higher Education Academy Fellowships can help identify lecturers with a particular interest in students' learning. Early career academics may often be more focussed on learning and teaching than research, but the EAP practitioner seeking collaboration must always be aware of hierarchies. A cautionary note is struck by Pitt et al. (2019: 74) in their own collaborations: if subject lecturers are 'not module or programme leaders, they have limited curriculum influence.' Networks developed through the other activities of an EAP centre can be beneficial in developing ISEAP and existing connections with disciplinary academics that relate to a pre-sessional or pathway provision can be exploited to implement ISEAP.

Despite the variety of paradigms for delivery and the advice from practitioners working in the field presented above, there are unfortunately no guarantees for effective provision. Meeting students' needs and running a smooth course are by no means a given. The remaining section of this chapter looks at running an ISEAP course by considering some of the common pitfalls and possible ways of overcoming them.

3.3 Course Delivery

Much of the content of this chapter has offered guidance and case studies leading to useful and rewarding collaboration. But many practitioners will be familiar with some of the common pitfalls of teaching ISEAP, not least being perceived as peripheral to learners' main area of study – despite efforts at embedding – and the attendance issues associated with this. This section firstly considers some case studies of where in-sessionals have not gone to plan despite appropriate needs analysis and careful preparation. It will then move to the practicalities of mitigating some of these aspects.

In a case study of in-sessional provision for international bachelor's students studying management at the University of York in the United Kingdom, Warwick (2007) judged the course to be a failure, 'well meant but misguided' as the title of the paper indicates. The major factor was attendance: three-quarters of the targeted students did not attend any of the sessions. The main reasons for this included a lack of mapping to core activities, it being set up as an optional adjunct, and an implied deficit through the targeting of international students. Its timing was an issue too, at the start of first-year studies; the course highlighted (and possibly exacerbated) differences at just the point when international students may have been trying to assimilate. Warwick (2007: 6) also identifies a perennial issue with ISEAP: 'attempts to help the students require them to spend more time studying,' a point echoed by Bond (2020: 73) in her discussion of poor attendance on in-sessionals; she noted that students were strategic in how they made use of their limited time. Where provision is specifically directed towards international students, there is also a likelihood that many will be spending a greater amount of time on reading, for example, than much of the cohort due to unfamiliarity with the discourse. These factors all impact in-sessional attendance.

Bond (2020) further reports that in their feedback, in-sessional students indicated that the course would be taken more seriously and better attended if it were credit-bearing. In considering in-sessional attendance, one must also be aware of the attitudes of the students. The preponderance towards entry tests such as IELTS, and teaching to the test, within some branches of EAP may have an influence in this regard. Students' attitudes towards in-sessional classes may be transactional, especially if they have already done a pre-sessional. Writing of EAP more generally, Turner (2011: 31) argues that, "[s]tudents seem to want to 'train' to reach the appropriate entrance level score or band rather than to engage with the language as an essential, and integral, part of their engaging with, and being assessed in, their subject of study.' Simply put, students may not attach the importance of language development to their academic performance that we do. They may conceptualise language classes mechanistically, as 'training' rather than an intrinsic part of their educational journey.

It may indeed be such a misconception of ISEAP that was a factor in the poor attendance Warwick (2007) describes. The failure of the course was partly due to how it was presented to students. Another case study, describing an ISEAP provision which floundered for entirely different reasons, is presented by Barron (2002); it concerns collaborative in-sessional provision for science students at the University of Hong Kong. In this instance, there was a breakdown in collaboration between EAP and science lecturers. There were logistical problems, such as the latter making changes to the course without informing the EAP parties, but more fundamentally there were epistemological and ontological divides partly instigated by a lack of reciprocity in the partnership. As Barron (2002: 304) puts it, 'the ontological superiority that Science teachers give to their scientific facts is not conducive to free negotiation.' In this collaboration, EAP practitioners' 'linguistic facts' were unable to compete with science's absolute facts. This clash was experienced by the students, who actually recommended terminating the course. One of our interviewees similarly noted some of the challenges of teaching EAP in science fields. As we have seen, a discourse-analytical approach is common in ISEAP, enabling a nuanced exploration of how meaning is produced. This is entirely appropriate for humanities and social science disciplines, but in contrast they argued that:

> In STEM [Science, Technology, Engineering, Mathematics] a lot of it is word-cloud stuff, corpus stuff: a list of technical vocabulary that is used and assumed knowledge in their discipline.

Thus, the role ISEAP can adopt in STEM contexts may be significantly diminished, less working with discourse and more focussing on vocabulary acquisition. In contrast, in applied disciplines, problem-based learning pedagogies may be employed, which can offer excellent collaborative opportunities, as in MacDiarmid et al.'s (2021) discussion of successful collaboration with the medical faculty at the University of Glasgow.

Returning to the factors these case studies present that inhibit the delivery of successful ISEAP courses, these were also prevalent in a number of our interviews. The recognition by course designers that students are time-poor and the desire not to overburden them means that there is usually no requirement for students to do any production for an in-sessional. Even without the need for teachers to mark work, the absence of students' work places a rather different burden upon them, to keep students engaged and attending. Referring specifically to writing, this characteristic of many in-sessionals was remarked upon by one interviewee as problematic:

> It's like teaching someone to learn to drive, but never actually being in the car. We teach them stuff but unless we see their writing – we ask them to then produce something – and, if they produce something, then someone needs to read what they produce.

3.3.1 Attrition

Marks (2019) makes a similar point about where the teaching of writing fits into Manchester University's in-sessionals. He relates attrition in student numbers to the essential issue of not having a loop between student production and teacher feedback. For much of the in-sessional curriculum he describes, students were not required to do any writing; and large class sizes meant that when they did, there was limited capacity for providing meaningful feedback. He notes, 'the lack of individual feedback may further disincentive the students to write in the first place' (Marks, 2019: 97). This is not an uncommon issue and put simply, some of the tensions inherent within much ISEAP can make it a turn-off in terms of student engagement.

Issues relating to attendance and attrition were raised by many of our interviewees. One of them was concerned that the provision was unable to reach the desired student groups:

> Because it's optional, we get what we call the 'worried well' who communicate very well verbally, communicate very well in their written work. Almost what they're asking for is just validation: 'just tell me I'm good enough.' Because it's optional, the students who've just scraped the entry requirements, they don't do these extra courses because they already feel pretty overwhelmed with all the stuff they have already. So they're very unlikely to sign up to these courses.

Also, where it is not possible to sustain a stable cohort of students week-on-week, continuity throughout the curriculum becomes a challenge; each week it becomes difficult to build on the work of earlier sessions. In the case described at Manchester, Marks (2019: 96) states that due to inconsistent attendance, 'most workshops are standalone in nature, making little connection to previous or later sessions.' This is a natural reaction to unstable cohorts, yet may not necessarily offer the best learning experience. Once again, a partial solution to this comes through closer embedding and mapping. In the case of ISEAP at Heriot Watt, Bell and Guion Akdağ (2019: 111–112) identified student attendance as 'clearly strategic and linked to assessment deadlines.' Time-poor students may need a strong extrinsic motivation to attend.

For a small minority of our interviewees, attrition was not seen as an issue. When asked about this, one practitioner replied:

You do see some attrition over the term, but on the ESAP provision we tend to be quite good at chasing it up and working with the departments to chase it up, so I think the provision and the attendance on that is normally pretty good, partly because we've got these things so up and running now that really the right students are on those modules, so by the time you get to the module starting, the students who need to be on it are on it and then they attend.

This suggests that good record-keeping and communication with disciplinary departments, as well as clearly targeting the needs of the students, is a key to success.

There is a sense though that the in-sessional teacher needs to be thick-skinned; they are not working with 'their' students in the same way as they would be on a pre-sessional or foundation course. In most settings, an in-sessional is not a high-stakes course which needs to be passed in order to progress. To a greater or lesser extent, attrition may be an intrinsic part of the ISEAP context. Some useful context was provided by some of our inter-viewees though, who noted attrition was also a trend on students' substantive programmes: in this context at least, it was not just an ISEAP problem.

3.3.2 Encouraging Attendance

Where in-sessional provision is pitched at international students who have completed a pre-sessional course, there is a need to build upon this and to differentiate ISEAP from it. This is where a connection between pre-sessional and in-sessional can be of great value, making the in-sessional a clearly de-fined part of these students' learning journey. The in-sessional can also fulfil an information-gathering role about academic practices across the institution to feed back into pre-sessional course design, stopping it from being siloed. Simple advice was offered by one interviewee:

The in-sessional lead knows what happens on the pre-sessional, so she knows not to repeat it but to build on it, but is also aware that not all of the students will have done the pre-sessional. If they're doing something similar, they know in their classes to say, 'we know you've done this on the pre-sessional; we're going to build on that.' It has to build, otherwise that's when you get students dropping out of in-sessional, when they say 'we've done this before, it's pointless.'

By simply highlighting the relationship between the two courses, teachers can enable students to see how their learning builds. It also deals with the potential for student ennui head-on by demonstrating to students how the ISEAP provision is unique.

Some institutions have tried to incentivise attendance on in-sessionals. As we have seen, for the most part courses are not credit-bearing, yet in one case a certificate of attendance was awarded to students. An interviewee explained its appeal to students:

> I think they love it! It has a mystique about it. If my friend has it, I want it. So it has a slightly superficial value, but I think students really do love collecting certificates.

They did note that this related closely to an institutional focus on extra- and co-curricular activities, providing opportunities for synergies with other awards. In the United Kingdom, undergraduates receive a Higher Education Achievement Record (HEAR) as part of their degree transcript. This is a recognition scheme for activities outside of students' core studies, including career enhancing activities. Some universities have made an effort to include in-sessional courses as 'HEAR-able' activities, aligning them with more strategic imperatives, career goals, and their graduate attributes. At the University of Sheffield, for example, successful completion of its Academic Skills Certificate can be recognised on students' HEAR (University of Sheffield, 2022). Such incentivising activities may work well with certain students, yet cannot be seen as equivalent to the sense of purpose that comes from well-mapped collaborative provision. This is not to say that the two are mutually exclusive though.

3.3.3 Communication and Record Keeping

Fundamental to a successful in-sessional is where lines of communication run smoothly in a mutually supporting environment. Not every practitioner works in a setting where ISEAP is highly valued, visible, and embedded. For many, this would require such fundamental structural change that they simply have to make the best of being an optional non-credit-bearing adjunct with the potential pitfalls this entails. To ensure relevance and continuity, decisions need to be made on:

- How best to reach and communicate with students, including those who have missed sessions to encourage and enable continuity;
- Record keeping on attendance and lesson content;
- Conducting course evaluations;
- Protocols for sharing information between EAP practitioner and disciplinary lecturer(s).

These structures help to ensure an in-sessional's clarity and relevance and should therefore enhance student engagement and attendance. One of our interviewees, reflecting on past experience at their institution, emphasised the importance of record keeping:

> We did write reports of in-sessional classes and send them to the department, about how students had progressed, obviously very brief outlines. But then we thought the department just filed them in the bin basically, so we stopped doing it. But I think it's worth keeping a record of not only attendance but how you see the students having improved – who you think has improved and in what areas.

Report writing is most obviously helpful in a context where these are not 'filed in the bin.' But overall good record keeping also has obvious benefits. Where collaboration or cooperation is effective, it provides evidence or cases to inform discussions about students' progress and curriculum development. It can also serve to highlight issues which may not have yet shown themselves for disciplinary lecturers.

We conducted an interview with an EAP practitioner and disciplinary lecturer together, who outlined how such aspects played out in their postgraduate context. The discussion exemplifies the importance of maintaining a line of contact, perhaps especially where the in-sessional lacks embeddedness. Even though they did not meet regularly, there was a high degree of respect from the disciplinary expert for the adjunct EAP provision:

> Year-long support really strengthens [students] along the way as they study their subject. As an academic, I can't show them previous students' essays and I don't have the time to tell them how to write. [The EAP teacher] can. They understand what I need. It makes my work easier and students don't just go to improve their language.

From this comment, it can be seen that the partnership can be identified as more cooperative than collaborative. Even where the EAP practitioner is taking care of literacy matters to enable the subject expert to focus on content, the relationship is still mutually supportive. Through regular communication about attendance and course content, the disciplinary lecturer has a good notion of what happens at ISEAP; they actively promote it and even set a formative writing task to identify student needs. Even though cooperation is ad hoc, it is an important factor for the success of the course:

> A lot of materials they use are actually from me. It would be a problem if they had to create a different set of materials. Students would say, 'erm, this is very different to my course.'

In this case, provision is far from embedded, yet is as relevant to students' learning as conditions allow. It is a situation where the subject lecturer recognises the role of ISEAP as something more than a language fix ('much more holistic support' in their words). Even the fact that provision is not embedded is considered satisfactory in this instance. There is no desire from the interviewees to make it compulsory or to further incentivise participation:

> The more compulsory mechanisms are there, the less students feel proactive to take responsibility for their own learning.

This conclusion may be partly because the students in this instance are postgraduates who have vocational experience.

3.3.4 The Loneliness of the ISEAP Practitioner

Having considered how liaison and mutual respect can aid in-sessional de-livery, it is worth drawing attention to settings where such cooperative re-lationships are absent. For some, teaching in-sessionals can be a lonely undertaking. One interviewee succinctly described a typical experience of an ISEAP teacher:

> You're on your own. Pre-sessional is very collaborative: if you're writing materials, you're writing them for 20–30 people, whereas on in-sessional, you're independent.

This independence is a double-edged sword. It enables autonomy, the ability to develop a course based on need as you see it, and the freedom to proactively seek collaborative partnerships. On the other hand, it can leave one feeling isolated and working within a vacuum, without the usefulness of a sounding board or another's perspective.

In the case of the interviewee adherent to Dogme ELT pedagogies (Thornbury, 2005), as discussed in Chapter 2, severely limited academic partnerships are mitigated through the creation of partnerships with the students. Rather than teaching meticulously organised lessons, the practitioner articulated this in terms of a 'joint exploration' with the students, seeking answers to their disciplinary investigations together in a way that aligns somewhat with the 'meddler-in-the-middle' (McWilliam, 2009) described in Chapter 1. They made particular note of the importance of the learning context:

> I think it's worth bearing in mind this is not for credit, it's in a lunchtime and some students said 'I don't want to come to another 'class'; I've got enough classes and I don't really want to give up a lunchtime for another lesson.

This comment underlines the sometimes overlooked social and community-building spaces that an in-sessional can contribute to. But it also provides the conditions for a collaborative learning experience in an adjunct, unembedded learning context. An in-sessional teacher may well be trusted as they are neither an insider or an outsider. The class may offer a more comfortable, and more reflective, learning environment than one which focusses on core content: students are less likely to feel judged in the same way as they might in their substantive classes.

Another of our interviewees described a formalised scheme for peer-observation with their EAP centre, particularly as an attempt to encourage supportive networks, so that in-sessional practitioners are not so isolated in their practice. They described this as follows:

> One of the things we're starting to do is to have critical friends as teachers. Teachers observe a particular session and then look at the materials and talk about the materials with the teacher as a peer-observation, peer-critique [...] so then it doesn't become this is one person's 'baby' and nobody else can touch it.

Concluding Thoughts

In conclusion, above we have tried to present practical advice for successful ISEAP needs analysis, conception, and delivery in a range of contexts, based on concepts, models, case studies, and our interviewees' comments. The end-of-chapter questions pick up on these themes and direct the reader towards considering them in their own setting.

Following this, Chapter 4, Changing Contexts in ISEAP, turns to institutional contexts and the effect these have on ISEAP. The institution has a very real effect on what is possible in our classes. As Pitt et al. (2019: 75) note about their situation at Middlesex, 'we have minimal airtime to make an impact.' The chapter will consider how an institution might seek to measure this impact, and how rapidly changing contexts of higher education can often affect practitioners' conditions. The nature of the ISEAP provision can be subject to higher decision making and rapid alteration despite all of the efforts of the EAP centre. This may not be in the best interests of students' learning. To exemplify this, one interviewee described how provision had changed in their centre:

> We were restructured a couple of years ago. As a result of that, the more department-specific modules were cut, so we now only offer generic modules, open to students from all disciplines.

The chapter will consider how neo-liberal forces are experienced on in-sessionals.

Chapter 3 Reflection

1. Work through the **Target Situation Analysis checklist** (section 3.1.1). What information sources do you have available to you in your context?
   a. Who are your informants?
   b. What are the desirable outcomes of the in-sessional for disciplinary lectures?
      i. Are these realistic in the time allocated for the in-sessional?
      ii. How can you manage expectations?
   c. Do you have access to examples of student writing?
      i. What does a discourse analysis of this reveal?
   d. Did you have the opportunity to observe any classes or lectures?
      i. What did you gain from your field notes?
      ii. What are the types of interactions?

      iii. How are ideas presented?

      iv. Do you have a deeper understanding of what counts as knowledge in the discipline?

2. Working with your students, work through the **Present Situation Analysis checklist** (section 3.1.2).
   a. Do your students' needs align with the department's?
   b. How can differences be negotiated?
   c. Is there any need for a 'rights analysis'?

3. The concept of a needs analysis suggests a deficit. How can you avoid some of the pitfalls of a deficit mentality in your own institutional context?

4. What resources do you have for the in-sessional? You may wish to consider:
   a. Time available for delivery;
   b. Staffing resources;
   c. Your reach – all students or targeting a group;
   d. Structures enabling work with other departments.

5. How large is your class? How does this affect ISEAP delivery? What can you do to prevent attrition?

6. What are the practicalities for collaborating in your context? Do you have:
   a. Access to necessary information?
      i. Programme documentation?
      ii. The virtual learning environment (VLE)?
   b. The means to reach and communicate with the students?

7. Are the learning outcomes agreed with the subject academics? Are they notional? How feasible is it for students to meet them within the timeframe for the course?

8. How can you best balance the three interconnected elements of:
   a. The available EAP resource;
   b. Department and university needs for the students;
   c. How the students articulate their needs?

9. How will you keep records of:
   a. Attendance?
   b. Record of work?
   c. Course evaluation from students?
   d. Course evaluation from lecturers?
   How will you implement these and which will you need to share?

10. Are there any opportunities for getting feedback on your in-sessional materials from disciplinary experts and/or EAP colleagues? What might be gained from this in your context?
11. Are the conditions in place to implement the CEM Model, including a powerful champion? If this is not practical, how might you make use of its underlying principles? Note any opportunities for:
    a. Contextualised provision;
    b. Embedding and timetabling sessions within a disciplinary module;
    c. Mapping to key dates and student activities.
12. How can you stage your ISEAP course in the time available to meet the key needs identified in your analysis?
    a. What are the key themes of each session?
    b. What is the relationship between the sessions?
    c. Do they interconnect, building session by session or stand alone?
    d. What if people miss a class?
13. Are there opportunities for peer-observation or peer-critique of materials with other EAP practitioners in your context?
14. Having delivered the course, how can you critically evaluate your own practice?
15. How will you institute any changes necessary? Do you need to negotiate with other stakeholders to do this? How will you approach them?

References

Barron, C. (2002) 'Problem-solving and EAP: themes and issues in a colla-borative teaching venture. *English for Specific Purposes*, 22:3, 297–314.

Bell, J.G. and Guion Akdağ, E. (2019) In-sessional Academic Skills (AS) provision using the CEM model: A case study at Heriot-Watt University. In Strandring, A. and Stansfield, G. (eds.) *Papers from the Professional Issues Meeting (PIM) on In-sessional English for Academic Purposes held at London School of Economics 19 March 2016*, 107–115. Available at: https://www.baleap.org/wp-content/uploads/2019/10/Baleap_Book_Interactive.pdf [accessed 1/9/22].

Benesch, S. (2001) *Critical English for academic purposes: Theory, politics and practice.* Mahwah, NJ: Lawrence Erlbaum.

Benson, C. and Anderson, K. (2019) A dissertation writing course for School of Education students at the University of Edinburgh. In Strandring, A. and Stansfield, G. (eds.) *Papers from the Professional Issues Meeting (PIM) on In-*

sessional English for Academic Purposes held at London School of Economics 19 March 2016, 85–94. Available at: https://www.baleap.org/wp-content/uploads/2019/10/Baleap_Book_Interactive.pdf [accessed 1/9/22].

Bond, B. (2020) *Making language visible in the university: English for academic purposes and internationalisation*. Bristol: Multilingual Matters.

Bruce, I. (2011) *Theory and concepts of English for academic purposes*. Basingstoke: Palgrave Macmillan.

Campion, G.C. (2016) 'The learning never ends': Exploring teachers' views on the transition from General English to EAP. *Journal of English for Academic Purposes*, 23:2016, 59–70.

de Chazal, E. (2014) *English for academic purposes*. Oxford: Oxford University Press.

Dudley-Evans, T. and St John, M.J. (1998) *Developments in English for specific purposes: A multi-disciplinary approach*. Cambridge: Cambridge University Press.

Hutchinson, T. and Waters, A. (1987) *English for specific purposes: A learning-centred approach*. Cambridge: Cambridge University Press.

Hyland, K. (2006) *English for academic purposes: An advanced resource book*. London: Routledge.

Jordan, R.R. (1997) *English for academic purposes: A guide and resource book for teachers*. Cambridge: Cambridge University Press.

MacDiarmid, C., Williams, A., Irwin, K. and Doonan, B. (2021) Integrating a Signature Pedagogy into a Pre-sessional: Impact on Pedagogy in ESAP. In MacDiarmid, C. and MacDonald, J. (Eds.) *Pedagogies in English for academic purposes: Teaching and learning in international contexts*. London: Bloomsbury Academic, pp. 169–183.

Macnaught, L., Bassett, M., van der Ham, V., Milne, J. and Jenkin, C. (2022) Sustainable embedded academic literacy development: the gradual handover of literacy teaching, *Teaching in Higher Education 11 March 2022*, 1–19.

Marks, R. (2019) 'Doing writing': Motivating students to write in in-sessional classes. In Strandring, A. and Stansfield, G. (eds.) *Papers from the Professional Issues Meeting (PIM) on In-sessional English for Academic Purposes held at London School of Economics 19 March 2016*, 95–102. Available at: https://www.baleap.org/wp-content/uploads/2019/10/Baleap_Book_Interactive.pdf [accessed 1/9/22].

McGrath, L., Negretti, R. and Nicholls, K. (2019). Hidden Expectations: Scaffolding Specialists' Genre Knowledge of the Assignment They Set. *Higher Education Research & Development*, 78, 835–853. doi:10.1007/s1 0734-019-00373-9.

McWilliam, E. (2009) Teaching for creativity: from sage to guide to meddler. *Asia Pacific Journal of Education*, 29:3, 281–293.

Meyer, J.H.F. and Land, R. (2003) Threshold concepts and troublesome knowledge: linkages to ways of thinking and practising. In Rust, C. (ed.) *Improving student learning - theory and practice ten years on.* Oxford: Oxford Centre for Staff and Learning Development (OCSLD), pp. 412–424.

Murray, N. and Muller, A. (2019) Developing academic literacy through a decentralised model of English language provision. *Journal of Further and Higher Education.* 43:10, 1348–1362.

Murray, N. and Nallaya, S. (2016) Embedding academic literacies in university programme curricula: a case study. *Studies in Higher Education*, 41:7, 1296–1312.

Pitt, A., Bernaschina, P., Celini, L., Dillon-Lee, F., Endacott, N., Lazar, G. Thomas, P. and Wilkinson, G. (2019) Embedding academic literacies and educational development. In Strandring, A. and Stansfield, G. (eds.) *Papers from the Professional Issues Meeting (PIM) on In-sessional English for Academic Purposes held at London School of Economics 19 March 2016*, 71–81. Available at: https://www.baleap.org/wp-content/uploads/2019/10/Baleap_Book_Interactive.pdf [accessed 1/9/22].

Shrives, L. and Bond, C. (2003) Consultancy in educational development. In Kahn, P. and Baume, D. *A guide to staff and educational development.* Abingdon, Oxon: Routledge.

Sloan, D. and Porter, E. (2010) Changing international student and business staff perceptions of in-sessional EAP: using the CEM model. *Journal of English for Academic Purposes*, 9:3, pp. 198–210.

Sloan, D., Porter, E. and Alexander, O. (2013) Yes, you can teach an old dog new tricks. Contextualisation, embedding and mapping: the CEM model, a new way to define and engage staff and students in the delivery of an English language and study skills support programme: a case study of Heriot-Watt and Northumbria University. *Innovations In Education & Teaching International*, 50:3, 284–296.

The EAP Archivist (2015) The CEMistry of EAP. *The EAP Archivist.* Available at: https://theeaparchivist.wordpress.com/2015/01/15/the-cemistry-of-eap/ [accessed 22/9/22].

Thornbury, S. (2005) Dogme: Dancing in the Dark? Available at: http://nebula.wsimg.com/22eaea86234146ac3105f57698b06b75?AccessKeyId=186A535D1BA4FC995A73&disposition=0&alloworigin=1 [accessed 2/10/22].

Turner, J. (2011) *Language in the academy: Cultural reflexivity and intercultural dynamics.* Bristol: Multilingual Matters.

University of Sheffield (2022) 301 Academic Skills Certificate. *Higher Education Achievement Report.* Available at: https://www.sheffield.ac.uk/hear-search/view?protocol=SSDCER&protocolVersion=1 [accessed 2/10/22].

Warwick, P. (2007) Well Meant But Misguided: A Case Study of an English for Academic Purposes Programme Developed to Support International Learners. *International Journal of Management Education*, 6:2, 3–17. Available at: https://s3.eu-west-2.amazonaws.com/assets.creode.advancehe-document-manager/documents/hea/private/ijme62warwick_1568036940.pdf [accessed 2/10/22].

Wingate, U. (2015) *Academic literacy and student diversity: The case for inclusive practice.* Bristol: Multilingual Matters.

Wingate, U. (2019) Introduction. In Brewer, S., Strandring, A. and Stansfield, G. (eds.) *Papers from the Professional Issues Meeting (PIM) on In-sessional English for Academic Purposes held at London School of Economics 19 March 2016*, 9–17. Available at: https://www.baleap.org/wp-content/uploads/2019/10/Baleap_Book_Interactive.pdf [accessed 1/9/22].

Section B:
In-sessional EAP:
Its Role Within the
Wider University

Chapter 4

Changing Contexts in ISEAP

Having so far surveyed the essential issues inherent in ISEAP, the pedagogical choices open to practitioners, and the practical, logistical considerations of provision, this chapter turns to the wider context of working in this field. Its focus is on the institutional shifting sands of the settings where EAP operates. Just as we can say that the experience of international students foreshadows the experience of other cohorts (Ryan and Carroll, 2005), so 'EAP units in universities act as a social barometer for predicting the future of other academics in such institutions' (Hadley, 2015: 4). EAP centres are particularly susceptible to socio-political changes as they affect the HE sector. The essential focus on change in this chapter looks at how ISEAP activities are affected by universities' embracing of neo-liberal strategies. This has implications for the funding of in-sessional courses and so the type of provision that is feasible. We have seen at the end of the preceding chapter how one interviewee's EAP centre rapidly moved from disciplinary-focussed ISEAP to general provision as a result of a restructure; this was in spite of the practitioners' views on the best approach for students' learning. But change is not only experienced top-down as a result of institutional drives; the chapter also considers other factors, for instance changes to ISEAP provision ushered in by the COVID-19 pandemic, not least a move to online pedagogies, and also how ISEAP responds to bottom-up change as movements towards decolonising the curriculum grow. This has implications for ISEAP, predicated as it is in many settings on acculturating students towards somewhat fixed notions of institutional norms. As these norms change, so must ISEAP.

4.1 Neo-liberalism: A Pervading Influence

The conditions of neo-liberalism are often central to EAP as it is experienced by practitioners, and in some contexts may even be its *raison d'etre*. The precarious nature of work, sub-optimal conditions, zero-hours contracts, EAP as a commercial imperative, and creeping privatisation within the sector are all symptoms of a neo-liberal framing of EAP activities. Yet a consideration of this has been largely absent from most EAP literature, an imbalance partly redressed by Ding and Bruce's *The English for Academic Purposes Practitioner* (2017), which dedicates considerable space to detailing how this context affects practitioners' professional standing. It is not the purpose of this chapter to provide the same level of detail, but to consider the implications for ISEAP. In order to provide a clear context for the discussion that follows, we adopt Hadley's (2015: 6) definition of the neo-liberal university: 'a self-interested, entrepreneurial organization offering recursive educational experiences and research services for paying clients.' Much of this chimes with the EAP experience: centres are often entrepreneurial, playing a key role in international student recruitment strategies; the common reliance on textbooks for teaching means students' experiences can be recursive. Furthermore, within this context students are positioned as 'knowledge consumers' and practitioners' 'pedagogic output must be justified as beneficial to the university through quantitative measures' (Hadley, 2015: 6). Where public funding for universities is weaker, it is inevitable that they will emulate corporate models in order to survive. So what are the implications of these tendencies for ISEAP?

Fulcher (2009: 135) surveyed EAP centres within U.K. universities and found that participants 'almost unanimously claimed that the institution saw their activities as primarily entrepreneurial.' Yet this hardly matches ISEAP's role in enabling students (international and increasingly home) to perform to their potential in their studies. He further notes that much of the activity of EAP centres in the United Kingdom has been taken over by commercial providers, but crucially these entities want little to do with 'less lucrative activities' (i.e. in-sessional) and have instead focussed on preparatory courses. Thus, ISEAP can occupy an anomalous position: an important part of the activities of a commercial centre, yet unlikely to be income-generating.

4.1.1 Funding ISEAP

Few would suggest the ISEAP is lucrative, but as the net of student recruitment has been thrown more widely, it is a necessary activity contributing towards student success. ISEAP is something universities mostly expect EAP centres to provide. This can be funded through a variety of means. Where directed specifically to international students, their fees may be top-sliced to provide it. Alternatively, academic departments may directly pay the EAP centre for its provision. Another model is for it to be 'free,' effectively supported by the surplus generated through an EAP centre's commercial activities. As Fulcher (2009: 135) notes, the variety of funding models for ISEAP suggests 'an institutional uncertainty with how to deal with this kind of international student support.' The variety of funding models is unlikely to be experienced by the students themselves though. In our interviews, just one participant spoke of the possibility of students paying directly for provision:

> We charge for any student who wishes to study more than their entitlement … we do have students who study for six hours a week and pay for the additional two hours.

Of course, where ISEAP is set up for all students, it is likely to be more substantially funded, as it is probably implemented with the support of a powerful institutional champion.

More often though ISEAP occupies a less clear position. Where the EAP centre is effectively positioned as a 'Student Processing Unit' (Hadley, 2015), in-sessionals may be a mere accessory to its main activities. But where a centre's positioning is more visible, interacting with the wider university – for example on collaborative ISEAP provision – its cultural capital will be that much greater. Indeed, Fulcher (2009: 137) notes in his survey that where an EAP centre's activities are more academically integrated with the wider university, it is less likely to be outsourced. While unlikely to be a major income-generator, ISEAP's visibility can help lessen the effects of neo-liberal forces. One of our interviewees spoke of the advantage of institutional visibility, but was also forthright about the benefits conferred by being an income-generating unit rather than sitting within an academic faculty:

> The biggest factor in how successful an EAP unit's going to be is money. So who controls the flow of the money? If you sit within a faculty the only reason you'll be tolerated is because there's an income stream from

pre-sessional. And that income goes straight into college and it supports high-prestige main degree courses. And you don't have control of the finances to use any surplus from fees to develop your in-sessional programme. So you're not viewed as proper academics and you're not given the financial autonomy you need to be able to develop a strong programme of in-sessional support for your students. And you're less visible to the institution as a whole. You're seen as being a part of that particular faculty.

The interviewee is under no illusion about the neo-liberal forces under-pinning ISEAP within the university. In-sessional activities are funded by commercial activities, but their focus is on having the resources available to create high-quality provision.

This alignment of an EAP centre's financial success to its ongoing stability is commonly articulated, but contrasting values can be seen in Webster's (2022) article on how EAP practitioners' academic identities were strength-ened through the production of written scholarship output. In this instance, the centre allocated scholarship time within its workload allocation model and actively encouraged outputs. Over a two-year period, he reports on the emergence of a 'can do' culture among practitioners, and importantly, how scholarship was 'seen to promote a stronger academic identity for the parti-cipants, leading to closer alignment with academics in the wider academy' (Webster, 2022: 10). Enhanced professional standing among colleagues, en twining EAP more fully within the fabric of the institution, may indeed help to make the EAP centre less subject to privatisation. The work of the centre is less likely to be technicist in approach and less likely to, as Hadley observed in many centres, 'use the same sets of prepackaged materials for all their learning objectives' (2015: 39). As we have seen, prepackaged materials are unlikely to fulfil in-sessional students' needs and are hardly appropriate in such situated learning contexts.

Indeed, it is often the kinds of detailed needs analyses and bespoke ma-terials development that can make ISEAP a costly undertaking. As we saw in Chapter 3, the resource-intensive nature of embedded delivery led colleagues at Middlesex University and elsewhere to get in, get on, and get out (Shrives and Bond, 2003), leaving disciplinary academics to take over responsibility for embedded literacy development. Limited ISEAP resources can then be ap-plied elsewhere. We quoted one of our interviewees in Chapter 3, who spoke about aspiring towards 'legacy relationships' between the EAP centre and disciplines. They gave further detail:

> We're trying to move towards having our sessions more embedded into the term and tied to a particular assignment. We're hoping that then we're going to have better collaboration with lecturers, and then we can say, 'okay maybe you guys can now start teaching this sort of thing,' to give them a little bit more agency rather than us swooping in and them saying, 'thank you very much.' We're trying to move to a model where we can step away and give the lecturers a bit more power and control after we've done an academic literacy intervention of some sort.

The intention is partly to make ISEAP less of a passive box-ticking exercise for academic departments, and instead try to cultivate a greater sense of investment in literacy development. But it is also because the EAP team's resources are small and it has to cast its provision as widely as possible. In this discussion, a participant from another university questioned 'getting out':

> I'm wary about that, because the minute you do that, you don't want them to start changing their EAP provider, do you?

The precarious nature of EAP in many universities is always at the forefront of an EAP practitioner's consciousness, and this leads to the crux of the matter. EAP centres mostly thrive or fail according to the income they generate; creating a surplus is as important as teaching quality in neo-liberal settings. In-sessional activities are much more likely to eat into this surplus than contribute to it, and may therefore lack full resourcing. This leaves EAP centres with a conundrum balancing effective use of resources with being seen to be providing a service in the university. As the first speaker then commented:

> Yes, it's a fine line: we don't want to do ourselves out of a job. We need to be here, right?

The next section turns to this issue: the precarious employment conditions affecting many EAP practitioners.

4.1.2 Precarity and ISEAP

In his study of EAP centres, Fulcher (2009: 139) argues that they can differentiate themselves through research-led teaching and a scholarly and questioning environment, amongst other factors. This relates closely to Webster's (2022) view of scholarship outlined above, and they are precisely the factors that collaborative ISEAP practices can contribute to and benefit from. However, it is impossible to ignore that precarious employment conditions are a concern for many working in the centre, what Fulcher (2009: 136) described as 'the slow but widespread de-professionalism in employment practices,' which have only continued apace since his time of writing.

Indeed, this became very apparent in discussions on the BALEAP JISCMail in early 2021. Instigated by a short thought piece titled 'Some thoughts on precarity and EAP status in universities,' over 30 replies were generated in the space of a few days, making this a hot topic for the forum. It was clear that many practitioners keenly felt the effect of neo-liberal employment practices or were worried about them. The topic of the thread turned to ISEAP, with some arguing that this is one of EAP's most academic endeavours and the one recognised most fully institutionally. One contributor explicitly made the case for the work being done to develop in-sessionals to be seen as scholarship:

> Chatting recently with in-sessional colleagues [...] about the preparation we do for a discipline specific EAP course, many activities we discussed could be classed as scholarship (e.g. analysing task briefs/lectures/previous student work, discussing expectations with subject teachers, reviewing previous years' lesson materials) which then inform the materials design/ lesson planning/classroom management 'teacher' skills many of us developed in TEFL. (9 March 2021)

Another contributor also made the connection between scholarship and ISEAP, instead referring to how enhancing scholarship within the EAP centre, and the visibility of this, helped give the centre a voice in a wider university issue, namely the disparity between international recruitment and broader internationalisation of the educational experience:

> [Enhancing scholarship activities] was used to highlight the disconnect between university strategies of internationalisation and of education and to suggest that Insessional provision was one way to help this connection. (18 March 2021)

Connecting ISEAP to more prominent issues within the university can provide opportunities to enhance its status and that of the EAP centre, and *may* in some way help offset job instability. Visible in-sessional work may enable university decision makers to see the quality and usefulness of its teaching and so resource EAP teams. It should be noted, however, that this idea was put to many of our interviewees and gained little traction with them. One interviewee said they did not see how in-sessional activities could help combat precarity, going on to add:

> Sometimes people prefer just the spoon-fed delivery side of things. There are a lot more [course] books now which are quite good. It makes it easier and some people are happy just following a course book. It's without intellectual stimulus, but not everybody wants that. But those that do are the ones you want to have teaching on an in-sessional, or developing an in-sessional.

The comment highlights a possible divide between EAP teaching per se and the development of academic literacy in students. However, once again a link is made between scholarship, or at least an active engagement with the specifics of teaching and learning in a university setting, and successful in-sessional activities. Chapter 6 will pick up this point in relation to how opportunities such as this can have a beneficial impact both on the practitioner and on ISEAP in a wider context.

In terms of raising the visibility of in-sessional, publicly articulating its relevance to prominent university strategies and agendas can help. As we have seen in Chapter 1, provision specifically for international students can be easily pigeonholed, and delivered separately from the main cohorts with minimal visibility. On the other hand, university strategies very often focus on widening participation, which involves enhancing the student experience, inclusivity, tackling attainment gaps, improving student wellbeing, employability, and limiting attrition. One of our interviewees made a comment that is hardly uncommon for practitioners working in EAP:

> A lot of people don't know we exist.

Yet they went on to describe how they had been able to raise the profile of in-sessionals and the EAP centre by explicitly associating it with some of these agendas. As previously highlighted in Chapter 1, this focus on students' wider needs enables a strategic repositioning of activities away from solely international students:

> If you start using words like 'inclusivity' and 'equality' and all that sort of stuff, you could get a non-native speaker saying: well, you know I need some help with my writing too.

And indeed some of the provision itself became more visible and embedded as a result, particularly as it was then 'packaged' along with other provision. They described how a disciplinary lecturer they collaborated with incorporated the in-sessional provision into a wider package of support:

> She created a zero-credit course to include employability skills, careers advice and academic skills. So she's slipped it in there and she's using the correct terminology: employability, that sort of stuff.

There may well be disadvantages with this kind of packaging, not least having insufficient airtime to meet students' literacy needs. However, in neo-liberal university contexts, it is expedient to align provision with the agendas, imperatives and terminology that are institutionally valued. This way, there is likely to be more investment in provision. Returning once again to the BALEAP JISCMail thread on precarity, one contributor made this point contrasting funding to support international students with other initiatives:

> Whereas funding has been found for all kinds of support for UK students under the widening participation initiative, there always seems to be a problem when it comes to footing the bill for international students. (17 March 2021)

Even without attaching ISEAP to a specific agenda, articulating provision in terms of working to improve students' resilience and self-efficacy can speak more readily to the wider university than, say, simply supporting international students.

4.1.3 A Repositioning of ISEAP

There is the possibility for EAP practitioners to widen their reach by training subject lecturers in more inclusive teaching practices, rather than solely focus their resources on students. The 'getting in, getting on, and getting out' model points towards this (Shrives and Bond, 2003). But also it may be expedient to reposition the academic discourse expertise inherent to ISEAP within a frame of learning development. That there is a need is suggested by Nicholls' (2019) conclusions based on a qualitative study of academic leaders' attitudes to students' language and literacy. She interviewed academic leaders responsible for teaching and learning strategies at a U.K. university. Although this is a small case study, its conclusions are likely to be relevant beyond its immediate context. Nicholls (2019: 14) concludes:

> [M]y findings indicate that academic leaders should agree clear lines of responsibility for students' language development. They should provide opportunities for academics to discuss what they expect of students' academic language.

If they enjoy the championing of academic leaders, EAP practitioners are ideally placed to support such a process. McGrath et al. (2019) similarly identified that disciplinary academics often lacked 'metacognitive awareness' of the literacy expectations inherent in the tasks they set, a similar observation to that of Lea and Street (1998). Of particular note is where McGrath et al. see an opportunity for EAP practitioners: they recommend a professional development role to enhance subject academics' awareness, 'starting with an appreciation of genre and the nature of academic literacy, the turf of the academic literacy specialist' (2019: 850). As we have seen throughout this book, collaboration is nothing new, but the writers present evidence that the nature of the collaboration should differ:

> The significance of our study is that it highlights the value of changing the direction of this collaboration. We show how input from academic literacy specialists (with their bricolage of expertise) can impact subject specialists' practice by providing a theoretical frame and (meta)cognitive tools to evaluate and modify their teaching.
>
> McGrath et al. (2019: 850)

It is not too unusual for academic literacy specialists to contribute to the certificates in learning and teaching offered by many universities for early career academics, yet it is much rarer for more experienced university colleagues to experience regular teacher training. This is perhaps where a newly defined role for EAP practitioners like this would meet resistance. The idea of a 'training' role was suggested to an interviewee who works in an EMI setting and enjoys close collaboration with disciplinary specialists. Their response suggested that this would be problematic:

> I'm sure they would really resist that, no way, and today even now if top management would say 'they will come and train you how to be aware of

language issues,' I don't think they would, especially if we used the word 'training,' no way, I don't think so.

They went on to explain how collaboration best works where discipline lecturers seek out collaboration with the EAP centre 'naturally' rather than this being imposed. They suggested that collaboration works best within a more standard ISEAP paradigm. But this is not to say that a repositioning of practitioners as learner developers, enabling perhaps a less precarious position in the neo-liberal university, is not possible. Rather, as ever in ISEAP, the institutional context is a key factor.

The collaborative opportunities of an in-sessional teacher mean that they may well have a clearer understanding of an institution's educational culture and practices than most disciplinary academics. They effectively act as 'eth-nographers of the university,' as one of our interviewees put it. Harvey and Stocks (2017: 60) note how their small-scale ethnographic study of inter-disciplinary and transdisciplinary master's programmes 'raised interesting points about the way the students' identities were intertwined with their interpretations of their writing assessments.' The assignments in question straddled different genres, highlighting essential ambiguities and uncertainties inherent to students' writing experience. As subject lecturers were interested in how students responded creatively to their briefs, little was offered in the way of modelling and guidance. ISEAP by necessity therefore involved both students and teacher collaborating in 'a co-inductive process of navigating unpredictable yet creative territories' (2017: 59). They conclude by noting that in-sessional teachers' unique vantage point puts them in a strong position of expertise within the institution, as more degrees embrace the creative synergies offered by transdisciplinarity, with opportunities to enhance subject lectures' understandings.

To conclude this discussion of a possible repositioning of EAP, it may be helpful to reflect on Turner's (2011: 35) use of the concept of the phar-makon to describe the role of EAP in how language issues are seen in-stitutionally. The concept refers to both a poison and a remedy, which might describe the line that EAP practitioners often need to tread: to have enhanced awareness of the poison of language's diminished role, but the agility to harness its positioning to positive ends. Perhaps most EAP centres do have an entrepreneurial, commercial – and often remedial – remit, but by becoming enmeshed within the institution, there is also the possibility to make a distinctive contribution to students' learning and the wider culture of learning and teaching. The affordances offered by the unique positioning of in-sessional activities in the university will be taken up more fully in Chapter 5: The ISEAP Practitioner.

4.1.4 Measuring the Effectiveness of ISEAP

The final aspect of neo-liberal institutions to consider is their tendency towards measurability. If it is increasingly the case that by undertaking higher education, students are making a substantial financial investment for their personal gain, then it logically follows that the educational impact should be quantified. As in any transaction, it is in the interests of the provider to ascertain whether they are providing value for money. In the United Kingdom, the Office for Students has shown just such an interest in the creation of the TEF (Teaching Excellence Framework) in 2016, which uses a variety of metrics in an attempt to measure the teaching quality of every institution. But as noted in Chapter 1, for the most part, ISEAP is very often occluded, sitting outside of institutional quality assurance processes, and is unlikely to feed into such national mechanisms. Nevertheless, it is not immune to measurability. Hadley (2015: 95) conceptualises measuring as 'quantitative efforts in neoliberal HEIs [higher education institutions] to demonstrate educational excellence and justify one's existence in the organization'; the implication of this for an in-sessional intervention is that if its effectiveness is not made visible through measurement, should it therefore exist?

As noted in Chapter 3, record keeping is recommended for pedagogical and collaborative reasons. As we saw, one interviewee mentioned keeping a record of:

> how you see the students having improved – who you think has improved and in what areas.

However, such a personalised or impressionistic view of student progress may not be seen as evidence of learning in a neo-liberal context. In a culture where the voices providing auditing and metrics are widely listened to, EAP centres may be called upon to supply a firmer demonstration of effectiveness. This may be especially the case where there is a champion or significant investment in ISEAP; key stakeholders may want to understand its worth in a way that justifies its costs.

This is not easy in ISEAP. Not least is the issue of how we understand student success. The expectations may differ enormously between senior management, the EAP centre and the students themselves. For some of the cohort, student success may be achieving exceptionally high grades (firsts or distinctions in the U.K. context); it may be that an in-sessional has a role in enabling some students to achieve this. At the other end of the scale, student success may mean simply not failing, remaining on their programme of study, not withdrawing from their studies. Or is student success related to the students' perceptions; in neo-liberal terms, are the consumers satisfied with the service? Hadley (2015: 100) highlights the challenges of benchmarking EAP courses; as one of his informants puts it, 'we never found a way really to measure how well we did …' This is especially true of ISEAP; given the highly contextualised nature, comparability is largely lacking. Another of Hadley's (2015: 100) informants emphasises the risks of not measuring though:

> People need to know what you're doing […] if you can't produce any evidence about what you do and how effective it is, then you become vulnerable to restructurings and hivings off and downsizing and God knows what …

It seems therefore there may be advantages to ISEAP having limited institutional visibility. Indeed, we have found very few examples of where practitioners have tracked student attainment having attended an in-sessional. At the University of Edinburgh, Benson and Anderson (2019) were able to compare a sample of grades of both students that had taken an in-sessional course with those who had not, and found no significant difference. This is not a surprise, as there are so many contributing factors to achievement; in-sessional attendance as a variable is difficult to isolate. Indeed, the writers did not find this disappointing, noting that the cohort attending the in-sessional were international students whose English was relatively low level. Given this context, no significant difference in grades might be seen as a resounding success.

A much larger scale tracking of in-sessional effect was undertaken by Pearce et al. (2021), who presented this at the BALEAP Biennial Conference at Glasgow University within a paper explaining Hertfordshire Business School's embedded provision for international students. Taking demographic factors into account, a large data pool showed a 7.4 percentage point increase in student grades among students who had attended at least 7 out of 11 sessions. They note that this does not account for other factors like 'student motivation.' Nevertheless, in order to make this measurement, the team made use of a statistician, a resource likely to be unavailable in most EAP contexts.

Many of our interviewees aspired to track students' progress, but for the most part did not have the resources to effectively carry out such a project. Two colleagues in a university's EAP centre reported on their own efforts. They had not yet tracked students 'mathematically or systematically,' but were beginning to make progress in this area:

> We are starting to get a tracking process in place, but that is something we need to work on really.

They did report successful tracking on one collaborative, embedded example of ISEAP provision though. As 'weaker' students were the target of the intervention, based on an initial placement test, the colleagues were able to compare students' outcomes at the end of the year, comparing the ISEAP group with the remainder of the cohort. The key finding was that there was parity between the two groups:

> That was evidence that the input evened things out, evened the playing field by giving those weaker students genre knowledge and skills.

Access to this kind of data – students' degree or module outcomes – can sometimes be difficult for EAP centres, and so this is a further instance of the benefits of having a champion. With regard to the wider objectives of tracking, these colleagues made an important point about how an EAP centre might demonstrate the value of its in-sessional provision:

> Also managing people's expectations – we're not trying to make these students the best in the cohort, that was never going to happen. It's like they are comparable to the rest of the cohort.

This obviously plays into a deficit understanding of ISEAP, but that may be a result of the institutional context. Demonstrating the key role a course can play in 'getting students over the line,' as they put it, is of value in a culture keen to evaluate student success. In order to measure the effectiveness of an intervention though, many of our interviewees relied on students' articulation of their learning through feedback mechanisms in lieu of having more concrete data. It is possible to present the case for an in-sessional's usefulness through such data. An interviewee at a different university expressed it thus with regard to particular awareness-raising activities:

The feedback from the students was like, 'this is great'; 'why didn't we have something like this before?'; 'we should do these earlier'; 'we should do more of these.' The [disciplinary] lecturer also asked them about their feedback and their experience and it was really, really positive. Now obviously we haven't had the grades from that yet, but I'm very much encouraged by the fact so many of these students found it very useful.

Student satisfaction is a key metric in neo-liberal contexts, so such evaluation is not without value, even if it is notable that actual grades were not available at the time of the students providing feedback. Authentic student voices articulating how useful they found the learning is enormously important (just as students' own articulation of their 'wants' is so important to a needs analysis). Subjective accounts have value, especially where statistical data is difficult to access or there are not the resources to enact a full tracking project. In addition, subject lecturers' own accounts are also likely to be valued. One of our interviewees, a disciplinary lecturer, articulated how they saw the effect of in-sessional provision:

Without statistics, I can possibly say that the in-sessional made a huge difference on those students' performance who were willing to engage with the sessions. We always say the best students probably don't go [and] the least performing ones don't go. Usually it's the ones in the middle who are most keen to go. For this middle group of students, I think the in-sessional really makes the difference to allow those in the middle to become distinctions. I can definitely see that, although I don't have the statistics.

Without access to the data, it could be said that this measurement of effect is still impressionistic. Nevertheless, as the subject lecturer is surely a key stakeholder in in-sessional provision, their view carries weight institutionally.

4.2 Affordances of Technology

In contrast with wider English language teaching, until recently there has been a relative paucity of EAP literature specifically related to technology enhanced learning (TEL). The second edition of Alexander et al.'s popular *EAP Essentials* dedicates just four pages to e-learning, noting that 'e-learning courses suffer from higher drop-out rates than traditional courses,' (2019: 123), perhaps as a result of challenges in community building. Indeed, surveys show students' overall preference for physical in-class experiences, particularly among international students (ICEF, 2020) as well as the absence of a need to truly embrace it, depending on the particularities of the institutional culture. Walker (2014: 319) describes higher education as an early adopter of digital tools, yet also notes, 'teachers do not make full use of the technologies available.' Her focus is on digital resources, similarity-checking software like Turnitin, virtual learning environments (VLEs), and other tools which can support in-class learning. The situation has moved on since her time of writing though, not least due to the rapid transformation in EAP learning contexts wrought by the COVID-19 pandemic.

As Blaj-Ward et al. (2021: 1) put it in their introduction to BALEAP's rapidly published *Narratives of Innovation and Resilience*, the pandemic ushered in 'an intense period of professional development as we learned in real time how online teaching and support could help us reach and sustain our students.' The newly imposed conditions led to EAP practitioners and academics worldwide rapidly embracing video-conferencing technologies. Software like Zoom, Blackboard Collaborate, and Microsoft Teams have enabled them to run classes remotely, with participants entering a virtual classroom from wherever they are.

For ISEAP, this may have more lasting consequences than other aspects of the university curriculum. In institutions where demand for physical space is high, it is the non-credited, adjunct 'cinderella' classes (Turner, 2011) that are more likely to continue to be delivered online, while others revert to face-to-face teaching. This is something of a double-edged sword. It enables a greater reach, freed from the limitations of physical room capacity. The barriers to attendance are lower too, with students being able to join the class remotely from wherever they are. Virtual classrooms also open up possibilities for collaboration among students in the class using collaborative whiteboards and free software such as Padlet, which enables shared access and posting to online bulletin boards. Blaj-Ward et al. (2021: 2) further note the opportunities opened up by this new context, including the integration of provision into degrees. Hendrie and Tibbetts (2021: 15), reflecting on how in-sessional provision had altered at the University of Bristol, note that in a physical classroom setting, students did not always identify ISEAP as an integrated part of their programme of study. The pivot to online provision removed this distinction: they found the 'opportunity to be embedded much more deeply in course provision' by being hosted on departments' own VLE pages. Online collaboration also enabled greater flexibility for team teaching with subject specialists. Moreover, they have hopes that their increased prominence will enable them to be seen as more established 'literacy experts' in their institution.

On the other hand, even with a greater reach and higher attendance, levels of student engagement are often much lower online. There may not be the same level of being 'in the moment' as there is in a classroom setting. Fatigue sets in more quickly. Small-group breakout work among students may not be as collaborative without the non-verbal cues gained from working in physical proximity to each other. Rather than trying to rely on replicating a room-based class in an online setting, many have found the ABC approach to online learning, developed at University College London (ABC-LD, 2022), a useful toolkit. Developed by UCL lecturers Young and Perović, the tool enables a rapid reconceptualisation of existing teaching across disciplines into an online environment. It is based around six principles: acquisition, collaboration, discussion, investigation, practice and production. It explicitly invites educators to consider which aspects of their course can be delivered asynchronously and which synchronously. This has implications for ISEAP in that it facilitates a move towards flipped lessons, where considerable work may be done by the students asynchronously in preparation for a synchronous taught session. In this way, the actual time students and teacher spend together may be capitalised on. This need for greater preparation may again have implications for engagement though, particularly for adjunct provision. Students may not be willing to commit such efforts to what may be percived as a low-stakes course. Whatever pedagogical approach is deemed appropriate, there is nevertheless the ongoing danger of ISEAP being side-lined as universities return to on-campus teaching, a mode of delivery that is generally students' preference.

For the most part our interviews focussed on the principles underpinning delivery over pedagogical practicalities. However, one of the interviewees spoke of an expedient utilisation of online pedagogies for general ISEAP provision in order to free up limited resources for deeper collaboration with departments:

> We have so many more tools now to develop asynchronous lessons and we have the ability, the skills now to do it. So we're thinking of making more of our generalised sessions more asynchronous to be able to then go into more departments and offer more of an embedded approach.

Another interviewee similarly suggested that their EAP centre was now in an advantageous position, having developed online approaches for much of its provision. EGAP provision, in particular, may be particularly suitable for one-off online sessions; in this way, EAP centres can allocate resources more fully to embedded ESAP provision:

> When COVID happened and we all had to go online, we developed other aspects of [existing EGAP provision]: webinars that were designed specifically for online provision, so we've got a nice set of those now, more stand-alone. We're in quite a lot of transition now as we see what it might look like post-COVID, what might stay online, what might revert back to a more traditional delivery.

There are clearly affordances to be gained from online provision, not least having developed a bank of materials and lessons which can be deployed or further developed for future iterations. This may have a sustaining effect on ISEAP delivery. Online pedagogies are clearly a factor in the changing HE landscape and offer some affordances for ISEAP, yet it was clear speaking to practitioners that collaboration and a more flexible learning environment are still highly valued as key. Therefore, the operationalisation of online teaching in ISEAP should still maintain its focus on bespoke, integrated language and literacy development. More generic, less integrated language and literacy provision should not necessarily be considered the natural consequence of delivering online.

4.3 Decolonising the Curriculum

A final area of change to be discussed here is one affecting higher education more broadly, as disciplines update students' reading lists by highlighting previously limited voices, and rethinking the nature of knowledge as it is studied. Decolonisation is a process that can be understood and interpreted in many ways, but in education, it can be seen as:

> an expression of the changing geopolitics of knowledge whereby the modern epistemological framework for knowing and understanding the world is no longer interpreted as universal and unbound by geo-historical and biographical contexts.
>
> Baker (2012: 2), cited by Ewing (2022: 130)

The epistemological framework under review is informed by Enlightenment notions of what constitutes truth and the types of knowledge pertaining to this. The Enlightenment elevated rationalism and the use of empirical evidence above other sources of knowledge (Hall and Gieben, 1992). There is an inherent Eurocentrism here, understandings that go to the heart of Western universities' histories. But increasingly, the 'truths' of rationalism are not seen as universal, and have increasingly come under questioning within HE and beyond. Yet its presence in EAP literature is limited. This is surprising, as the work of EAP is mostly aiding international students' transition to a new academic culture, with its implications of assimilation to dominant norms, rather than transforming these from outside. As student populations become increasingly diversified and the role of EAP wider, not least as ISEAP widens its reach, so strategic agendas highlighting attainment gaps and equality of opportunity impact its approaches. This was recognised by one of our interviewees, who highlighted the connections between inclusive teaching practices and not making assumptions about particular students' traits. They stated their intentions as:

> taking a developmental approach, challenging the deficit model and also thinking about all of that in relation to international students who are, for the most part, still most of our audience, although we're open to students from anywhere. And thinking about how that connects with decolonial pedagogies and not stereotyping those students and making assumptions about what they can and can't do, how they do or don't think, or practices in their previous educational cultures. So I think for me the overarching principles are about equality, diversity and incusion really and just making sure that we're that we're inclusive, making sure that we're not making assumptions about particular people, practices or cultures.

Such an awareness is implicit in critical EAP approaches, yet can only become more prominent as the nature of the institutions in which we work change, too. Ewing (2022: 129), writing about an EAP-informed provision at Goldsmiths, University of London, argues that enabling every student with the right to speak and be heard requires 'continually unlearning and re-learning our identities as educators.' Working within this paradigm, ISEAP is not only enabling students to adapt towards disciplinary ways of knowing and writing, but also affirming students' own individual, decolonising context.

Vaghefian (2020) relates this issue to structures inherent to institutions. Referring to her own university context, which she reports has an attainment gap whereby international and Black and Minority Ethnic (BAME) students are generally awarded lower results, its in-sessional classes are designated as 'English classes.' She argues that this has remedial connotations for international students, and that the language policies of the university need to be reconsidered to reframe how these are presented to students. She recommends a focus on inclusive and critical ISEAP pedagogies in line with the university's wider strategic efforts to decolonise its curriculum. Importantly, she notes that the process of decolonisation is longitudinal, without a clear end point; its work encompasses not only pedagogies but reformulating institutional systems.

ISEAP's situation is as important in this regard as ever. In the settings above, both universities are arts-centric and London-based. In multicultural contexts, the discourses of decolonisation are probably more prominent. We quoted an interviewee, working in a South African context, in Chapter 1:

> There's a big drive for multilingualism at the moment in universities generally; the decolonisation agenda is also important, which we think about in a large part of our curriculum development.

In the South African context, it would be unsurprising if it were otherwise. They continued by explaining how this impacts the teaching of ISEAP:

> If you talk about truly decolonising the curriculum then we have to talk about the university structures, the whole system. But in an attempt to get to that point the first thing we did is we looked at our texts, to use texts and topics that are more linked to the South African context and to the students' context. [...] We're trying to activate prior knowledge but also prior experience, their lived experiences, and their previous literacies as well, and bringing that into the classroom, to say 'what do you know?'; 'where are you at?' Having texts by local authors, the South African situation, the Global South.

The choice of topics and texts in turn informs the ISEAP pedagogies and practices, and naturally aligns closely with critiques about the hegemony of English (e.g. Phillipson, 1992) and questions about the role of English language teaching in supporting and giving oxygen to this process. This naturally has implications for EAP practitioners and questions about the extent to which universities' internationalisation agendas are attempting more than to simply recruit international students (Jenkins and Wingate, 2015). Even in contexts where decolonisation appears not to impact ISEAP, it is likely to become prominent as university populations become more diverse – in student and staff bodies – and as institutions seek to redress injustices and enhance attainment. The more EAP practitioners are able to collaborate and understand how disciplinary knowledge is constructed, the more prominent these discourses will become to EAP practices. One of our interviewees stated how decolonisation agendas are central to their EAP practice:

> I think there is so much space in EAP for [decolonising pedagogies]: we are constantly asking people to think about vocabulary, but also reading as an active process and using an interpretive framework, but whose interpretive framework are we requiring them to use? It's most likely not their interpretive framework but some sort of legitimised way of seeing and understanding and being in the world, so it's picking apart a wide range of assumptions that make their way into the writing that we ask them to do.

She relates her approach to critical discourse analysis (Fairclough, 2010), a deconstruction of the foundations of discourse conventions. This links nicely to much EAP pedagogy, of looking beyond dictionary definitions and to engage in the debate that surrounds concepts. This is perhaps the next logical step, to look beyond a narrow Eurocentric framing. Even where ISEAP is closely aligned with disciplines with more fixed epistemologies, such as sciences and engineering, which may be less suited to such a critical approach, space can be made in the classroom for students to reflect on their own experiences and backgrounds, to compare these with the valued expectations of the discipline. There is no reason why students' experiences should not be central to their learning and this may differ widely from perceived norms. Framing decolonisation in this way, it can only occupy an ever greater part of many EAP discourses.

Concluding Thoughts

This chapter has moved beyond the scope of Chapter 3's focus on logistical matters to consider wider, more macro-level influences on how ISEAP practices are developing. These influences are significant for anyone working in universities today, and indeed the examples from our interviews above demonstrate that all of these issues highlighted – neo-liberalism, precarity, COVID-19 and the subsequent move to online delivery, and decolonisation of the curriculum agendas – have in some way all exerted an effect on ISEAP. The reflection section that follows this chapter focusses on these questions and is aimed at developing a personal appraisal of how these issues may affect practitioners in their own specific context.

Chapter 4 Reflection

Here are some questions that invite you to reflect on the macro aspects detailed in the chapter related to ISEAP.

1. How are in-sessionals funded at your institution?
   a. In what ways do structural factors affect provision?
   b. What are the implications for delivery?
   c. How does this affect staffing?
2. Do you see collaborative in-sessional work as part of your scholarship? Why/Why not?
3. Are there any opportunities that you can see where in-sessionals can bolster your standing within your EAP centre and/or university?
4. Look at your institution's mission statement and teaching and learning strategy.
   a. What are the main agendas?
   b. Can ISEAP be aligned with any of these?
   c. Is there a champion who may help enable this?
5. Are there opportunities for you to train disciplinary lectures in academic discourse matters? Are there ways for you to share your expertise on genre and academic literacy?
6. How do you measure the effectiveness of your in-sessional provision?
   a. Do you have access to data that offers tracking opportunities?
   b. Can student and lecturer feedback be a way of measuring effectiveness in your view?
   c. Are you able to attain disciplinary lecturers' feedback on the effectiveness of ISEAP?
7. What are the provisions for online delivery of ISEAP?
   a. What is being delivered online and what is not?
   b. Are there potential dangers attached to this, such as a risk of sidelining ISEAP?
   c. How could you avoid this in your context?
8. Are you aware of a decolonisation agenda in your institution?
   a. How can you make your classes more inclusive to all participants?
   b. In choosing texts, are you able to make choices about whose voices are heard?
   c. How does your ISEAP setting enable you to put students' lived experiences at the heart of their learning?

References

ABC-LD (2022) *ABC Learning Design @ UCL*. Available at: https://blogs.ucl.ac.uk/abc-ld/ [accessed 2/10/22].

Alexander, O., Argent, S. and Spencer, J. (2019) *EAP essentials: A teacher's guide to principles and practice*. (2nd ed.). Reading: Garnet.

BALEAP JISCMail (2021) *Some thoughts on precarity and EAP status in universities*. For tutors/lecturers in EAP (English for Academic Purposes) BALEAP@JISCMail.ac.uk.

Benson, C. and Anderson, K. (2019) A dissertation writing course for school of education students at the University of Edinburgh. In Strandring, A. and Stansfield, G. (eds.) *Papers from the Professional Issues Meeting (PIM) on In-sessional English for Academic Purposes held at London School of Economics 19 March 2016*, 85–94. Available at: https://www.baleap.org/wp-content/uploads/2019/10/Baleap_Book_Interactive.pdf [accessed 1/9/22].

Blaj-Ward, L., Hultgren, K., Arnold, R. and Reichard, B. (2021) Narratives of innovation and resilience: Introduction. In Blaj-Ward, L., Hultgren, K., Arnold, R. and Reichard, B. (Eds.) *Narratives of innovation and resilience: Supporting student learning experiences in challenging times*, pp. 1–5. Available at: https://www.baleap.org/wp-content/uploads/2021/02/BALEAP-Narratives-of-innovation-and-resilience.pdf [accessed 2/10/22].

Ding, A. and Bruce, I. (2017) *The English for academic purposes practitioner: Operating on the edge of academia*. Cham, Switzerland: Palgrave Macmillan.

Ewing, S. (2022) Decolonizing research methodologies: Practicalities, challenges and opportunities. In Day, A., Lee, L., Thomas, D.S.P. and Spickard, J. (Eds.) *Diversity, inclusion, and decolonization: Practical tools for improving teaching, research, and scholarship*. Bristol: Bristol University Press, pp. 125–139.

Fairclough, N. (2010) *Critical discourse analysis: The critical study of language* (2nd ed.). Abingdon, Oxon: Routledge.

Fulcher, G. (2009) The commercialisation of language provision at university. In Alderson, J.C. (ed.) *The politics of language education: Individuals and institutions*. Bristol: Multilingual Matters, pp. 125–146.

Hadley, G. (2015) *English for academic purposes in Neoliberal Universities: A critical grounded theory*. Cham, Switzerland: Springer.

Hall, S. and Gieben, B. (1992) *Formations of modernity*. Cambridge: Polity Press.

Harvey, S. and Stocks, P. (2017) When arts meets enterprise: Trans-disciplinarity, student identities, and EAP. *London Review of Education*, 15:1, 50–62.

Hendrie, P. and Tibbetts, N. (2021) In-sessional EAP in the time of COVID: Adapting in-sessional EAP provision, delivering online tutorials and refining the course evaluation process. In Blaj-Ward, L., Hultgren, K., Arnold, R. and Reichard, B. (Eds.) *Narratives of innovation and resilience: Supporting student learning experiences in challenging times*, pp. 13–22. Available at: https://www.baleap.org/wp-content/uploads/2021/02/BALEAP-Narratives-of-innovation-and-resilience.pdf [accessed 2/10/22].

ICEF (2020) New insights on how international students are planning for the coming academic year. *ICEF Monitor*, https://monitor.icef.com/2020/05/new-insights-on-how-international-students-are-planning-for-the-coming-academic-year/ [accessed 27/09/2022].

Jenkins, J. and Wingate, U. (2015) Staff and students' perceptions of English language policies and practices in 'International' universities: A case study from the UK. *Higher Education Review*, 47, 47–73.

Lea, M.R. and Street, B. (1998) Student writing in higher education: An academic literacies approach. *Studies in Higher Education*, 23:2, 157–172.

McGrath, L., Negretti, R. and Nicholls, K. (2019). Hidden expectations: scaffolding specialists' genre knowledge of the assignment they set. *Higher Education Research & Development*, 78, 835–853. doi: 10.1007/s10734-019-00373-9.

Nicholls, K. (2019) 'You have to work from where they are': Academic leaders' talk about language development. *Journal of Higher Education Policy and Management*, 42, 1–18. Available at: http://shura.shu.ac.uk/25135/36/Nicholls_YouHaveTo%28AM%29.pdf [accessed 15/9/22].

Pearce, D., Stamps, H. and Sloan, D. (2021) Optimising online Academic English support for large international student numbers using the CEM model. *BALEAP Biennial Conference 2021 at the University of Glasgow*. Available at: https://www.youtube.com/watch?v=yKLHQd2HbAs [accessed 18/9/22].

Phillipson, R. (1992) *Linguistic imperialism*. Oxford: Oxford University Press.

Ryan, J. and Carroll, J. (2005) 'Canaries in the coalmine': International students in western universities. In Carroll, J. and Ryan, J. (eds.) *Teaching international students: Improving learning for all*. London: Routledge, pp. 3–10.

Shrives, L. and Bond, C. (2003) Consultancy in educational development. In Kahn, P. and Baume, D. (eds.) *A guide to staff and educational development*. Abingdon, Oxon: Routledge.

Turner, J. (2011) *Language in the academy: Cultural reflexivity and intercultural dynamics*. Bristol: Multilingual Matters.

Vaghefian, S. (2020) The problem with 'English Class': Embedding as a tool for decolonisation. *Trinity College London*. Available at: https://resources.trinitycollege.com/teachers/english_language/webinars/the-problem-with-english-class-embedding-as-a-tool-for-decolonisation [accessed 27/09/2022].

Walker, A. (2014) Technologies. In de Chazal, E. (ed.) *English for academic purposes*. Oxford: Oxford University Press, pp. 319–339.

Webster, S. (2022) The transition of EAP practitioners into scholarship writing. *Journal of English for Academic Purposes*, 57, May 2022, 101091, 1–12.

Chapter 5

The ISEAP Practitioner

This chapter will examine the implications of being involved in ISEAP for practitioners. Moving into ISEAP from other EAP contexts may require specific adjustments, on top of what may be seen as a rather challenging transition for many practitioners from teaching in general ELT settings to EAP (Alexander, 2012; Bell, 2022; Campion, 2016; Ding and Bruce, 2017). Operating in the in-sessional context places practitioners right at the 'textface' (Tuck, 2018), accompanying students as they develop their academic language and literacy in situ. This is clearly quite a different prospect for EAP practitioners than teaching on pre-sessional or foundation courses. As Chapter 2 suggested, when it comes to pedagogy, to a certain extent EAP practitioners should be prepared to develop their competence 'on the job' (Bell, 2022). Moreover, from our interviews for this book, it is clear that certain attributes or skills may need to be developed for an EAP practitioner entering into in-sessional contexts, and these often go beyond purely pedagogical concerns. Even within the teaching practice in this area, however, there are specific issues related to conceptualisations of knowledge and expertise that require examination. ISEAP typically places the practitioner in less of an authoritative teacher role than other EAP settings, and arguably in a less clearly defined one. Being integrated within the substantive teaching programmes of the university and collaborating with non-language specialist academics leads to a shift in the ISEAP practitioner's own perceptions of their positioning and status in ways

DOI: 10.4324/9781003193715-8

which do not necessarily apply in broader EAP settings, such as working on a pre-sessional. This may also require further reflection and self-orientation. Beyond teaching, setting up and operating in-sessional language provision, as the previous chapter discussed, also requires a willingness to adapt to play a variety of roles to fit in with the context of the contemporary university. As ISEAP is arguably a more challenging and less straightforward arena to operate in than pre-sessional or foundation contexts, this may mean that it is not a suitable or desirable area of practice for all EAP practitioners. However, in this chapter we also suggest that there are a number of benefits and affordances for a practitioner's personal development in ISEAP, which may well outweigh the challenges.

The chapter begins with a focus on what it is like to enter ISEAP contexts for the first time, whether transitioning from English language teaching (ELT) or from experience of working on other EAP provision. It considers key challenges in terms of expertise and knowledge, the positioning and status of the ISEAP practitioner, and the implications of this. Then it explores the different roles and personal attributes that operating in this sub-field of EAP demands. Through reference to our interviews, we explore how all of the above impacts job satisfaction and how practitioners see themselves, their place in EAP, and their place within the academic community when specifically working in ISEAP contexts.

5.1 Transitioning into ISEAP

As should be clear now from what has preceded, ISEAP is not simply about language teaching. It is a sub-field of English for Academic Purposes (EAP), which itself derives from the wider field of English for Specific Purposes (ESP). EAP is distinguished from more general forms of English language teaching chiefly because of its degree of specificity, and a much more clearly defined purpose of instruction (Alexander, 2012; Bell, 2022; Campion, 2016; Ding and Bruce, 2017). For teachers in ISEAP, the target situation (as referenced in the needs analysis in Chapter 3) is not just about effective communication in academic contexts, but also being able to effectively function in diverse specific academic contexts. This may in fact be quite a range of contexts, as very often ISEAP practitioners work across a suite of different discipline areas and are expected to tailor provision to each one. Alternatively, where seconded into departments, for example, there is also a greater incentive for teachers to delve even deeper into understanding specific discourse communities. In addition, in ISEAP contexts teachers are not preparing students to enter future academic courses; rather they need to take account of the fact that the students are already members at the time of their interaction with them. All of the above points have important implications in terms of how the ISEAP practitioner is positioned in relation to their learners, how ISEAP courses are taught, the role of disciplinary knowledge, and what is understood to be the ISEAP teacher's remit.

All in all, this is what makes ISEAP such a complex, challenging, and also rewarding area to practise in. It does, however, mean there may be many initial questions related to expertise and role for a practitioner new to this area, which could portray it in a negative light as a particularly demanding niche area of EAP. Once in practice, the specific issues of ISEAP mentioned above may still impact on confidence levels, as one of the interviewees' comments we report below illustrates. Also, in terms of how practitioner identity develops, experience of working in this area may lead to changed perceptions of status and identity. There is little published research specifically focussed on transitions into ISEAP, so we start here by considering the transition practitioners make into EAP and then consider what our interviews with practitioners working in the field tell us about the more specific context.

As noted in Chapter 2, Bell (2022: 5–6) observed that there was a lack of research into exactly how practitioners teach in EAP contexts in general, but a larger body of literature on the transition from teaching in more general ELT contexts to EAP. Fitzpatrick et al.'s (2022) study also acknowledges this and tries to remedy the dearth of research by investigating EAP teaching expertise as perceived by practitioners themselves. In their study, they noted that:

> research suggests that EAP practitioners' academic status and teaching and research roles vary, quite considerably, across different contexts, leading to ambiguity about who EAP practitioners are and what roles and responsibilities they hold. (Fitzpatrick et al., 2022)

The majority of those they interviewed as part of this study cited EAP-specific knowledge as having the most significant influence on their personal development (Fitzpatrick et al., 2022). Chapter 2 of this book examined the key theories of EAP teaching and evidence from our interviews demonstrated the wide range and complex nature of what informs ISEAP practice, in line with the findings above. We noted that a number of our interviewees, when asked about their underlying pedagogy, picked aspects from across the range of the 'pillars of EAP', mentioning other more general concepts, techniques and modes of delivery, and often cited theory associated more typically with general ELT contexts. At the start of this chapter, then it is worth considering more closely how practitioners use or develop what they know from prior teaching and learning experience as they transition into EAP, and then more specifically into ISEAP contexts.

The ELT to EAP trajectory has been identified as the most common for EAP practitioners in the U.K. context (Ding and Bruce, 2017; Bell, 2022). Indeed, it is one common to both the authors of this book and many of those we interviewed. The move from teaching general English to EAP is often seen in a positive light, contributing certain aspects of expertise, despite the subsequent challenges practitioners may face to adapt pedagogy and practice to a more specific, academic environment. And there may even be an initial period where a significant difference between general English teaching experience and EAP are not fully appreciated, as one of our interviewees from a U.K. university context put it when discussing their move into working in a university context:

> I had seen my role as EFL [English as a foreign language], but it became EAP – largely through responding to learner needs, but that's where my proper career started.

The comment that EAP is where this practitioner's 'career really started' suggests a key identity shift. This may not be a sudden, drastic change, but more of a gradual evolution. By responding to the exigencies of the context, noted here as 'learner needs', this practitioner's own concept of their professional identity began to change. The quote suggests that working in EAP contexts did not require an immediate adjustment away from ELT, also that when adjustments came this was the result of a realisation on the part of the practitioner themselves. Indeed, as suggested in Chapter 2's discussion of pedagogies, being a reflective practitioner and having the willingness to continually make adjustments as one goes is a vital attribute of working in EAP (Ding and Bruce, 2017; Bell, 2022).

In terms of the content of teaching, while reviewing the literature of 'transition studies' that examine the move from ELT to EAP in general, Ding and Bruce observe that in EAP:

> the theme emerges that the pedagogical focus is no longer centred on specific features of language, but rather on larger units of language such as texts and on the discursive influences that surround the texts in both their creation and their processing. (2017: 103)

This suggests there is an important distinction between teaching general English and EAP in terms of the language component of what is taught, and to sum up what is needed for a transition, Ding and Bruce suggest knowledge development for EAP practitioners lies in two key areas: discipline-specific practices and expertise in discourse analysis (2017: 107).

Unfortunately, in some circumstances, as has been observed previously in this book, even in the situated context of ISEAP, practitioners are still often treated as no more than language teachers and their situation may still set them up in what is essentially no more than a language skills provider role. For example, one of our interviewees stated that due to department and institutional pressure in their ISEAP context they were still expected to base their syllabus for university-based academic English provision on learning aims derived from the Common European Framework (CEFR). CEFR is a framework typically used in language education across (mostly European) languages to distinguish between beginners (described as A1, A2 level), through intermediate (B1, B2) to more proficient users (C1, C2). Our interviewee commented:

> Learning objectives were given to us, twenty arbitrary points from CEFR.

The choice of the word 'arbitrary' is notable here. As discussed in Chapter 2 and elsewhere in this book, pedagogy in the ISEAP area is ideally not informed by a language-based approach and what may be seen as a deficit concept of fixing language problems. Developing language proficiency in students is not enough; what is needed is a wider focus on fully contextualised academic literacy development (Wingate, 2015). As previous chapters have suggested, however, this function of EAP practitioners is not always understood by institutions and a literacy development focus may not be enshrined in how courses are set up. As a result, practitioners themselves may have little control over course design.

However, beyond these particular examples of language focussed provision, there may actually be some positive crossover from ELT to EAP, in terms of teaching practice. Campion (2016), in a study of practising EAP teachers, notes that some of her respondents felt that in terms of teaching methodology, the skills needed are practically the same as for an ELT context (2016: 66). Bell (2022) suggests there is definitely room for some 'methodological transfer' from general language teaching backgrounds into EAP, even if there is also scope for some 'slaying of sacred cows of ELT' (2022: 8). For example, he questions whether certain key tenets of ELT classroom practice, such as the student-centredness of teaching, might be subject to reappraisal in academic contexts, allowing for slightly more teacher-centred approaches at times (2022). In in-sessional teaching in ESAP contexts, where the teacher is cast in a role of non-expert within discipline-based teaching, this might not seem to tally. Yet, what one of our interviewees said would appear to corroborate Bell's point:

> In in-sessional there is a need for quality input; it's different from other EAP teaching – teachers do talk more in the classroom. It's still interactive, but there's more teaching talking time … content knowledge comes from the student, but knowledge of the genre comes from the EAP practitioner – it isn't the case that the students can do it for themselves.

This quote also shows that there is specific expertise that language teachers bring to the EAP/ISEAP context and this is expressed in the form of genre and discourse analytical expertise. Moreover, it is interesting to note the description of ISEAP as requiring 'quality input' as a distinguishing feature. Another interviewee's comment reiterates the point above about what constitutes ISEAP practitioner knowledge and expertise:

> The whole team have a common background in applied linguistics and TESOL – we are all good at text analysis. We all look at texts as linguists.

A notable difference between ISEAP and other EAP contexts is the potentially higher degree of discipline specificity in in-sessional. This suggests another point to consider in relation to knowledge and expertise: the role of student knowledge in the classroom. In a sense, students are more expert than the language teachers in the ISEAP context in terms of the subject matter, and this has implications for the balance between teacher and student input. The implications of a knowledge sharing set-up does not necessarily suggest the need for a higher level of teacher-led instruction or teacher talking time as our interviewee put it. Wette (2014), in a study of EAP teaching practices in New Zealand where some of her interviewees were working in in-sessional contexts, talks of teacher-led 'assistance' in terms of teacher input. She notes, in a nod to Systemic Functional Linguistics (SFL)-informed genre practice, that:

genre-based pedagogies require explicit teacher-led assistance in the stages of the teaching-learning cycle that involve familiarising students with the genre, analysis of exemplars and guided text construction, with all three potentially involving modelling strategies. (2014: 62)

The above example suggests scaffolding and co-construction, techniques associated with genre theory and in particular the learning-teaching cycle and SFL-based instruction (Purser et al., 2020). Relating this to the previous comments from our interviews, a knowledge gap in the classroom is implied, but not the idea that to close that gap requires direct teacher input in terms of explicit instruction, as might be the case when teaching grammar rules in general English, for instance. Instead, co-construction and assistance suggest more of a knowledge-sharing experience and a less direct teaching style.

One teaching approach cited in EAP, and which is explicitly referenced by the BALEAP TEAP framework (2022) is that of the 'meddler-in-the-middle' (McWilliam, 2009). As discussed in Chapter 1, this may be a very useful concept for understanding the role of the teacher in an ISEAP context. In terms of what goes on in the class, McWilliam conceptualises the meddling teacher as being somewhere between the 'sage on the stage,' i.e. the arbiter of knowledge, and the 'guide on the side'; merely facilitating the learning process (McWilliam, 2009). The 'meddler' role places emphasis on the student centeredness of the learning process but involves the teacher actively intervening in student discussions, asking challenging questions that shape the learners' developing understanding of concepts and structures (McWilliam, 2009).

A key point about teaching in ISEAP contexts is the need to strike a balance in terms of positioning in the teaching role, so McWilliam's meddler role would then seem to fit in well here (McWilliam, 2009). Bell (2022) acknowledges that given the cohorts we teach in EAP contexts, learners certainly do not come to class as 'empty vessels,' as might be construed for teaching beginners in an ELT class say, and notes that teachers need to work on more 'of an equal footing' with students in EAP contexts (2022: 6). Again in embedded discipline-specific settings, this aspect would only be heightened. In pedagogical terms, referring back to Chapter 2, if what is implied by 'assistance' in Wette (2014) might be construed as fitting with a broadly genre-based or SFL paradigm, then the 'equal footing' comment in Bell (2022) could perhaps be seen as fitting in more with an Academic Literacies informed approach. (See Chapter 2 for a fuller discussion of the knowledge base of EAP).

Much of the actual teaching expertise, i.e. classroom management techniques that practitioners may have practised in their prior ELT teaching experience can still be drawn upon once teaching in an EAP setting. Moreover, experience developed while working in varied language education may also have instilled confidence in the practitioner as an adaptive classroom teacher. In fact, as noted in the previous chapter, having this solid background of teaching practice may actually be a point of distinction for ISEAP practitioners operating in the wider academy. One interviewee, who has an EAP background but is now involved in the staff academic development programme of a U.K. institution, observed that those with a strong ELT teaching background coming to work within the main teaching programmes of the university have potential to make a significant contribution to HE pedagogy because:

> we bring teaching excellence ... variety, interactivity, inclusiveness: the stuff we know helps students to learn.

Ding and Bruce refer to the transition to EAP from ELT as a 'well-trodden path' (2017: p.98). Indeed, in terms of the qualifications often needed to practise in EAP, Ding and Bruce (2017) observe that entry to EAP practitioner roles in U.K. universities is typically by way of what they term 'adopted' qualifications such as the DELTA (Diploma in English Language Teaching to Adults) or a master's degree in TESOL (teaching English to speakers of other languages). In their study, Fitzpatrick et al. slightly expand on this: they identify the most common basis for EAP teachers in terms of formal qualifications to be 'CELTA, DELTA, TEAP and Master's level study (MA TESOL and MA Applied Linguistics),' but comment also that these should be 'seen very much as starting points,' suggesting there is a need for something extra to be developed (Fitzpatrick et al., 2022). In the literature the availability and take up of formalised TEAP (teaching English for academic purposes) courses has often been discussed, usually with the conclusion that as yet this is very rarely a 'way in' to the EAP profession or that the critical mass of TEAP trained practitioners is rather low (Campion, 2016).

A couple of our interviewees explicitly mentioned teaching qualifications specifically in relation to ISEAP teaching. One discussed how they had plans for encouraging staff who worked on ISEAP provision to 'upskill' to having a DELTA. This suggests that the staff members in this case might have a master's in TESOL or Applied Linguistics, but not an ELT teaching qualification. Moreover, it suggests that for them having a DELTA is perceived as a mark of a high level of language teaching expertise in the ISEAP sector. It might be construed therefore that there is a strong link between ELT qualified status and ISEAP practice; however, the interviewee also acknowledged that 'you can't have someone with just a DELTA doing this.' Therefore, they clearly perceive the requirements for ISEAP teaching to have a firm basis in, but also to require more than, expertise in English language teaching to adults.

In a large post-1992 U.K. university context, where unusually ISEAP activities are coordinated through the university library rather than an EAP department, another interviewee told us:

> I was very keen on recruiting people with EAP experience, preferably DELTA and with university experience. EAP people thus support librarians in the faculty with learning and teaching … One librarian has done an EFL course; some librarians have done a TEAP course.

This reveals not only that ISEAP practitioners might enter practice from another, non-ELT route (in this case through working in the university library). The interviewee adds a further factor: 'university experience.' Their comment also demonstrates that TEAP, in this case at least, is seen to perform a function in bridging a gap in expertise for non-language teaching background staff.

Another interviewee at a post-1992 U.K. university also discussed ISEAP practitioners who did not come from an ELT background, but definitely had university experience. They had 'trained up' PhD students with no formal language teaching qualifications to deliver some elements of their ISEAP provision. The interviewee weighed up what the potential shortcomings with that approach to staffing were:

> I don't think it's necessary to have that experience of 20 years as a language teacher … but if you think you can just train anyone to do it … What we got from training students and understanding which elements are linguistic and what might be something else … you can't just give that to someone else. There is a benefit to having an experienced teacher doing the role.

What the comments from our interviews above suggest and corroborate from the literature is that there is certainly not a straightforward transition from ELT to EAP to ISEAP in every case. EAP, and we suggest ISEAP in particular, requires something far beyond language teacher expertise. There are other key components that are perceived as necessary beyond language teaching, but the definite advantage to having a solid basis of language teaching experience for working in this context is widely acknowledged.

5.2 Teacher Expertise

One of the key concerns practitioners might have regarding their expertise when transitioning into ISEAP in particular is a lack of knowledge and experience in the specific target context. As noted above, an ELT background can provide a solid basis of teaching and a master's in TESOL or applied linguistics can provide a basis in text analysis; however, more specific knowledge and even different forms of knowledge are needed in EAP (Ding and Bruce, 2017: 99). As Campion notes, it has previously been observed that:

> ELT prioritises delivery over content because anything counts as content, and in fact teachers pride themselves on being able to create lessons from nothing. Teachers feel deskilled when they move to teaching EAP because content is the priority.
>
> (Alexander, 2007: 8, quoted in Campion, 2016: 62)

This question of knowledge and expertise forms a key part of what may render the transition into teaching and operating in the area of ISEAP daunting to the newcomer. One practitioner we interviewed suggested that some members of staff at a large university were hesitant to work on in-sessional courses for postgraduate students as they themselves did not have a master's degree. Our interviewee said they felt their colleagues' reticence was understandable as for them teaching in an in-sessional context would cause 'discomfort.' Indeed, a number of our interviewees appeared to suggest that due to the perceived challenges of in-sessional teaching, ISEAP is not necessarily an area of EAP practice that suits all.

More generally speaking, much of the literature on ELT teacher transitions into EAP (e.g. Alexander, 2012) has been characterised as focussing too much on the challenging and negative aspects of entering into EAP contexts. Some have suggested that this has created a 'deficit novice practitioner' paradigm with so many reports focussing on shock and fear of those new to EAP (Ding and Bruce, 2017: 137). Bell (2022), however, likens this transition to a feeling that a 'rug has been pulled from under them' (2022: 8). This echoes the perception of the 'deskilled' feeling (Alexander, 2007, cited in Campion, 2016).

Campion (2016), however, downplays this shock-of-the-new aspect, suggesting that making such a clear distinction between novice and experienced EAP practitioners is unhelpful. Instead she suggests adopting more of a focus on the developmental arc of becoming a practitioner, pointing out there is no 'magic moment' where EAP expertise or competence is achieved. Indeed, Bell (2022) discusses the commonly occurring phenomenon of EAP practitioners 'learning on the job,' as a necessary part of a gradual developmental process.

Both Alexander (2012) and Campion (2016) in their studies of EAP practitioners note that it takes time to feel confident. As Campion reports on the interviewees in her study:

> Learning to teach EAP took them a considerable amount of time, and occurred through a wide variety of means. What has emerged is a symbiotic view of education and experience, where teachers undergoing further education and training feel that they benefit from a firm basis of practical experience on which to draw. (2016: 67)

ISEAP can be perceived as even more challenging than other areas of EAP in this way, and some EAP practitioners may prefer not to work in this area for a number of reasons. As one of our interviewees noted:

> [In in-sessional teaching] you need to be flexible. For new lecturers, this can be a challenge – to respond to what students come up with.

The quote above underlines the importance for developing confidence and flexibility, presumably as a result of experience in ISEAP contexts and therefore it has an aspect of 'learning on the job.'

5.3 The Status of ISEAP

It is important to make a reference at this point that we found in our interviews a tendency for more experienced EAP practitioners to be favoured over newer members of staff for in-sessional teaching positions. For example, one of our U.K. based interviewees observed that many EAP practitioners enter into a permanent EAP teaching position by way of pre-sessionals, but typically do not work on in-sessionals from the start. They suggested that they personally had needed to 'earn their stripes' by working on a preparation programme first in their institution.

We asked some of our other interviewees who are in management positions in their EAP departments whether they made a distinction in terms of the level of experience of their teaching staff who get to teach in ISEAP. One interviewee from a Turkish institution told us:

> We don't have the same teachers teaching the pre-sessionals and in-sessionals, but this doesn't mean that the door is closed to them, for those who are interested to move on to in-sessionals … the majority don't because they see them as a bigger challenge, … and also with these at the end of the day you are responsible; you are on your own.

The idea here is that there is more work to do and more responsibility for practitioners operating in ISEAP in this context, but it is also implied that there may be less support and, a more positive corollary, more autonomy.

Another interviewee from a U.K. university made a specific point about teaching in ISEAP related to the cohorts that are taught, which may also be a factor which discourages some practitioners already working within EAP from seeking to work on in-sessional courses:

> One of the big things in in-sessional is it's not your students: you're not only dealing with the academic staff as a peripheral being, but you have to remember that for the students you are offering help within that space and not adding anything to that burden. And it's a different orientation to having your own fee paying students who are there for you, so a lot of people get excited about it, [but] a lot of people don't.

This last quote clearly suggests that ISEAP is not for everyone. It also relates to the unique positioning in terms of the ISEAP teaching role, working 'as a peripheral being' here echoing Ding and Bruce's concept of EAP 'operating on the edge of the academic world of universities' (2017: 107).

One interviewee we spoke to commented that 'in-sessional is the more exclusive area of EAP' and, as we have seen, may be the preserve of more experienced staff within an EAP centre. The following quote from a practitioner working in a large university in the U.K. reveals this as a controversial issue within EAP:

> I have to be hugely careful about the idea that somehow in-sessional is more difficult, more valuable [and] requires higher training to teach, because I've seen it used against me [...] But there is an informal hierarchy

of higher status EAP and lower status EAP and it's not one I'm entirely happy with. I would hope that we can empower and train teachers to teach what we do; yes, there is a certain period of getting used to particular contexts but I am positive about tutors' ability to learn to teach in in-sessional contexts. I don't think it just has to be teachers who taught it 20 years ago who have to teach it.

Moreover, once working within ISEAP contexts there may be distinctions made as to what specific provisions a practitioner may work on. The following quote from another interviewee from the U.K. also suggests that ISEAP expertise is usually seen as something that needs to be developed gradually in EAP practitioners when they are in those settings:

> We tend to start inducting people into in-sessional by having them teach on one of the big business school courses where there is more control of the materials and usually they get on really well with it and can maybe go further in that direction.

It is worth speculating in light of what our interviewees' comments reveal that being a practitioner in specifically ISEAP contexts may then require a further transition within EAP, an extra degree of specialisation and challenge. It also suggests, however, that the discussion of the status of those who work on in-sessional programmes may reveal that there is a barrier preventing entry to this area of practice imposed from within EAP itself.

The comments reported in this section so far should absolutely not be taken to suggest that those who work in ISEAP do so exclusively; typically practitioners will also teach on other EAP programmes at the same time. Simultaneously working across EAP programmes, e.g. pre-sessional and in-sessional, can be beneficial as there is possibility for crossover and informing course development in both directions. However, the quotes below from two interviewees, both from the same U.K. university, highlight again how tensions or a perceived hierarchy between these different provisions within an EAP department may exist. One told us:

> There is a development group working on the pre-sessional course and assessment – they want an in-sessional perspective to understand assessments. Bubbles can be detrimental. In-sessional teachers need to know what [students] have done on pre-sessional assessments to know what they need to work on further … This all needs to improve a bit,

teachers do make connections, but perhaps sometimes we see pre-sessional and in-sessional as entirely separate areas.

The other practitioner from the same institution suggested that this connection between pre-sessional and in-sessional is not necessarily a straightforward one, and differences in how the programmes are organised may explain some of the reasons for the separate nature of the two provisions. They commented on how the in-sessional provision relates to pre-sessional in their department:

> Our [provision] is siloed. It depends on the way the pre-sessional is run; it has more of a language school mentality. For the pre-sessional these are *our* students, for in-sessional they are *their* students, but actually they are all University of [X] students ... There is a lack of awareness of the complexity of what we do on in-sessional and how that could inform pre-sessional.

Clearly, then, this section has shown ISEAP may not only entail an extra level of complexity and challenge for those entering it, but not all of this is down to teaching expertise or experience; often it appears there are organisational barriers within EAP too.

5.4 Discipline-Specific Knowledge in ISEAP

In the sections above, one of the key points made was that transitioning into teaching in ISEAP contexts could be perceived as daunting due to the disciplinary specificity involved and that practitioners need to develop confidence in dealing with that particular aspect. It is also suggested that there is an essentially non-expert role imposed by working in ISEAP contexts and that there is a different balance between what learners know in this context as opposed to other EAP settings. In order to discuss the question of discipline-specific knowledge and what that implies for the role of the ISEAP teacher, we begin this section with three examples where interviewees commented on their perceptions of their role in their relation to specialised knowledge within the context of teaching law students. One of our interviewees, from a large U.K. institution, suggested:

> Even though I believe you should be able to teach on any discipline, some of the stuff in Law is just beyond me, so I recognise the need to

carefully allocate staff to courses where they have the right knowledge base to contribute.

Another interviewee from another U.K. university who had developed and published specific EAP materials for law students was asked 'How do you know the limits of your expertise?' They replied that in the preparation of their materials:

> I spent a lot of time [...] on referencing. This is one of my learning objectives. I don't know it 100 percent, but I can tell you if it's right or wrong – with law referencing I'm looking for consistency.

The referencing system typically used for academic law programmes in U.K. university settings, OSCOLA, is notoriously difficult to master. The relations between what an ISEAP practitioner needs to know and what the content lecturer knows, and how this is perceived by students is also referenced by a third ISEAP law 'specialist,' who told us what they tell their students in relation to disciplinary specificity:

> I introduce you to a little bit of OSCOLA, but I'm not an expert – so you go and ask the librarian, or the lecturer, for a bit more.

These three quotes, all located in the same discipline-specific field of ISEAP, raise a number of questions about how ISEAP practitioners see their remit in terms of disciplinary specificity. Relating to the first comment, is it necessary or desirable for ISEAP teaching staff to have a knowledge background or at least some experience in the field of study they work with? From the two latter comments on law referencing, what level of disciplinary knowledge should an ISEAP practitioner be expected to master? Consequently, is there a line between what language practitioners and content specialists 'teach' and a need to avoid crossing it?

Although some of our respondents did mention that they were embedded, or at least had started to become embedded, in a particular discipline in which they themselves had prior knowledge, this is typically not seen as the norm, nor is it seen as a necessity. A head of in-sessional teaching at a U.K. university commented at length on this point:

> Sometimes we have people who have a musical background and they could work with music, but although it would be great and you might

have an aspiration to have something that you could draw on, I'm not sure that is really needed. It's not a bad thing for a student to have to communicate what they have problems with in writing, etc., and at the end of the day whatever they are studying, what the students have to produce and be assessed on will require the same type of support, so if someone is being too descriptive in their writing and not showing enough critical evaluation that could be the same in engineering, opto-engineering and English … You could have any of the tutors working in my centre working in those areas, saying ok, what is it that you are required to do, where is the criticality coming in, what do you think your tutors are looking for? You can draw on their understanding: what are you trying to frame here; are you looking for perspectives or different solutions to a problem? … When you have worked out what they [departments] need, you can come from a variety of backgrounds and you can still help those students, maybe if you have an engineering background, or a fashion background, but you would have to have a lot of different tutors on your books in your centre. You're going to have a lot of people … You just need tutors to have that agility, to understand quickly.

The quote above makes a strong case for non-discipline-specific backgrounds actually being preferable in ISEAP practitioners. It also suggests what the ideal teacher's role in an ISEAP classroom should be, recalling the discussion of working on a more equal footing with students in in-sessional contexts discussed earlier in this chapter. The interviewee also highlights the need for agility, which will be discussed later in this chapter as one of the key attributes required of practitioners working in ISEAP.

So, prior disciplinary knowledge on the part of the ISEAP teacher does not have to be a prerequisite. But by working in close contact within a specific discipline area over a period of time, should it be developed further? The opening chapter discussed the issue of secondment into departments as one approach to ISEAP. The secondment model does, however, tend to only happen in larger institutions where there is a large teaching staff, avoiding what the last interviewee described as the need to have a lot of teaching staff 'on your books.' In the U.K. context, most of our interviewees linked the secondment approach in particular with the University of Leeds, which is not the only institution to do this, but is well known within the U.K. sector as having a model of discipline-specific EAP, both at pre-sessional and in-sessional level (Whong and Godfrey, 2022). Secondment can facilitate the development of discipline-specific EAP scholarship, as can be demonstrated by the fact that EAP practitioners working there were able to research and publish accounts of their practice and knowledge about student writing gained directly from prolonged contact within these situated contexts, Whong and Godfrey's (2022) edited volume being a case in point.

Chapter 6 will return to this question of the affordances related to the disciplinary positioning of ISEAP for research purposes. In terms of the implications of working in a secondment system on practitioner knowledge though, one interviewee (who works in a semi-seconded system) did not seem sure their presence within a specific department as a seconded ISEAP practitioner would necessarily imply becoming a disciplinary expert:

> I wouldn't see myself as getting into the subject … I understand my position in the course … But maybe in a couple of years' time I'll feel more knowledgeable in the subject. Maybe I'll feel 'I know this course, I know this subject matter,' but then I might have a tendency to overstep.

'Overstepping' suggests again that there is an intrinsic question about limitations of the ISEAP practitioner role, and also the boundary between content lecturer responsibility and language teacher responsibility is seen here as potentially problematic and a need for caution is implied.

In terms of subject content knowledge, in the previous section, the idea of shared teacher and student input was introduced as a potentially distinguishing feature of ISEAP instruction. In ISEAP contexts, the teacher is often positioned slightly differently compared to other EAP contexts. An interviewee mentioned earlier in this section, a head of in-sessional who suggested that there was no need for discipline-specific backgrounds such as music to be applied when allocating staff to departments, went on to make a more detailed comment on how this issue can be resolved in actual teaching practice:

> I don't think you need to be a specialist. I don't think as long as you can work in partnership with your students and you need to get your students to explain to you as much as you are explaining to them, hopefully then a lightbulb goes on. And between you, you gain some recognition, you understand something from them and they understand a lot from you, and then can move forward so they get the point. I don't think it needs an engineer to teach engineers.

This last quote seems to enshrine much of what we felt practitioners told us about the ideal conceptualisation of the role of the ISEAP teacher. Essentially it involves occupying what might seem like a slightly unorthodox teaching position, a non-expert role, applying what practitioners bring in terms of language expertise and experience of discourse analysis to a 'partnership' with the learner. The quote above also chimes with the intention behind the key function a 'meddler' should perform in the learning process, i.e. challenging students to reach their own understanding (McWilliam, 2009).

The questions posed above by the examples of the practitioners teaching law students and the comment about overstepping a line reveal an underlying concern with the positioning of ISEAP teachers in relation to the content specialist lecturers they work with. If the practitioner working in ISEAP must take care not to overstep the line between what they teach and what the content lecturer teaches, or must refer students to contact a librarian or lecturer if they need answers to questions related to certain discipline-specific literacy issues, what exactly is the contribution of the ISEAP teacher to learning in context-specific areas? The sections above have suggested that something beyond language teacher knowledge and classroom expertise is significant to the formation of the ISEAP teaching role. What ISEAP teachers bring is not just language teaching to support learning, nor is it merely reinforcing content taught by the content lecturer; instead, it lies in the area of academic literacy development (Wingate, 2015), in an integration of language use in practice in specific-discipline areas (Bond, 2020).

One of the key points to note in order to understand better how this may appear in practice relates to the concept of 'tacit knowledge' (Elton, 2010). This means knowledge, key to understanding how to operate effectively within an academic discipline, is not typically explicitly communicated by 'knowers' in that sphere and therefore remains essentially implicit and unclear. Content lecturers are knowers in this sense as they are situated fully within the discipline-specific context. McGrath et al. (2019) comment that there are several inherent obstacles to content specialists being in a position to effectively teach disciplinary literacy related to their own subjects. This is despite the fact that they are the ones fully immersed in disciplinary literacy knowledge:

> Awareness of having knowledge does not mean that the knower can explain the process by which that knowledge was gained, and representation poses the problem of how tacit knowledge can be elicited and communicated. (McGrath et al., 2019: 836)

On the other hand, from their position as semi-outsiders, it is here where ISEAP practitioners play their key role: in facilitating knowledge sharing and discovery with students, as the quote below from one of our interviewees suggests:

> One of the things that we as EAP practitioners have is the ability to understand academic discourse and being able to analyse student samples and to distil and break down what was invisible before and make it visible to students. That's what our real strength is.

5.5 Positioning of the ISEAP Practitioner

What then should characterise the ideal relationship between EAP practitioner and content teacher in ISEAP contexts? Taking one example, we interviewed a content lecturer and an ISEAP language specialist who work closely at a U.K. university. Theirs may be an ideal relationship based on Chapter 1's consideration of how the dimensions of cooperation and integration work to provide the fullest expression of integrated academic language and literacy provision in practice. They reported, for instance, that they met regularly over the duration of the course and, before the academic year started to discuss the content of the highly tailored EAP provision that the ISEAP practitioner had set up. Although the language specialist was not fully integrated into the module, feedback and advice appeared to be flowing between them in both directions.

In the interview, we asked what they thought was the students' perception of their respective positioning. (The question is reproduced at the top of this quote, and the ISEAP practitioner below is referred to as A, the content lecturer as B):

Is the line between expert (B) and non-expert (A) hard to perceive for students?

A: I don't think so! Only a blurred boundary if you start to try to teach it, students rarely expect subject knowledge from me [...] It might be about clarifying feedback or about writing. I can't answer questions about jargon, but mostly they don't ask, and most students have more knowledge than me, as they have worked in the field: they quickly know you don't know much.

B: A's already getting there, but they're quite right: students understand the practical aspect, but not how to articulate practical issues in an academic way and this is where A can help.

This reveals an interesting aspect of positioning of the ISEAP practitioner in the eyes of the students: they may not actually have expectations of expertise related to the subject matter from them (*'they don't ask.'*) Moreover, this lecturer appears to really value their colleague's contribution and understand very clearly what is in the academic language and literacy expert's purview:

> They [ISEAP practitioners] have a middle way: sometimes they are an instructor; sometimes they are a learner of a new subject, an easier, more empathetic position when they see students' problems. Problably at some stage they have the same questions ... This is where the academic from the language centre builds into their understanding and skills, combined with their understanding of my subject and so helps the students share their understanding in a very complex and very subtle way. It's not as simple as 'here's a text then you'll be fine.' There's a lot of effort that goes into understanding and digesting the subject and then sharing with students, I think that probably works well: in their essays I can read that, it's down to the individual, but thank you A for taking time and effort to understand my subject.

As previously stated, the relationship and the understanding between the language academic and content academic here was mutually supportive; the thanking of the colleague at the end is particularly heart-warming. The end of the quote also suggests that the content lecturer has seen tangible evidence of the effectiveness of the language practitioner's contribution to learning.

Unfortunately, in our interviews, practitioners often reported much less understanding of the role of integrated language specialists coming from the content lecturers they worked with. For example, an ISEAP practitioner working in a university in the E.U. told us their perception was that the subject academics there were generally not concerned with students' language or misconceptions they may have because of language, and suggested their attitude towards academic literacy development was typically, 'read this paper, see how they do it; you do the same.' On the other hand, this practitioner described their own practice as much more systematic, but, in rather an unspecified way, suggesting they essentially concentrated on 'fostering certain skills.'

Another example from a U.K. context below shows how not having a successful level of integration with a content specialist can have a detrimental effect on ISEAP practice and potentially creates more work for the practitioner:

> When I had to set up UG [undergraduate] law, they were very adamant about everything that they didn't want to happen and they weren't really very helpful. There was a lot of tension around it at the beginning and I did what I thought would be a straw-man outline, and there are loads of books on writing for law, and then I had to find examples. I bought books to save myself time and I worked around their anxiety around examples. That's one of the biggest things: they want you to teach but they don't want any of their examples used, but they are unnecessarily wary of that and you have to do a lot of lateral thinking.

Positioning with relation to the subject lecturers is a key factor when setting up ISEAP provision, and thankfully it is not always as problematic as it appears in the particular case above. For example, when asked what characterised successful EAP provision, another interviewee stated:

> What I have noticed is learning more about the discipline and the way communication is happening directly from the lecturer, directly from the academic, rather than us having to work it out for ourselves. Which is fine: we can do that detective work ourselves. But it's when we're starting to get more and they're highlighting certain things: that to me is an indicator of collaboration, when we're invited to their student liaison committee or we're part of their assessment processes.

The final part of this quote also suggests certain 'indicators' of a successful relationship with subject lecturers. ISEAP practitioners did perceive having a positive relationship with content specialists and getting their input as key to developing successful ISEAP provision, as another interviewee from a different university in the U.K. makes clear here:

> If you've got collaboration with lecturers, and you're party to conversations about how they think and talk about knowledge in their subject, you're better placed to explain that to students.

This is essentially seeing a positive relationship with content specialist collaborators as not just facilitating ISEAP practitioners' access to disciplinary knowledge, but also playing a key role in aiding their process of understanding it. The same interviewee went on to explain how much of a successful relationship was down to them and how it even led to being more of a 'critical friend' to disciplinary teaching staff, in the sense of what is often perceived as the ideal relationship between content lecturer and language specialist (e.g. Bond, 2020; Wingate, 2015; McGrath et al., 2019). They explained:

> Because I'd built rapport with fashion lecturers and I wasn't just someone in and out for a one-off session, they started to trust me as a colleague. I was reached out to, to help with writing assignment briefs. It was not a formal part of the job, but it came out of collaboration, organically; we can really help with that.

The comment above also demonstrates the practitioner's perception of their own role and what is within their potential remit; it stretches towards aiding lecturers. Even if this is not part of the formalised arrangement, 'we can really help with that.' The concept of formal and informal arrangements where ISEAP practitioners find themselves in an advisory role to content lecturers will be discussed in more detail in Chapter 6.

This chapter has previously mentioned how teaching in ISEAP contexts requires a different teaching approach due to specificities of the cohort and suggested that this may be a distinguishing feature of ISEAP as a subfield within EAP. Another important question relating to positioning is how students perceive the role of practitioners in ISEAP contexts and what typically characterises that relationship.

According to an interview with two colleagues, comparing how students perceive their content lecturers and language practitioners working in embedded ISEAP contexts, it appears there is a beneficial positioning and potentially closer relationship:

> You've got a little bit more relationship with the student: you don't give them marks, they don't have to impress you really. You're not somebody that doesn't know anything about the module, so you're in a nice place where you can give them constructive feedback that can make a difference.

This suggestion of being in a 'nice place' as an ISEAP practitioner perceives the positioning as being ideal for delivering effective teaching. The positioning is neither the same as the lecturer, nor exactly on the same level as the students themselves, but places the ISEAP practitioner somewhere in the middle.

This interviewee went on to explain that students on modules where they were not providing embedded provision, including some 'home' students, also came along to their one-to-one sessions to ask for advice on writing:

> They come to us because of our language and academic skills expertise ...
> *Their colleague added:*
> On the pastoral side, the module leader might not care the same way. You're someone who cares, you don't have to be the world's best teacher, but I say 'yes I'll look at your draft' ... Home students want to get a first; they think you've got that insight – it's true, you do – you can tell. I never say if it's going to pass, but you can tell them things that will enhance the submission.

The quotes above might seem a little reductive in terms of what constitutes ISEAP expertise, but they do reveal another important aspect of the unique positioning of the ISEAP teacher: their perceived approachability and insight as a partial insider. The importance of the pastoral function of EAP in in-sessional contexts (as noted by Bond, 2020, for example) is also significant. Another interviewee from a U.K. context made the following memorable observation of how their students saw them, which seems to be defining their practitioner identity largely in terms of performing a key pastoral function.

> I'm a 'fluffy signpost' – I'm a nice person: I can help you to get help. [It is] a massive part of our role.

Again, this highlights a greater degree of perceived approachability from students towards EAP practitioners in comparison with content lecturers. It also suggests another facet of the role of an ISEAP practitioner, i.e. someone within the institution with knowledge of how learning in the particular university context works and possible sources of help when students are unsure.

This section has shown how the positioning of the ISEAP teacher both in relation to lecturers and to students contributes to the development of a useful and perhaps even intrinsic figure within today's complex higher education learning landscape. It is also important for individual practitioners to consider their unique positioning when developing self-conceptions, and the reflection at the end of this chapter will come back to this issue as an aid to understanding practitioner identity, together with a focus on specific roles and attributes which are developed through working in these contexts, which is the focus of the following section.

5.6 Roles and Attributes of the ISEAP Practitioner

As Ding and Bruce (2017) note, a number of researchers have suggested that being an EAP practitioner involves occupying a variety of roles. Dudley Evans and St John, for example, suggested there were five key EAP roles which encompass teaching, course design, materials development, evaluation (which includes assessment), and research (Dudley Evans & St John, 1998). Ding and Bruce later observe that Basturkmen (2014) added two more to this list: a role in content learning in language and being an intercultural mediator (Basturkmen, 2014, cited in Ding and Bruce, 2017: 118).

Based on what has been discussed in the section above, extending these lists to include the pastoral aspects of the ISEAP role might also be in order. Moreover, a consideration of the somewhere-in-the-middle positioning of the language teacher in ISEAP and implications for knowledge and expertise as discussed previously, might suggest the need to think of a range of alternatives to the term *teacher* to better describe the ISEAP role. In terms of how the role relates to disciplinary knowledge and practice, another conception might be as a mediator between content lecturer and students.

One interviewee suggested they felt they had a role as a contact point for lecturers from across different faculties and departments within their institution. This may occur in this area of practice as a result of ISEAP practitioners working in collaboration with more than one department within an institution. This could perhaps be referred to as go-between for academic staff in the university.

Ding and Bruce (2017) note a distinction between two broad types of EAP practitioner roles: what they refer to as TEAPs, whose activity largely resides in teaching EAP, and (citing Hadley, 2015) BLEAPs, or 'blended EAP practitioners', who may also take on more managerial or professionalised aspects (2017: 119). In this rest of this section, we will consider various roles and attributes that are typically required of ISEAP practitioners and link them to broadly to TEAPs or BLEAPs.

Several of our interviewees mentioned attributes they themselves developed in the course of their ISEAP practice which could be categorised as BLEAP characteristics, as they are organisational or managerial, interpersonal, or, in some senses, entrepreneurial in nature. In all contexts, attributes which we often heard repeated, in relation to both pedagogy and practice, were agility and flexibility, both important characteristics for various roles within the ISEAP practitioner's area of practice. For example, in relation to course design and teaching, i.e. a more TEAP context, one of our interviewees from a large university in the United Kingdom told us that in their experience a significant difference between ISEAP and other EAP contexts can be expressed in terms of how willing one has to be to work with ambiguity and insecurity in ISEAP:

> With the pre-sessional there is given material, it is there for you. You might inherit an in-sessional course, but at some point you'll have to make something from scratch because of out-of-date materials, or assessments have changed, or it's new. … What do we need to offer a new group of MA students? Liaise with people in departments, get them to understand what you can do and what you can't do, and if you don't get the necessary information you need, you need a workaround: you still need to produce a course even if you don't get information from the department.

This interviewee went on to spell out the implications of this for the ISEAP practitioner, which might add to the perception of ISEAP as an area of challenge and volatility, which could deter some EAP practitioners from wishing to work in this area:

> Preparation can be hand to mouth. You might only be doing materials a week ahead; there may not be another way, and a lot of people don't like working like that.

The need for agility in course design and having to develop materials at short notice is not uncommon. Indeed another interviewee from an Australian university noted that subjects are constantly changing (in this context, *subjects* refers to what are usually termed *modules* or *units* of programmes in the U.K. context). Also, where a degree course may suddenly no longer be offered or totally new assessments are introduced, all this means that ISEAP practitioners are often 'designing as they go.'

In terms of attributes, key skill areas in more of a BLEAP sense when developing in-sessional provision typically involves the need for interpersonal skills and perhaps even what might be termed entrepreneurial skills. Part of the necessity for this is connected to seeking greater visibility of what is done in the ISEAP context and to preserve or enhance its status and legitimacy. A head of an EAP department at a U.K. university commented that connections across the wider university often require a great deal of sustained effort, 'helping people to continuously understand what we do and why it's important.'

Moreover, another interviewee from a northern European university commented:

> It's continual work to, not legitimise ourselves, but institutional visibility is constant work. People come and go and for this institutional work you need connections, and to maintain these, to work at them, for our work to work.

In terms of dealing with setting up provision with specific departments, another ISEAP practitioner from a U.K. institution where large-scale in-sessional provision has been developed also commented on the relentless nature of this work and the need to adopt a promotional role. This appears to be necessary here, even in the case where a course with a partner department has already been established:

> Every year I have to remind them [the partner department] that it [the provision] exists, and then they reply very positively and we slowly start. It's a bit like herding cats but we scoop up all the names for the course and that led us to suggesting, and to them being enthusiastic about, setting up a dissertation writing provision for the summer term.

This interviewee notes that this way of approaching negotiation for a course involves building on existing partnerships and always being prepared to develop new courses. Indeed, they also went on to stress the need for quick thinking in an ISEAP management role, and being constantly ready to exploit any new possibilities that arise to develop or extend provisions. Agility is therefore a key requirement for what we might term the 'entrepreneurial' nature of a BLEAP-like role, as can be seen in this further quote from the same interviewee:

> I think one thing that helps us is being quite proactive and going for any chink of a possibility. During the pandemic there were different admissions criteria brought in and I and the colleague who supports the postgrads in the [name of department] were very proactive in agreeing to create a bridging course before the students started and then linked this to the in-sessional.

What lies behind this need for a flexible, proactive entrepreneurial stance to ensure the continuation and the success of an in-sessional provision often comes down to what has been termed the neo-liberalisation of universities and its impact on the environment in which ISEAP has to operate, as discussed in Chapter 4. This can be a challenging role for ISEAP practitioners to inhabit. One of our interviewees who had developed a very strong relationship with the business school in the university where they worked suggested that all the postgraduate work they were involved in was due to them carefully developing a positive relationship with a content lecturer. They suggested that to set up successful ISEAP, a practitioner really needs 'emotional intelligence and diplomacy.'

However, there is also an element here of what might be simply termed 'collegiality' across the university. The deployment of interpersonal skills may be something which occurs quite naturally rather than a role which needs to be consciously adopted. There is clearly still a place for more informal communication and human interaction across the university as a way of developing relationships, as another interviewee from a U.K. context explained:

> [Collaboration with content lecturers] was the most successful and rewarding thing I did. It happened organically. It happened because of going to yoga with one of the lecturers. That's how it all started, it evolved naturally; you don't want to wait for a diktat from Senior Management, you just need to collect evidence, have a champion and present [it] to them.

This example, in the first line, also illustrates another key point which is significant to our discussion of the ISEAP practitioner role: the often perceived rewarding aspect of working in ISEAP, and that is discussed in the section that follows.

5.7 Rewards and Challenges

The highly complex and contextually governed area of ISEAP practice may well appear rather daunting to those with little prior experience. As has been demonstrated so far in this chapter, working in in-sessionals may cause EAP practitioners to question their expertise. It can challenge their concepts of knowledge in terms of what a teacher brings to the classroom. It can involve potentially problematic positioning within the university and may require the development of new skills and attributes when transitioning from other EAP contexts. Moreover, somewhere along the way it is necessary for the time spent in ISEAP practice to translate into a perceived level of experience by others and a growing sense of confidence in one's own capabilities.

At a personal level, therefore, there are plenty of challenges for the EAP practitioner operating in ISEAP contexts. Yet despite this, many of our interviewees explicitly and enthusiastically commented on just how rewarding working in this context can be.

One of the key themes that emerged was how working in this area allows the practitioner to connect different aspects of their own academic experience when they were a student to ISEAP practice and draw on this in their interactions with students. This may also help in the process of developing confidence in this specific teaching context, as for example the quote from one of our interviews below suggests:

> Yes, I talk about my own study experiences, especially with humanities and social sciences students. With pre-sessionals you can have a sage-like persona, yet now [in in-sessional] they're in the context and maybe more familiar with subject matter. At first I was intimidated, yet when I read their end-of-semester-one assignments, I realised how much I could do for them. Drawing on my own writing and experience of working and researching and delivering presentations, talking to students about my experience: it builds more of a rapport, even though I work in a different discipline.

It is interesting to note above how the ISEAP work allowed this practitioner to bring elements of their experience of developing their own academic literacy into their teaching in a way that is less likely to occur when teaching in other EAP settings. Being involved in the specific context also made them reflect on how their learning through teaching in this context might inform their teaching in other non-integrated EAP programmes, like a pre-sessional:

> Learning how students respond to tasks, how language works now, especially online, could feed into pre-sessional development more, with more awareness of what's going on in the university. How are assessment practices changing? This should be reflected in the pre-sessional to have context validity.

However, one of the key challenges which our interviewees note with working in ISEAP is summed up by the following quote from a practitioner; this is the case of someone who essentially works as a one-person ISEAP unit at their U.K. institution:

> [There is] ambiguity about what I'm doing, what I'm meant to be doing, how I'm meant to be doing it, much more so than in other jobs I've done. I think I provide a very useful service, but no one, apart from the students, is interested. The school's very grateful, we're supporting high-paying international students. But in terms of the operations, I could be running a terrible set of courses here and I don't think anyone would really care.

This shows that ISEAP work can be discouraging, as described in Chapter 1 as 'the loneliness of the ISEAP practitioner'. However, the flipside to this is the level of freedom that may be enjoyed. A practitioner working in an Australian context told us:

> The best bit about our job is the autonomy, it's up to me to make up my job. There is a lot of time to try out new things and it's challenging but interesting.

This may be particularly noticeable in comparison to other areas of EAP; for example, one interviewee from a university in the United kingdom who had worked on both pre- and in-sessional provision commented that pre-sessional by comparison appeared more 'centralised, controlled and standardised,' and suggested that this could 'sometimes engender a private language school ethos.'

This point is also reflected in the example below. In this case, the relative level of freedom provided by working in ISEAP is linked to an appreciation of feeling more like a fully fledged member of academic staff at the university where they work:

> I'm able to behave like other people who work at the university. There's a lot more autonomy, no one is expecting you at your desk if you're teaching across campus. That's not a bad thing, if you're working at a university: you want to feel you're working at a university.

The academic identity of the ISEAP practitioner is an interesting aspect to discuss here. There was a clear sense in many of the interviews that this lay below what is perceived to be particularly rewarding about working in this context. Beyond this however, and a point that will be further discussed in relation to research opportunities in Chapter 6, ISEAP contexts provide practitioners with an almost unique vantage point as they are located in situ where academic language and literacy is in development. What is more, they are, in the case of fully integrated ISEAP models, placed right within the disciplines, allowing them to develop greater understanding of an area or an overview of a number of areas of disciplinary specificity. Again, an example from the interviewee who had set up in-sessional provision after meeting a subject lecturer at a yoga class:

> Embedded work is thoroughly rewarding: having the space to really get entrenched in the discipline, to try to understand how it works, to form a collaborative rapport with lecturers. I pushed for team-teaching with the lecturers. It was amazing, I loved it, it's ideally how I would like it to be.

Indeed, another U.K.-based interviewee described how the comparative academic freedom of working in ISEAP afforded them opportunities to really put into practice what they were researching in terms of their own EAP practice:

> [That's] one of the things I love, it's scary at the start: you ask 'what am I doing?' But it's the first time in ages I've been able to read stuff and use it to inform my course design and no one's going to stop me. [There's] potential for exploration and discovery.

Concluding Thoughts

This chapter has covered different aspects of what ISEAP means for the practitioner working in this field of practice. It has considered how practitioners arrive in this context and questioned what expertise means here. It demonstrated that ISEAP is often seen as a specialised and somewhat exclusive area of EAP practice, in fact identifying that it is not typically an area of practice open to newcomers to EAP. It has been suggested above that questions of the ISEAP practitioner's role and positioning help form a slightly different identity compared to working in other EAP contexts. However, given that many practitioners in the field probably teach across a range of EAP activities, an ISEAP experience may simply refine an overall sense of their professional academic identity. Finally, this chapter suggests that, for many, in-sessional is seen as a particularly rewarding yet challenging area to work in; an interesting aspect of this is that for those who find it rewarding, ISEAP confers more of a sense of being an academic and is perceived as allowing for more freedom for pedagogical innovation and experimental practice than other EAP contexts.

As we have reiterated in every chapter of this book, ultimately context specificity is all in the realm of ISEAP. This guide is not prescriptive; we attempt to illustrate the options and possibilities that exist and suggest ways in which to navigate them by promoting reflection. That holds especially true for the most personal aspect of ISEAP: practitioner identity. Consequently, the exercise that follows takes each of the key themes presented above and suggests a series of questions to aid personal reflection.

Chapter 5 Reflection

In this chapter, we discussed the following aspects that relate to ISEAP practitioner identity:

1. Transitions into ISEAP
2. Expertise and knowledge
3. Positioning and status in relation to:
   - lecturers you collaborate with
   - in-sessional students
4. Roles and attributes
5. Challenges and rewards of ISEAP

In the table that follows, note down your initial ideas for each one of the above categories to create a practitioner profile and to help you start examining your own values and beliefs about ISEAP. There are extra guiding questions in each box to help. You can write your ideas in the right-hand column.

Topic	Your answers
Transitions: how did *you* arrive in ISEAP? (i.e. was it from an ELT background or other?) Did any of the accounts or points made in the chapter above resonate with you?	
Expertise/knowledge: What do you see as your key qualifications for teaching in ISEAP? What do you bring? What is your attitude towards 'knowledge'? (Again, do any of the accounts above resonate for you in particular?)	
Positioning/status: Consider how you are positioned in relation to: • content lecturers • students • other EAP contexts and colleagues • the wider university	
Roles you may play in ISEAP: Is yours mainly a TEAP or a BLEAP role? Do you relate to any of the roles mentioned in the examples in sections 5.5 or 5.6 of this chapter?(e.g. the pastoral role in teaching, being a mediator between lecturers and students, being a go-between for lecturers from different departments) Are there any other roles that you feel you fulfil in ISEAP in your experience?	
Attributes (for example, flexibility, agility): Which personal attributes do you feel are most important for being an ISEAP practitioner? Which attributes do you already have which you bring to ISEAP?	
Challenges: List up to three of the key challenges you perceive related to working in ISEAP contexts.	**Key challenges of ISEAP:** 1. 2. 3.
Rewards: Now list up to three key rewards (you can get ideas from the chapter, but keep it personal).	**Key rewards of ISEAP:** 1. 2. 3.
Last box: Up to you! At the end of this chapter, how would you sum up what you see as your identity as an ISEAP practitioner?	

References

Alexander, O. (2012) Exploring teacher beliefs in teaching EAP at low proficiency levels. *Journal of English for Academic Purposes*, 11:2012, 99–111.

Basturkmen, H. (2014) LSP teacher education: Review of literature and suggestions for the research agenda. *Ibérica*, (28), 17–34.

Bell, D. (2022) Methodology in EAP: Why is it largely still an overlooked issue? *Journal of English for Academic Purposes*, 55:2022, 1–11.

Bond, B. (2020) *Making language visible in the university: English for academic purposes and internationalisation*. Bristol: Multilingual Matters.

Campion, G.C. (2016) 'The learning never ends': Exploring teachers' views on the transition from General English to EAP. *Journal of English for Academic Purposes*, 23:2016, 59–70.

Ding, A. and Bruce, I. (2017) *The English for academic purposes practitioner: Operating on the edge of academia*. Cham, Switzerland: Palgrave Macmillan.

Dudley-Evans, T. and St John, M.J. (1998) *Developments in English for specific purposes: A multi-disciplinary approach*. Cambridge: Cambridge University Press.

Elton, L. (2010) Academic writing and tacit knowledge. *Teaching in Higher Education*, 15:2, 151–160.

Fitzpatrick, D., Costley, T. and Tavakoli, P. (2022) Exploring EAP teachers' expertise: Reflections on practice, pedagogy and professional development. *Journal of English for Academic Purposes*, 59:2022, 101140.

Hadley, G. (2015) *English for academic purposes in neoliberal universities: A critical grounded theory*. Cham, Switzerland: Springer.

McGrath, L., Negretti, R. and Nicholls, K. (2019) Hidden expectations: Scaffolding specialists' genre knowledge of the assignment they set. *Higher Education Research & Development*, 78, 835–853. doi: 10.1007/s10734-019-00373-9.

McWilliam, E. (2009) Teaching for creativity: From sage to guide to meddler. *Asia Pacific Journal of Education*, 29:3, 281–293.

Purser, E., Dreyfus, S. and Jones, P. (2020) Big ideas & sharp focus: Researching and developing students' academic writing across the disciplines. *Journal of English for Academic Purposes*, 43, 100807. doi: 10.1016/j.jeap.2019.100807.

Tuck, J. (2018) *Academics engaging with student writing: Working at the higher education textface*. Abingdon, Oxon: Routledge.

Wette, R. (2014) Teachers' practices in EAP writing instruction: Use of models and modelling. *System*, 42:2014, 60–69.

Whong, M. and Godfrey, J. (Eds.) (2022) *What is good academic writing?: Insights into discipline-specific student writing (new perspectives for English for academic purposes)*. London: Bloomsbury Academic.

Wingate, U. (2015) *Academic literacy and student diversity: The case for inclusive practice*. Bristol: Multilingual Matters.

Chapter 6

Beyond ISEAP

This chapter concludes the book by looking beyond in-sessional provision itself to consider how its practices may be creating new paradigms, both within institutions and beyond. This book has demonstrated in all the preceding chapters how complex the realm in which ISEAP exists is, and has shown numerous examples of how practitioners working in this area are pushing the traditional limits of EAP. We suggest therefore by way of conclusion to the book that ISEAP can be seen as an emergent, hybrid sub-field of practice evolving with and within the wider context of developments in HE practice and pedagogy. Interconnections, interrelationships, and interdisciplinarity are all features of this complex environment in which practitioners work. Chapter 4 discussed some of the complications of the wider context where ISEAP often resides and considered the forces acting upon it. Then Chapter 5 examined insights from the perspective of how such aspects might impact on the practitioners themselves. This final chapter shifts focus to consider how ISEAP practice itself may contribute to the development of HE pedagogy and practices and its potential as a field of research. In other words, for those involved in ISEAP, beyond considering how they themselves might need to adapt their teaching style or cultivate certain attributes to be able to operate effectively in contemporary university settings, we now suggest they might also consider what their own impact on their context is or could be. The chapter considers the huge potential offered by the unique vantage point of ISEAP practice and suggests there is plenty of scope for practitioners

DOI: 10.4324/9781003193715-9

to develop further through researching academic language use and literacy development up close from within its discipline-specific habitats.

6.1 The Boundaries of ISEAP

Approaching this book with the idea of ISEAP as an interesting and under-explored area of EAP, and one that is developing in interesting ways, we found that our interviews with practitioners demonstrated the value of attempting to map ISEAP pedagogy and practice at this particular moment. Firstly, it appears that more disciplinary-informed in-sessional practices are ubiquitous now, at least in higher education in the U.K., and thus this is in some ways becoming more of a distinguished subfield of EAP practice in its own right. As discussed in our introduction, in her book *Academic Literacy and Student Diversity: The Case for Inclusive Practice*, Wingate (2015) suggested that even though EAP centres may have purported to be delivering integrated language with content – academic language and literacy development – very often they were working within an outmoded deficit skills model. Although we cannot claim to portray a fully comprehensive picture of ISEAP practice here, it should be clear from what we have presented from our conversations with practitioners that although the ways ISEAP is delivered is often mixed and very reliant on contextual factors, there are plenty of examples of fully collaborative, integrated practice in the field. Everyone we spoke to was at least aware of the benefits of moving towards a contextualised integrated academic language and literacy development focus and away from a deficit model of de-contextualised skills provision. Indeed, many sought to move in this direction, if they were not there already. Therefore, our first conclusion can be that it appears that sector-wide the ideal model of ISEAP provision is acknowledged to be broadly in line with an integrated academic language and literacy approach, working in collaboration with content lecturers and informed by disciplinary specificity.

As we also mentioned in the Introduction, Wingate collaborated with Tribble to investigate the type of in-sessional support being delivered in the U.K. context by searching university websites for mention of courses for international and home students, but reported that they were only able to find details at a relatively small sample of universities and requests for further details produced only a handful of responses (research carried out by Tribble and Wingate, reported in Wingate, 2015: 46). We set out with the idea to expand on this somewhat by holding more in-depth conversations with practitioners working in ISEAP, not only in the United Kingdom but beyond. However, as in Wingate (2015), we must also admit the limitations of our research. At best, we are only providing a snapshot of the sector; we cannot claim a representative sample. However, we hope the insights that we have reproduced in the form of quotes from those conversations along the way will serve to enlighten the reader as to what actually goes on in practice and that this will prompt others to take up the challenge of investigating ISEAP more thoroughly or more in depth. We have not attempted to map all ISEAP here, but at least to put ISEAP firmly in focus.

Perhaps the most common statement made by our interviewees when we approached them was that it was high time for a book to explore the world of ISEAP, as it remains a more occluded practice area by comparison to pre-sessional or foundation provision. The quote from an interview with a practitioner who had recently attended the 2021 BALEAP Biennial Conference before they spoke to us exemplifies this:

> You don't really know what goes on in different places. We don't know what we do; pre-sessional is more visible in assessments and outcomes. There was a question at BALEAP: what is there to stop in-sessional teachers from doing what they like, if you don't have mechanisms or a forum to discuss and agree common approaches? Nobody knows [what is going on] in other institutions or even within our own institutions. I sometimes feel like people in institutions or even departments when they ask, 'oh, do you do that?'

As another interviewee commented, ISEAP is naturally 'so integrated, so collaborative – it's therefore more invisible, and in a way it's good that it's invisible.' But that is not very useful for practitioners starting out in this area or who are developing new provision.

One way in which ISEAP as a practice area could become more visible and develop more openly is by practitioners connecting across boundaries to share knowledge and advice. Interviewees typically welcomed the idea of a book looking specifically at this area in order to promote more inter-institutional knowledge sharing. The quote from an interview from a U.K. context below shows, however, that practitioners do sometimes connect with one another across institutions:

> You do hear from others. [name of another UK institution] got in touch about a year and half ago, they said 'we're thinking about running CEM

modules but there is no formal information.' So you are consolidating that in the book, a model that can be followed.

The CEM model (Sloan and Porter, 2010) was presented in Chapter 3. As discussed throughout, however, this guide is not intended to be a prescriptive one. Given the highly contextualised nature of ISEAP practice it would be impossible to suggest a framework or a pedagogy that works across all contexts. There is simply so much complexity and diversity in terms of where ISEAP is delivered and how practitioners respond to their context that we believe that the development of models would be best generated to fit specific contexts by informed and reflective practitioners.

The other point raised in the last quote about practitioners connecting with each other beyond their own institutional boundaries, however, is something we would fully endorse. A number of recent developments in the wider field of EAP suggest that the typically obscured area of in-sessional practice is drawing increasing amounts of attention to itself. For example, one of the authors of this book has been involved in discussions around the set-up of a possible BALEAP Special Interest Group (SIG) dedicated specifically to in-sessional EAP (at the time of writing, the proposal for this was being prepared for submission to BALEAP for ratification). It is to be hoped that initiatives like this, beyond raising the visibility of ISEAP within EAP, might enable more cross fertilisation of ideas, and engender opportunities for mutual support and sharing of practice between practitioners from different institutions.

In our interviews, we noted a number of examples where practitioners were already taking the initiative and reaching out to each other from one institution to another. The use of group emails such as the BALEAP JISCMail, or encounters with other practitioners at conferences, often provide informal springboards for inter-institutional collaborations. For example, one interviewee from a U.K. institution commented on their use of the shared email list to get an idea of what went on in other institutions:

> The reason I have been emailing BALEAP [is] to try to get some numbers. This is about the relationship between engagement and success. We're putting together a proposal to get better central funding [for ISEAP provision].

As in the earlier example of a practitioner from one institution approaching another about the use of the CEM Model (Sloan and Porter, 2010), the example above shows an ISEAP practitioner reaching out with a need for logistical information, in this case for the specific purpose of putting together a funding proposal. This reflects ongoing uncertainty about how ISEAP is funded and set up, as there is typically not a precedent for this within a single university. On the other hand, other interviewees told us they had connected with colleagues at other institutions in order to become more informed in pedagogical matters, in particular related to working with disciplinary-specific genres. One interviewee told us they had been working on a project with a colleague from another university from another part of the United Kingdom who also taught creative arts students, with the purpose of:

> Trying to find out why design assignments are a pot pourri, they are hybrid genres.

Given the way ISEAP provision was set up in their own institution they were not embedded enough in the discipline to allow for a detailed enough analysis or seek closer collaboration with content lecturers in this, a consequence of them being required to operate in a more generic EGAP model due to lo-gistical constraints. This is an example where cross-institutional relationships can produce answers to pedagogical questions when in one's own institution the necessary information is not easily accessible and there is a lack of research in such highly discipline-specific areas. In the case of creative arts disciplines, hybrid genres are a prevalent feature of the context (as noted by Carr et al., 2021 for example). Given the lack of published material on delivery of ISEAP in this context or published analysis of particular sub-genres, developing such connections with those working in other institutions may provide a vital source of information. Moreover, there are other practical as well as social benefits of networking with ISEAP practitioners from other universities and developing cross-institutional relationships.

Carr et al. (2021) offer a good example of the possibilities of cross-institutional collaboration for research in ESAP practice. In this study, four practitioners working at different institutions in the United Kingdom, all in creative arts contexts (including fine art, design, music, and architecture), collaborated in a joint autoethnography, sharing narrative accounts of their practice with each other, exploring the 'lived practical experience and ped-agogies of EAP practitioners working with and in the creative disciplines' (Carr et al., 2021: 154). This study yields a large amount of rich data, not only on practitioners' reflections of working with genre-specific issues in this area, but also their experiences of collaborating with content lecturers and in-tegrating their ISEAP practice (2021: 165–7). There is also an illuminating discussion about the significance of the importance of location in terms of the kinds of spaces where creative arts students learn, with implications for communication with learners and practitioners' own feelings and observations about being integrated as teachers into this discipline-specific space (Carr et al., 2021). This aligns with the underlying principles of the CEM Model (Sloan and Porter, 2010), with its emphasis on provision being embedded and mapped, even if not implemented as such. Moreover, it demonstrates the potential of working in ISEAP to make observations about what would otherwise be unexplored areas of research.

Perhaps studies like this could serve as an inspiration to ISEAP practitioners who might like to investigate practice if they identify a specific disciplinary field worth exploring across two or more university contexts. Indeed, a collaborative, ethnographic approach like this could be a useful model to emulate, as the resulting study provides some deep insights into what we have identified as the shadowy world of ISEAP practice. And as the authors state:

> Willingness to go outside the EAP department and think creatively to access resources has been a key component in successful collaboration, and allowing time to do this and seek collaboration opportunities is one of the main ways in which departments and institutions foster and support important interdisciplinary and cross-institutional educational development.
>
> (Carr et al., 2021: 166)

Beyond joint initiatives like this, another way in which ISEAP expertise can cross-pollinate from one institution to another arises when practitioners themselves move jobs, taking their knowledge and experience from a con-textualised setting in one institution into another. We had two clear examples of this in our conversations. One head of an EAP department in a large U.K. university, who had been in charge of in-sessional provision in their prior university, told us that they were able to apply lessons learned there to the new context (again stressing the agility which is characteristic of practitioners who develop in ISEAP settings, as identified in Chapter 5). They explained how they demonstrated the known efficacy of a model of in-sessional pro-vision in presenting it to university management at the new institution:

> In terms of a pedagogic vision, it was very well received. So I've been able to take what I learned at [prior institution] and develop it into a

vision at [current institution]. That was very well received … not only by the university but by colleagues in the department that I run.

Another interviewee working in the European Union told us how they had been forming a network of language professionals working in in-sessional language teaching in university contexts from different countries, and had taken that project with them from a university in one country to a completely new one. This is a transfer of a more tangible nature, but as in the previous example, it illustrates the importance and value of the individual ISEAP practitioner themselves, operating in the heart of institutions. Moreover, in line with the attributes discussed in Chapter 5, it demonstrates the value of a proactive approach and presumably the development of strong interpersonal skills and confidence in one's own abilities.

The most developed example of connection between practitioners from one institution to another came in the form of what those involved themselves referred to as a 'critical friendship.' A critical friend has been defined as:

> A trusted person who asks provocative questions, provides data to be examined through another lens, and offers critiques of a person's work as a friend. A critical friend takes the time to fully understand the context of the work presented and the outcomes that the person or group is working toward.
>
> (Costa and Kallick, 1993: 50)

This critical friendship developed out of the role of external examiner. As previously mentioned in this book, formal external examiner arrangements between universities for in-sessional EAP are not common. The practitioners came from two different institutions in different parts of the United Kingdom and they established a series of regular online meetings and a 'reciprocal relationship' discussing matters relating to how they ran the in-sessional provision in their respective universities. In the following extract from our interview with them, they describe how their professional relationship functioned. The relationship is less like a formal external examiner one and more like cross-institutional peer observation. They told us that one of them:

> Chose a particular issue, which we talked through. The other person just asked critical questions … then we would go back and analyse it. We had one person talking and then the other one asking critical questions, then

taking it away and then writing up a reflection ... to make it a reflective practice of management.

They adopted a formalised model of dialogic reflection, and when they spoke to us they said that it was an arrangement they planned to continue (it was a process which had begun during COVID-19 lockdown) and possibly extend to include other colleagues working on in-sessionals in their institutions, and so it might become a means of generating ongoing scholarly discussion beyond institutional boundaries.

The instances of cross-institution ISEAP discussed above may not seem like much, and the examples from interviews quoted here often just start from informal chance encounters or from a short-term instrumental need. However, they clearly go towards fulfilling a role of providing collegial support, whether in areas of practicalities, pedagogy or practice. This can be extremely valuable in the context of the hidden nature of ISEAP and the potential loneliness of the ISEAP practitioner. As previous chapters have shown, ISEAP can be a challenging area of practice, dealing with constant change as a matter of course, so establishing connections like these, perhaps facilitated by networks such as special interest groups, might be one way in which ISEAP opens up more in the future. It is hoped then that it may become less of an intimidating and obscured field.

6.2 The Spread of ISEAP

One area of the spreading of ISEAP (i.e. expanding beyond its original remit) that was often reported in our interviews was where ISEAP practitioners, as a result of their collaboration with content specialists, have developed their role beyond purely teaching students. Bond (2020: 192) suggests that 'there is a strong argument for collaboration between educational development, EAP and content teachers to encourage a sharing of knowledge and good practice.' We discovered many incidences of informally sharing good practice in our interviews, but also heard of several examples where ISEAP practitioners were working directly with lecturers, not just as team teachers but in an advisory role or even as trainers. McGrath et al. (2019), as previously mentioned in Chapter 4, provide an example of how the kind of knowledge and experience that an ISEAP specialist can develop, which they term 'a bricolage of expertise,' can be applied, advising content lecturers on aspects of their practice.

We found numerous examples of ISEAP stretching beyond its teaching remit to encompass such roles in our interviews with practitioners, suggesting this is already quite a common and natural progression of working in an ISEAP context. For example, an interviewee in a U.K. university stated how this kind of arrangement may arise as a natural progression in a relationship with a collaborating department in integrated ISEAP:

> You can end up with a learning and teaching hat on too, looking at assignment briefs, being a sounding board to the module leader as well.

The discussion of wearing different hats fits well with the discussion of roles one may play in the context of being an ISEAP practitioner, as discussed in Chapter 5. In this case, what was occurring appears to have been fairly informal. However, in other instances, we spoke to practitioners who had developed more formal, established arrangements. In an Australian context, for example, where EAP in-sessional courses were set up so that admission was based on students taking an institution-wide language test (discussed in Chapter 1), practitioners reported that they came to have an institutional role, advising departments on aspects of their marking related to language issues. This situation confers extra status and responsibilities on the practitioners as essentially they become perceived as the key language experts across the university to be consulted in discussions around teaching and learning policy. Our interviewees told us that this included reporting directly to the university vice chancellor and senior management team on occasion. More than just increasing the visibility of ISEAP practitioners within the university, this also had the effect of making the university more visible to the practitioners involved. As they stated, 'having to make connections across all units of the university, we found people we didn't know existed!'

In the ISEAP provision of one of the authors of this book (University of Bristol), the ISEAP coordinators have been involved in a formal arrangement involving summative assessment within a particular provision. This has involved co-writing assessment criteria on master's degrees, which contain both a 'technical mark,' marked by engineering tutors, focussing on content, and a 'language mark' assessed by the ISEAP tutors. The language mark assesses areas of language related directly to the learning outcomes of the integrated ISEAP sessions taught within the master's course. In another provision, there is also a project involving co-writing of assignment briefs and marking criteria for assessing group presentations, and it is hoped that this will include joint standardisation and moderation processes with content lecturers in the future. Caulton et al. (2019) report on EAP practitioners co-marking with disciplinary experts, finding that the values of the two parties aligned closely, but would benefit from greater collaboration to enable both to comment on language and content – that both are symbiotically related in communication, a point emphasised by Bond (2020). We did not hear of many more specific instances of working with content lecturers on jointly assessed summative assessment in a similar way from our interviews, but it is certainly an area in which integrated language specialist teachers could naturally extend their remit beyond providing taught content.

The opportunities for such arrangements to happen, as has been discussed throughout this book, are very much dependent on the specific context of how the EAP centre is postitioned in individual universities. It may seem optimistic, but extension of the ISEAP role into all aspects of the modules where the practitioners' work (including summative assessment) would seem to be a natural progression. In this way, language and content practitioners would be working together in a fully integrated model. Moreover, this could be seen as the optimal arrangement, set up as institutional policy. As one of our interviewees from an EU-based institution commented:

> Wouldn't it be great if every programme had a language expert, who could take on part of the curriculum discussions formally?

Another interviewee based in Australia told us that some EAP specialists are routinely involved in working with content lecturers in their university in the area of assessment practices:

> There's an old colleague of mine attached to my faculty, Arts and Social Sciences, and also others attached to other faculties. They work with lecturers to redesign the wording of the assignment tasks, maybe sit in on a lecture, maybe give a tutorial ... they are part of a whole programme called Embedding English Language.

It is not completely clear if these colleagues come specifically from an EAP centre; however, they are identified here as language experts operating in an in-sessional context, and so this can be taken as an example of what the remit of ISEAP practice might aspire to include. This interviewee was also consulted at an institutional level themselves. Due to the compulsory national requirements related to English language standards in Australian HE contexts, there is a definite need for their expertise, again at a higher, pan-institutional level. As the quote below demonstrates though, there is also a sense of the need for them to be proactive in order to make such opportunities happen:

> As an academic you have to make yourself sit on certain committees. I ended up being on the courses accreditation committee, which was extremely high powered and the committee was full of big shots, heads of departments, etc., and here's me as a lecturer. But I was invited to be in it as a language expert. So we had to look at applications from faculties for new courses. And a part of the elaborate documentation we had to provide was information on English language standards.

It is interesting in light of the discussion on practitioner identity in the previous chapter how, even though this practitioner is clearly deeply embedded institutionally and accepted as an expert at institutional level, there are still signs here of their own insecurity about status, as evidenced by the comment 'here's me as a lecturer.' Nevertheless, it is clear from the context above that this practitioner is highly qualified and experienced and very adept at the role. Moreover, it can be supposed that their experience of authentic disciplinary language use (developed through ISEAP practices) is a key factor in their suitability for this role.

In other examples from our interviews, it was clear that ISEAP specialists were also developing other types of courses beyond integrated language and literacy provision. For example, one interviewee in a U.K. institution told us what they were currently working on:

> I'm developing a course on intercultural communication as that is where we need to be to work with the whole university, and to work with different nationalities. There is a feeling that staff would benefit too. Probably a lot of us do that. I find that now I really have to stress the importance of language and that this isn't just an add-on. They [stakeholders] cannot separate academic skills from language or separate writing from language. I'm having to point out to people: I don't think you can do that.

Beyond the stretching of the scope of this practitioner to include intercultural communication, the second part of the quote recalls much of the discussion in Chapter 4 related to raising the profile of ISEAP work and articulating one's provision. The extra responsibility for advocating best practice in integrating language and content, and disseminating this message across the wider university, is also a key recommendation for what EAP practitioners in general should see as part of their remit, according to Bond (2020). For example, she states:

> [T]he development of inclusive, language aware teaching practices needs to be an accepted norm within the training and development of good HE teachers across all the disciplines, with support materials and development for continuous professional learning (CPL) readily available.
>
> (Bond, 2020:192)

One of our interviewees from a Scandinavian university suggested that part of their work involved providing workshops for lecturers, the focus of which they described as 'awareness raising, giving them tools,' and this was related to academic literacy development. These workshops were set up partly in the hope that they would encourage content lecturers to incorporate elements from academic literacy-informed practice into their content teaching repertoire. The interviewee commented that this intervention also had another function: it showed their university colleagues what EAP practitioners do (and so this aided the visibility of their own practice). The interviewee stated that this was useful as it helped to correct misconceptions of their role that they just 'fixed students' grammar,' as well as raising the profile across the university of academic literacy as an important concept within HE pedagogy.

The interviewee below from a non-U.K. context suggested in an earlier quoted example that in their view, more of an explicitly shared responsibility and proactive involvement from all parties is required in terms of explicitly developing learners' academic literacy:

> We have done a lot of work to teach the other colleagues in the subject, professors, in that it's impossible: we cannot be the only ones who teach [English] and you can't just expect the students to be taught it [at the EAP centre] and that'll be okay. It needs to be enforced through your classes, through your feedback, through your consciousness about language issues. We are open to cooperation and we are open to any projects that ensure that this is happening.

Importantly, the final line of the quote above shows that beyond being an advocate for the role of language and literacy work, there is also an openness on the part of the ISEAP practitioner to extend their provision to other collaborative projects which may arise.

Another example of this proactive approach, this willingness to get in-volved, can be seen in what another interviewee in a U.K. context told us. They work closely with colleagues from health sciences in an undergraduate context in their university and explained how an interesting extension be-yond the usual remit of ISEAP teaching practice arose naturally as a result of a series of team-taught sessions:

> It's targeted at the students but team-taught with the academics, who said this is great, you know we have a real issue with consistently giving feedback within our team. Would you be able to do a similar session with our staff? So we have 40 senior academics in the school and I'm going to deliver a session with our centre as assessment specialists on something very similar to that. So it does lead to other things. So there is all sorts of value that comes out of in-sessional provision. It goes beyond the classroom.

This is an interesting example as it not only extends ISEAP expertise to a non-EAP area, articulating feedback effectively, but also the cohort for this is the content lecturers themselves rather than students. Therefore, the role of the ISEAP practitioners has developed to incorporate an element of teacher training across boundaries in the university on more general HE pedagogical aspects.

The issue of training, or rather the choice of the term 'training' itself might be seen as problematic for some, as discussed in Chapter 4, with its im-plication of a narrow focus compared with the wider associations of 'edu-cation' – and as a result this may not be explicitly communicated as the focus of stated development plans for ISEAP provision within institutions. As a practitioner working in a South African university commented:

> My 5 to 10-year plan is to have a third branch which works with lecturers and, I don't like the word 'trains,' but talks about how to incorporate academic literacy into their modules.

To sum up the lessons from the last few examples, the spread of practitioner expertise and their role being widened to involve aspects of advising content lecturers appears to be quite common, and often arises naturally as a con-sequence of working in close collaboration with them in the context of ISEAP courses.

One other movement in spreading the remit of ISEAP practitioners that we noted in our interviews was a tendency for practitioners to move into operating within academic staff development work. This area may involve projects, initiatives, and courses related to teaching practice for the benefit of all teaching staff at a university. These include working with departments dedicated to staff development within U.K. universities. Examples of this from our own institutions are the Teaching and Learning Innovation Centre (TaLIC) at Goldsmiths, University of London (TaLIC, 2022) and the Bristol Institute for Learning and Teaching (BiLT) at the University of Bristol (BiLT, 2022). The remit of these centres lies in training academic staff in institutions, as HE lecturers may well enter into a teaching position in a university with no formal training in how to teach. For example, the BiLT website lists a number of course options that include academic and professional development opportunities such as the Postgraduate Certificate in Academic Practice (PGCAP) or courses leading to Advance HE Higher Education Academy Fellowship accreditation (BiLT, 2022). The TaLIC website states: 'We work in partnership with Goldsmiths' staff, lending our support and expertise to the shared goal of excellence in teaching and learning' (TaLIC, 2022). The mention of 'excellence' here echoes the TEF or Teaching Excellence Framework, carried out by the U.K. government's Office for Students (Office For Students, 2022). The TEF is intended to measure the effectiveness of teaching at U.K. universities and is used to audit U.K. institutions. Its influence on universities is considered generally to have less weight than the REF, a similar exercise related to research and research output, but both can be considered examples of practices applying metrics to attempt to establish some form of standardisation. As Ding and Bruce (2017) point out, both of these can be considered instances of the increased 'marketisation' of the HE sector (2017: 20), which has previously been discussed in Chapter 4.

There are similarities between the work of academic units like TaLIC and BiLT with ISEAP; both operate within an interdisciplinary context where, as in the TaLIC website quote above, there is a key focus on collaboration and shared goals. This type of context has been classified as a 'third space' within institutions, the term denoting environments that 'do not sit easily in formal organisational structures and can be both ambiguous and uncertain' (Whitchurch, 2015: 1). There are also similarities between staff who work in ISEAP and in academic development, and Whitchurch comments that applying the concept of third space can enable 'exploring groups of staff in higher education who do not fit conventional binary descriptors such as those enshrined in 'academic' or 'non-academic' employment categories' (2015: 1).

Not surprisingly, then, there are often informal links between the two that develop within university ecologies.

One notable example of crossover to academic development from ISEAP was noted in an interview with a U.K. practitioner. This occurred in the context where they themselves inhabited two roles within an EAP centre and in academic staff development. The following quote from the interview explains how this dual role has led the practitioner to asprire to bringing their language specialist colleagues over to lead workshops in staff development, making use of their particular expertise:

> We want to put certain resources together to support staff. Different people will be allocated to teams and they will feed into a bank which departments can then draw on, maybe setting up workshops or to deliver workshops or doing something with those resources themselves to take on an away day. The first thing I said: well there's nothing there about international students and there's nothing specifically about critical thinking, although I can see how that would fit in with subject area knowledge. But no one is actually working on that particular area. That is going to be crucial and I'm looking at ways in which I can bring in people from [the EAP centre] and looking at ways I can bring in CPD.

In terms of what the content of these sessions might involve, the interviewee went on to explain that there would be something on teaching international student cohorts, perhaps unpacking with non-language specialist staff what IELTS scores actually mean, intercultural communication and dealing with academic integrity issues.

In connection with the last item listed above, another interviewee told us how the expertise drawn on in outreach projects of this kind demonstrates the ISEAP specialist's wide-ranging knowledge of genre and communication in the discipline:

> One of the things we looked at was professional ethics and how that would relate to academic integrity – communication was at the heart of it, but also intellectual property ... The example of an engineer using the same source code for two different employers, which was in a case study on the course: we discuss this case and do some synthesis writing and do a critical summary of four different experts and learn about academic integrity in that way.

This example is also a good one for demonstrating innovation and creativity as well as the ease of working in interdisciplinary and transdisciplinary contexts, which all mark out ISEAP practitioners with the experience of particular discipline-specific contexts as specialised educators within institutions, whose expertise is not just language related. What is more, it appears from the previous examples there is potential for ISEAP practitioners not only for working on student-based initiatives, but also in academic and professional staff development contexts.

Finally, as Chapter 1 observed, there may very often be a perception on the part of ISEAP practitioners that they are the subordinate partner in a collaborative ISEAP context due to preconceptions about expertise and knowledge. The following quote from an interviewee in a European university is a refreshing take on this, suggesting that given the complex and mutable nature of contemporary HE pedagogy, all educators are in some ways equal:

> We're not experts but we contribute … I don't think anyone's an expert in teaching. We're all tweaking, trying to get better.

6.3 The Potential of ISEAP

Beyond the developments within HE pedagogies which have already been mentioned, the following section turns to consider ways in which practitioners working in ISEAP might actively exploit their unique positioning and expertise within university contexts.

6.3.1 Impact and Visibility in the Institution

There is a sense, considering the relatively recent developments in the United Kingdom of the TEF and centres within institutions focussed on teacher training for lecturers, that HE pedagogy continues to be a developing area of practice. Moreover, ISEAP practitioners, with a language teaching specialisation, are very often not the only agents operating in the transdisciplinary third space between departments collaborating in teaching. Also in this area, as Chapter 1 discussed, there is often a separate, more general academic skills provision, particularly in U.K. contexts, often based in the library and typically delivering workshops on issues such information literacy, referencing, and perhaps some generic ideas about approaches to organising and planning writing. There can at times be an overlap with ISEAP with what they contribute in terms of academic literacy (and occasionally even more language-based content); as discussed in Chapter 3 the relationship between ISEAP and such study skills centres is not always harmonious.

One interviewee, for example, told us that although they had the opportunity to get involved in a large-scale project developing a MOOC (Massive Open Online Course) with the business school, they had not automatically been included in the project, whereas the study skills team had. This demonstrates again the possibility for creating impact on the university, but also that having impact often still involves a need to negotiate what ISEAP's contribution can actually be in an area of university activity. Moreover, the territory may be contested with other agents in the interdisciplinary space.

This chapter has mentioned a number of ways in which ISEAP practitioners have become more embedded in institutional-level projects. Even where the status of the ISEAP provision itself is more established, this has still often only come about at a cost, based on a constant need to strive for recognition and vie for opportunities when they present themselves. The quote from an interviewee from a U.K. university below, demonstrates this point:

> We've worked hard to make it so. We go on committees. We promote what we do, and to be scholars, to engage in research. EAP practitioners often complain of feeling undervalued. At [name of university] I've never felt less than anyone's equal. We have so many skills and are often engaged in scholarship, we're a lynchpin. We mediate between lecturers all the time. We should be seen as highly important and skilled. EAP should go everywhere.

In fact, this practitioner suggested there was a need to go beyond networking and getting involved in programmes and committees; they actually stressed the value of continuously 'being a nuisance' in order to participate actively at institutional level, and be able to articulate the value of their practice area and ensure visibility.

One way in which ISEAP practitioners can add to their perceived value as teaching specialists in the university context in the United Kingdom is by engaging actively with institution-wide schemes such as the HEA (Higher Education Academy) Fellowship scheme, under the auspices of Advance HE (2022). Both of the authors of this book are Senior Fellows (SFHEA) for example, and involved in assessment and mentoring of colleagues for the Fellowship from various departments across their institutions. A number of our U.K.-based interviewees mentioned that they had also had Fellowship status and one commented on its perceived value in terms of conferring status on them as operators within their institution, especially when the visibility of the EAP centre may not be optimal and the onus is on them to reach out to content lecturers:

> HEA recognition helps, it's really important. They don't really understand [the EAP centre], who we are, whether we are qualified or not. That [HEA Fellowship] helps a lot in being valued more.

As mentioned above, involvement in high-level committees at university often comes about as a result of practitioners being involved in embedded in-sessional contexts. This can in turn raise the profile and status of EAP departments. In this way, a by-product of ISEAP is that it often serves as a conduit for developing greater recognition within an institution and places EAP practitioners in more visible collaborative roles with other academic departments. As one of our interviewees, a director of an EAP centre, said, although the in-sessional part of what an EAP centre does is not typically a fund-generating part of its activities, it is an important 'extra layer' for both staff and students across the university, suggesting that there is a possibility of reputational damage if in-sessionals are not part of a centre's portfolio. At another U.K. university, an interviewee confirmed the importance of ISEAP as part of what an EAP centre does, and how in-sessional provision with one department had directly resulted in them being involved in other projects, which were in fact income generating:

> In-sessional is our *raison d'etre*, you have to keep on reminding people of that. It doesn't bring in the money, in fact it can be seen as a drain on resources, but we wouldn't exist if we didn't make that provision … And it is something that has improved the status of EAP – contacts in the department have led to other things, for example to development of a [name of department] summer school, which does bring in money, so it is increasingly seen as important. Yes, in-sessional is a drain, but a necessary drain.

Heads of department at large U.K. universities that we interviewed mentioned involvement in university committees related to assessment and feedback and even attempts to get institutional buy-in to have academic language and literacy provision delivered by EAP practitioners expressly included in every course. Such a move would not only expedite the development of new provision and allow for involvement in a whole range of new initiatives, it would also confer more agency for EAP practitioners within institutions and opportunities to articulate the value of their provision as a whole. As one of the U.K. heads of department commented:

> I think it's important to be able to articulate our value on our own terms as well as through plugging into other things.

6.3.2 Research Opportunities in ISEAP

One respect in which ISEAP practitioners may struggle with perceptions about their status within institutions relates to the fact that typically, unlike their content specialist collaborators, they are not employed in posts that are considered to be research active. As Chapter 1 pointed out, this may be due to the location of the EAP centre itself. For example, if it lies in an adjunct service unit within the university, rather than an academic centre, it is less likely that scholarship or research time will be included in the EAP practitioner's contract. In the U.K. context, the REF (Research Excellence Framework) is now an established feature of the HE landscape for lecturers, with an express requirement for them to publish in order to strengthen the rating of the department and that of the wider university. It is highly unusual for EAP practitioners to be included in the REF. In one way, this could be seen to be advantageous in terms of the comparative lack of pressure on them to try to fit research into typically busy teaching schedules compared to content lecturers. However, being a 'non REF-able' member of faculty is also a potential barrier to acceptance and accumulating greater agency and capital within institutions. One interviewee, a programme lead for the in-sessional provision offered by their centre, suggested that due to this fact they were often excluded from discussions with other faculty-level programme leads in committee meetings, for example.

A number of our interviewees have completed PhDs or EdDs, even if doctoral study is typically not the norm among EAP practitioners. One of our interviewees, working in ISEAP in a mainland European institution, commented that their perception was that having a doctorate, rather like having an HEA Fellowship in the United Kingdom, played a significant role in convincing other departments to accept them as valid partners within the university context. Moreover, in this case the subject matter of their doctoral study also had the additional value of communicating the importance of language in the academy. They even reported that other lecturers had been surprised to note that it was possible to do research into the area of student writing practices in HE contexts. Again, this confirms that an advocacy role, communicating the importance of integrated language and literacy within institutions, is a key responsibility that comes with the role of being an EAP practitioner (Bond, 2020).

However, again in light of the discussions in Chapter 4, if the positioning of the EAP department itself is problematic, having higher-level academic qualifications is not necessarily an advantage. One of our interviewees, a PhD candidate, reported feeling extremely frustrated with their current situation within their EAP centre and with their perceived status within the university as a whole. They also commented on the fact that their head of department was not actually an EAP practitioner themselves:

> In terms of our voice, I feel a lot more jaded. Our director has no understanding of how to teach language or how to teach international students. We can feel that they'd like us to be a support service; we don't fit with the REF output, i.e. [the university's] research themes; therefore, they are [changes in the quote requested by interviewee] not interested in us doing pedagogic research.

This demonstrates that not only can a lack of research opportunities be a real barrier within institutions, but also shows how desire to develop any kind of research as an EAP practitioner may also be denied by the context in which one works. Clearly, this can be a cause of anxiety and distress.

Even if there is no official requirement to be formally research active, it is generally accepted by most EAP centres that there should be opportunities for EAP professionals to participate in scholarship activities. Ding and Bruce (2017: 111) define scholarship as activities relating to 'developing and refining one's overall knowledge of practice in EAP.' Despite the previous interview example, the majority of EAP departments (based on our research and experience) actively encourage scholarship in this sense, as this quote from an ISEAP practitioner in the United Kingdom shows:

> [The centre] very much supports scholarship. You're encouraged to do HEA Fellowship and go to conferences. They give some time for scholarship, and it's very important to do scholarship if we want to improve our status within the faculty. This involves being active in conferences, and in [the university's] internal conferences and projects.

Moreover, apart from having time dedicated to such activities within their own department, EAP practitioners may have other potential sources of support for scholarship and even for doing some research. In this chapter, we mentioned a practitioner who had transferred from a role based purely in EAP to an academic staff development role within their institution. They suggested that there may be funds available from staff development initiatives at university level for research and continuous professional development (CPD) and that practitioners can exploit these to develop their research ideas on a small scale. They commented that this typically has a very positive effect in terms of contributing to a more positive practitioner identity and fostering greater job satisfaction:

> I think there are opportunities that people don't realise to get little bits of money to do things. It's where you can actually make life a bit more interesting because you're doing something that you enjoy doing: you can work on something that you're in control of. No one is telling you what to do. You can work on it, you might even get some money, you might get to a conference; you might even get to publish in a journal somewhere. We do scholarly work and we do go to conferences; you can come back and say 'I did this'. It doesn't even necessarily need to be published, it doesn't need empirical evidence, you can say 'I've done this, I put something in for a conference and I got some good feedback.'

This quote has a reassuring quality, suggesting that possibilities for a small scale, perhaps action research for example, may be accessible in every institution. This is something Webster (2022) demonstrates, in his description of how an EAP centre reaped the benefits of encouraging scholarship amongst its practitioners. Participating in more formal research is something that Ding and Bruce (2017) and Bond (2020) both urge practitioners to get involved in. Apart from the need to be an advocate for the role of language in the institution and for developing their own self-efficacy, it can also contribute to a practitioner's sense of fitting in to the academic environment they are working in, as the interviewee from the previous example went on to say:

> [There is] a whole pressure around you in [disciplinary] departments to be researching and that's the pressure in universities. And everybody thinks they are highly important in the work they do. So maybe we have a bit of an attitude problem ourselves in that we live up to other peoples' images

of us and don't say 'hey we're significant players as well'; maybe our research isn't as scholarly, but it's still important.

The first part of the quote from this practitioner mentions the importance of practitioner freedom, which was discussed in Chapter 5 as a significant contributing factor to a sense of ISEAP practitionership being a rewarding occupation. Other interviewees cited some research opportunities that working in ISEAP contexts had brought them and this was typically linked to a perception of freedom to operate in terms of pursuing their own ideas and interests.

The quote below from an interview with an ISEAP practitioner in a mainland European university is a good example of this. The practitioner in question has had opportunities in their role for both setting up an international conference and for writing discipline-specific English textbooks and was very pleased with the opportunities that working specifically in an ISEAP context had brought them. The question from the interview is also reproduced at the start:

Q. *So in a sense you're free agents?*

Yes, I quite like that, and we've met colleagues – through conferences, through Erasmus [a European Commission scheme which in this case enabled ISEAP collaboration] – the kind of freedom that allows us to be in control. It allows us to experiment, we're not tied to an approach. If you have an idea, you may not really be allowed usually, but this has enabled us to produce books, and for me to create my own stuff.

The above example shows someone developing their own identity as a practitioner as a result of growing within the ISEAP context. The resultant boost to their sense of self-efficacy from having opportunity to try things out, in a way that perhaps more formalised areas of EAP practice would not allow, is evident. Moreover, this person is clearly in a much more positive position than the earlier quoted interviewee who mentioned feeling jaded in their department with an unsympathetic director.

A key point about working in an ISEAP context is the potential not only for creating one's own scholarship and research opportunities, but for developing joint research in collaboration with the content lecturers. An interviewee from an Australian university told us that their ISEAP practice had also afforded them this kind of collaborative research possibility:

> We partner with people in faculties doing joint research projects. We come along with our applied linguistics and language education background, working with a business or health professional ... I have co-authored with a nursing academic, something that arose out of a student focus: seeing a problem, trying to find a way to solve the problem and realising that I can't solve it by myself and the faculty people can't solve it by themselves.

The final part of that quote gives us a nice example of a very balanced and equitable situation in terms of the relation of the ISEAP practitioner to the content lecturer. This chapter previously mentioned Carr et al. (2021) as an example of a cross-institutional ISEAP practitioner collaboration, but unfortunately examples of joint research projects like this with content lecturers were not commonly referred to in our interviews. This is clearly one area of development in ISEAP research with the potential to go beyond the institution, which we can only hope will become more evident in the future.

Their positioning within the university in some ways conveys a unique vantage point to ISEAP practitioners, as stated in the previous chapter. This allows them to see academic language and literacy development up close. Therefore, it should certainly yield more opportunities for research to inform all who are concerned about what actually goes on in university learning contexts. Such research could take various forms: ethnographic research, discourse analysis within specific genres or action research, with practitioners investigating their own teaching or reflecting on their status as third space agents within the university, for example.

A published example of collaborative research between EAP practitioners and content lecturers is the collection of discipline specific examinations, *What is Good Academic Writing?* (Whong and Godfrey, 2022a, 2022b). In the introduction to this compendium of EAP practitioner and joint EAP and content practitioner accounts of discipline-specific written genres, the editors note the challenges for EAP practitioners related to their circumstances in terms of doing research and getting published. They urge that in future initiatives like theirs become 'the norm' (Whong and Godfrey, 2022a). Although they explain that originally their plan was for all the studies in the collection to be the result of a 'match' between a content specialist and a language specialist, demonstrating 'a happy marriage of EAP and content tutor expertise,' the published result does include a number of sole EAP practitioner-led studies (Whong and Godfrey, 2022b: 24). They do however suggest that if such collaborative content-language specialist research practices are encouraged more generally, this could then lead to a better understanding and sharing of the 'metalanguage' of genre analysis for content lecturers and maybe even result in some ways in a 'blurring' of the lines between content and language tutor expertise (2022b: 24–25).

A key point to note here is that the collaborative research project was an EAP centre-supported one. It was not specifically ISEAP, but still it suggests how enshrining research and publication projects as normal practice within EAP departments is often necessary for such initiatives to work and for practitioner research to get to publication and therefore achieve dissemination beyond the boundaries of its own context. It could, therefore, be a useful model for departments to enable ISEAP practitioners working across a range of disciplines within a university to exploit the affordances of their unique practice area to the fullest.

Concluding Thoughts

This chapter, by way of conclusion, is an attempt to draw on ideas from the two preceding chapters to consider where this area of practice is going, looking within and beyond ISEAP's established habitat. It has suggested a number of ways in which ISEAP is evolving, developing its remit, and reaching out across boundaries within institutions and between institutions. As a follow-up to this in the final reflection section of the book, we encourage practitioners to ask themselves the following questions we have considered here:

- What impact are ISEAP practitioners and ISEAP practice having on HE institutions?
- In what ways is ISEAP developing and spreading?
- Where might it go?

Chapter 6 Reflection

The questions below are related to the content of the chapter and focus on crossing three boundaries that an ISEAP practitioner may face: to ISEAP practitioners in other universities, to others within your institution beyond your centre, and finally the potential contribution of ISEAP to the development of HE pedagogy on a larger scale.

Reaching across university boundaries to other ISEAP units in other universities:

1. What do you think you could learn from ISEAP practitioners working in other contexts?
2. What would you share about your practice?

Within your own university:

1. How does what you do as an ISEAP practitioner currently have an impact on the wider university?
2. What connections do you personally have across departments?

… and beyond:

1. How do you see university education developing in the next ten years? Can you list at least three key trends?
2. How can ISEAP contribute to these trends in the next ten years? How can it respond, but also how can it have agency in these areas?
3. What are the wider purposes of ISEAP and where is it going?

References

Advance HE (2022) Fellowship [online] Available at: https://www.advance-he.ac.uk/fellowship. [Accessed 1/10/22].

Bond, B. (2020) *Making language visible in the university: English for academic purposes and internationalisation*. Bristol: Multilingual Matters.

Bristol Institute for Learning and Teaching (BiLT) (2022) University of Bristol. http://www.bristol.ac.uk/bilt/ [Accessed 01/10/22].

Carr, C., Maxwell, C., Rolinska, A. and Sizer, J. (2021) EAP teachers working in, with and through the creative arts: An exploration. In MacDiarmid, C. and MacDonald, J. (Eds.) *Pedagogies in English for academic purposes: Teaching and learning in international contexts*. London: Bloomsbury Academic, pp. 153–168.

Caulton, D., Northcott, J. & Gillies, P. (2019) EAP and subject specialist academic writing feedback collaboration. In Gillway, M. (ed.), *Proceedings of the 2017 BALEAP Conference: Addressing the State of the Union: Working Together = Learning Together*. Reading: Garnet Education.

Costa, A. and Kallick, B. (1993) Through the lens of a critical friend. *Educational Leadership*, 51:2, 49–51.

Ding, A. and Bruce, I. (2017) *The English for academic purposes practitioner: Operating on the edge of academia.* Cham, Switzerland: Palgrave Macmillan.

McGrath, L., Negretti, R. and Nicholls, K. (2019). Hidden expectations: scaffolding specialists' genre knowledge of the assignment they set. *Higher Education Research & Development*, 78, 835–853.

Office for Students (2022) About the TEF, https://www.officeforstudents.org.uk/advice-and-guidance/teaching/about-the-tef/

Sloan, D. and Porter, E. (2010) Changing international student and business staff perceptions of in-sessional EAP: Using the CEM model. *Journal of English for Academic Purposes*, 9:3, 198–210.

Teaching and Learning Innovation Centre (TaLIC) (2022) Goldsmiths, University of London. https://www.gold.ac.uk/talic/ [Accessed 01/10/22].

Webster, S. (2022) The transition of EAP practitioners into scholarship writing. *Journal of English for Academic Purposes*, 57, May 2022, 101091, 1–12.

Whitchurch, C. (2015). The rise of third space professionals: Paradoxes and dilemmas. In U. Teichler and W.C. Cummings (eds.) *Recruiting and managing the academic profession.* Dordrecht: Springer, pp. 1–19.

Whong, M. and Godfrey, J. (2022a) Introduction: The good writing project. In Whong, M. and Godfrey, J. (eds.) *What is good academic writing? Insights into discipline-specific student writing.* London: Bloomsbury Academic, pp. 1–8.

Whong, M. and Godfrey, J. (2022b) A collaborative scholarship model of EAP research and practice. In Whong, M. and Godfrey, J. (eds.) *What is good academic writing? Insights into discipline-specific student writing.* London: Bloomsbury Academic, pp. 9–30.

Wingate, U. (2015) *Academic literacy and student diversity: The case for inclusive practice.* Bristol: Multilingual Matters.

Appendix: Standard Questions for Interviewees

Practice

- How do you see the status of in-sessionals within your EAP department?
- Is ISEAP seen as a specialisation or treated in a special way within the EAP provision that you offer?
- Do you adopt a different pedagogical approach compared with other EAP teaching?
- Would you like to share any examples of excellent practice?

EAP practitioners

- Are staff required to have a specialisation in the subject area they teach in for in-sessionals?
- Do in-sessional lecturers develop their own relationships with collaborating departments?

Students

- Do you teach home and international (L1 and non-L1 English) students together?
- Are your courses optional or embedded?

- Do you conduct needs analysis as a fundamental part of developing course design? (If so, what is your approach to this?)
- Do you evaluate transfer from IS to their performance in substantive programmes? (If so, how do you do this?)
- Are there any issues, such as engagement or attendance? How have you sought to resolve these?

Relations with subject lecturers

- Do subject lecturers *collaborate* or *cooperate* freely with you? What access are you given to materials, course docs, teaching information, lesson observation, etc.?
- How are EAP lecturers treated by subject lecturers? Is this the same across the board – or are some departments/lecturers more willing to collaborate than others?
- What do you think subject lecturers know about your centre's EAP practice?
- Are in-sessionals seen as a fix to a problem? (from their point of view, or from yours?)

Institutional role

- How visible is in-sessional provision within the University?
- Are you seen as a support service?
- Do you have a 'champion', i.e. someone who promotes you within the institution?
- Does in-sessional provision align with any University strategies?

Logistics

- How large is the in-sessional provision? (e.g. number of courses)
- Does in-sessional provision come under your own auspices or is it embedded within departments?
- Do you apply any specific QA processes to your ISEAP?

Index